# Nostalgic Design

**Pittsburgh Series in Composition, Literacy, and Culture**

David Bartholomae and Jean Ferguson Carr, Editors

# Nostalgic Design

Rhetoric, Memory, *and* Democratizing Technology

**William C. Kurlinkus**

University of Pittsburgh Press

Published by the University of Pittsburgh Press, Pittsburgh, Pa., 15260
Copyright © 2018, University of Pittsburgh Press
All rights reserved
Manufactured in the United States of America
Printed on acid-free paper
10 9 8 7 6 5 4 3 2 1

Cataloging-in-Publication data is available from the Library of Congress

ISBN 10: 0-8229-6552-6
ISBN 13: 978-0-8229-6552-7

Cover art: "Existentialism" by Aaron Cahill
Cover design: Melissa Dias-Mandoly

This book is about using nostalgia to reach toward more democratic, inclusive, innovative, meaningful, and human designs.

For Dad, Mom, and Krista

# Contents

Acknowledgments

ix

Why Nostalgia? Why Here? Why Now?

3

## Part I. Identifying Nostalgic Conflicts

**Chapter 1.** Nostalgic Design:

Between Innovation and Tradition

17

**Chapter 2.** Nostalgic Resistances:

Remembering as Critical Redesign in Everyday Workplaces

47

## Part II. Mediating Nostalgia

**Chapter 3.** Nostalgic Deliberations:

What I Mean When I Say "Democratizing Technology"

77

**Chapter 4.** Nostalgic Mediations:

Asking the Right Questions in Vaccine Communication

106

**Chapter 5.** Nostalgic Negotiations:

Adapting, Adopting, and Refusing Client Expertise

138

## Part III. Designing for Nostalgia

**Chapter 6.** Nostalgic UX:
Designing for Future Memories

165

**Afterword.** From English Major to Designer

195

Notes

213

References

223

Index

251

# Acknowledgments

Much like the modes of democratic design featured in this book, the process of building *Nostalgic Design* has been a collaborative one, and a nostalgic collaboration at that.

Looking back, I'd like to thank first and foremost my family. To Krista Kurlinkus, my colleague at the beginning of this project and now my wife, who bore with me, taught me to rock climb, took care of me, came up with the concept of the nostalgic other, and challenged my ideas by telling me how they would work or fail in her practice as a professional technical writer. Can we go on vacation now? To Dad, Dave Kurlinkus, my consummate copy editor, who has read hundreds of drafts over the years—thank you. To Mom, Ann Kurlinkus, who has always been interested in and pushed me to consider how writing and design pedagogy might work in her fifth-grade classroom— thank you. And thanks also to my three brothers, Joe, Charley, and Ted, for constantly making fun of me throughout this process.

Thanks to my mentors at Ohio State: To my dissertation chair, Cindy Selfe, who gave me the leeway, critical apparatus, and chance to explore something weird like nostalgia. There's a reason why your words echo throughout this book. To Nan Johnson, who challenged me to keep rhetoric close to my heart and improve my writing (and was willing to say, "This is where your writing flows. And this is where it clunks."). To Louie Ulman, who brought an old typewriter to my PhD exam and said, "What about this?" and who is still providing me with examples of nostalgic technology in the news. To Beverly Moss, who helped me know literacy and community. And to Susan Delagrange, whose suggestions, research on wonder, and multimodal publishing have been an inspiration.

In earlier years, at the University of Illinois, thanks to Gail Hawisher, who introduced me to the field of writing studies, then computers and writing, then Cindy Selfe. I wouldn't be here without you. Like so many of us in rhetoric and composition, I also had a strong writing center director, Libbie Morley, who helped me through my first writing studies research—thank you. Thanks also to Spencer Schaffner, who showed me that English professors could study cool things like graphic novels and bird watching. To Peter Mortensen, who let me sit in on my first graduate writing studies course. And thanks to W. David Kay, whose lessons on Baldesar Castiglione during those Renaissance literature courses have stuck with me to this day.

At Penn State, thanks to Stuart Selber, who gifted me my first course on rhetoric and technology and let me write about nostalgia and graffiti for the first time. And thanks to Cheryl Glenn and Jack Selzer, who taught me about rhetoric.

Of course, before all of these trainers, thanks to my high school English teacher Tom Reynolds, who taught me to enjoy style.

Thanks to those colleagues at the University of Oklahoma who read drafts and walked me through publishing questions: Susan Kates, Roxanne Mountford, Bill Endres, Sandy Tarabochia, and Ron Schleifer. Thanks also to the Department of English, the University of Oklahoma, and especially my chair, Daniela Garofalo, for helping me get time off for research. And thanks to OU's College of Arts and Sciences for a much needed Junior Faculty Summer Fellowship.

Thanks to the University of Pittsburgh Press and especially David Bartholomae and Jean Ferguson Carr, editors of the Pittsburgh Series in Composition, Literacy, and Culture. A sincere thanks also goes to my editor, Josh Shanholtzer, for the wise advice and setting me up with two amazing readers, whom I also thank for their editorial comments.

Thanks to the design and photo contributors of this book: Daina Taimina, Todd Matthews, Fiona Raby and Anthony Dunne, Thomas Brisebras, Stacie Osborne, and Anna Citelli and Raoul Bretzel.

Thanks to Parlor Press and David Blakesley for letting me republish selections of chapter 6, which formerly appeared as "Memorial Interactivity: Scaffolding Nostalgic User Experiences" in Liza Potts and Michael Salvo's collection *Rhetoric and Experience Architecture.*

Thanks also to those friends in grad school who kept me sane: Jake Hughes, Lindsay DeWitt, Katie DeLuca, Lauren Obermark, and Chase Bollig. And to my volleyball team, now—especially Mark Norris and Sandy Tarabochia—who continue the tradition of helping me put the books down, if just for a minute.

And, finally, thanks to the research participants of chapters 2 and 5: Donna, Jo, Kit, Lux, Mason, and Grant. There wouldn't be a book without you. Thanks for being generous with your time and for saying such smart things that writing about you felt like writing with you.

# Nostalgic Design

# Why Nostalgia? Why Here? Why Now?

When I tell rhetoric, technical communication, and literature colleagues that I'm writing a book on nostalgic design, they usually say, "Oh." If I'm particularly lucky, "Oh, wait, what?" Longing for protractors, typewriters, and Super Nintendo, many of them tell me stories about their favorite piece of retro tech. Others wonder at the oxymoronic nature of the term—Isn't nostalgia, a regressive emotion, the opposite of design, an innovative act? If they know something about technology, they usually guess that I research skeuomorphs (those digital replicas of physical objects like the trashcan icon and desktop interface) or that I help hesitant users get over their love of the past so they'll adopt new tech. After all, "One way of overcoming the fear of the new," renowned designer Donald Norman advises, "is making it look like the old" (*Design* 159). But that's not what I mean (or, as you'll see, it's a small part of the work). Rather, nostalgic design is both a thing and an act, each entangling making in this era where nostalgia—*pride and longing for lost or threatened (personally or culturally experienced) pasts*—is booming. From craft revivals of knitting, brewing, and home repair; to endless reboots of film franchises; to international rises of anti-immigrant nationalism, it's undeniable that twenty-first-century citizens long for ever-colliding pasts. In response, nostalgic design is a perspective and a method that argues that carefully negotiating such conflicts of memory can lead to more democratic, inclusive, innovative, meaningful, and human technologies by asking:

1. Why are citizens of the twenty-first century so nostalgic for old technologies, traditions, and ways of knowing the world?
2. How can innovators who are concerned with creating inclusive futures better engage traditional communities that are resistant to novelty and (because of this hesitancy) habitually left out of the design of the world?
3. What can designers learn from the ways that technology users at the edges of progress weild nostalgia to contest new designs and reshape their lives?

4. And, in light of such defiance, what does the democratic design of technology pragmatically look like in our current nostalgia boom?

Moreover, as *things*, nostalgic designs call users' and designers' attention to the way memory and tradition are structured around them. If, as designer Richard Buchanan observes, design is fundamentally rhetorical because "all products—digital and analog, tangible and intangible—are vivid arguments about how we should lead our lives," then nostalgic designs are arguments about how users should relate to the past ("Design" 194). From Instagram's retro photo filters, to Confederate Civil War memorials, to the slow food movement, such arguments reorganize time, trigger nostalgic ruptures, and ideally spark conversations in which citizens consider: *What am I nostalgic for? Why? To which ends?* And *How does my nostalgia differ from my neighbor's?*

Perhaps more often, however, we experience longing internally, assuming everyone else's ideal past is just like ours. Nostalgic designs ideally fracture this assumption by asking users to pay attention to the diversity of pride and longing that surrounds them. Sometimes, in the wake of a contentious election or a hot button social issue, such rifts are uncomfortable. Eyes riveted to social media, we realize that friends and family are actively remembering history in a different light than we are. In the wake of the 2016 U.S. presidential election, for instance, "the great unfriending" occurred: a wave of democratic voters unfriended Facebook contacts who celebrated the election as a positive event to remember into the future. "I unfriended my brother and sister-in-law today," says Facebook user Laura Fitch in the *Chicago Tribune*, "not because they were being particularly obnoxious, and I already knew they were Trump supporters, but because seeing their posts and 'likes' just serves as a sad reminder of how little we have in common" (Lindner). But learning to traverse this thorny experience is vital to democracy. It forces us to engage opinions outside ourselves, the vox populi, as logically proceeding from some personal or cultural past. As an *act*, then, nostalgic design is a method of democratic making wherein designers analyze these point breaks, identify the innumerous longings therein, and carefully mediate them into innovative futures.

To illustrate this process, in this book I bridge the fields of design studies, memory studies, and rhetorical theory to argue that rhetorical analyses of nostalgia can tell designers what different communities of users love about the past, miss in the present, and wish to recover in the future. Through textual probes and personal interviews, I tour the conflicting nostalgias of several U.S. techno-cultures, from young knitters and anti-vaccination protesters to physicians and graphic designers, because (despite misconceptions that technology is principally future oriented) all citizens imagine good futures from what they esteem about good pasts. When designers address these memories and traditions, democratic designs thrive. But when nostalgic ideals are ignored, users are excluded, citizens feel isolated and attacked, they attack one another, and designs sputter out. To see the process of nostalgic design in action, in this book we'll consider questions including:

- Why has there been a rise in feminist knitting in masculine digital workplaces, and what can designers learn from such resistant nostalgic underlife? (Chapter 2)
- How do the fields of rhetoric and design theorize deliberative democracy/ making? What do the two have to learn from one another? And how might the constitutive force of nostalgia undergirding each ground the search for democratic technologies? (Chapter 3)
- How do designers mediate the conflicting technological traditions of their different users? How, for instance, can nostalgic design help physicians respond to the longing for a more "natural" medical existence of parents who refuse to vaccinate their children? (Chapter 4)
- How do practicing designers adapt, adopt, and refuse client nostalgias to create a transactive memory system that promotes smooth collaborations? (Chapter 5)
- How can studying nostalgic experiences (from crafting mixtapes to annotating a family bible) create longer-lasting user bonds in an age of disposable tech? (Chapter 6)

## What Is Nostalgia, Anyway?

Contemporarily, nostalgia has gotten a pretty bad rap. At best it's dismissed as an empty longing for an artificially sweetened past, and at worst, a propagandistic roadblock that halts progress. Folklorist Susan Stewart personifies such rejection when she defines nostalgia as a "social disease[,] . . . a sadness without an object, a sadness which creates a longing that of necessity is inauthentic because it does not take part in lived experience" (23). Historian Stephanie Coontz styles devotion to such inauthenticity as "the nostalgia trap." But nostalgia's seventeenth-century roots were intensely real, medical, even life altering. Physician Johannes Hofer coined the term in 1688 to explain the severe homesickness of Swiss mercenaries. The word is a portmanteau of the Greek *nostos* (to return home) and *algos* (pain/sorrow), and, as Hofer depicts, the feeling led to anorexia, insomnia, fever, and even suicidal depression, only cured by going home. Such life-changing medical definitions of nostalgia are still culturally (though not often medically) studied in refugee and military populations today (Ritivoi; Akhtar; Jones, "From").

Hofer's corporeal definition (which lasted well into the nineteenth century) was more a homesickness for lost spaces than it was a longing for time, but over the centuries this distinction between home and past blurred, spawning the type of temporal longing we know today. We see this switch, for instance, in the fin de siècle designs of Romantic authors and artists (from William Wordsworth to William Morris), who long for rural, pastoral, and handmade pasts as a proactive check to the Industrial Revolution. Contemporarily, sociologist Hartmut Rosa calls this critically aware desire for slow rhythms in the face of cultural and technical upheaval *entschleunigung*, deceleration: "[T]he 'tempo of life' has increased, and with it stress, hecticness. . . . We don't have any time although we've gained far more than we needed before" (xxxv). Constantly answering work emails at home, learning new tech, replacing obsolescent devices—to counter social acceleration, citizens look back for better solutions and more authentic selves.

Responding to such cultural observations, then, over the past decade nostalgia research has become increasingly scientific, again, focusing on the emotion's homeostatic function. That is, as social psychologists like Tim Wildschut, Clay Routledge, and Constantine Sedikides have tested, when life-changing events happen (getting divorced, being fired, moving across the world) people look back to known times and the positive identities therein to stabilize their lives. And it works: "Those in the nostalgia condition reported less attachment anxiety and avoidance, higher self-esteem, and more positive affect. . . . [W]hen people encounter self-threats, rather than countering directly the specific threat, they have the option of eliminating its effects by affirming essential, positive aspects of the self" (Wildschut et al. 989). As distinct from Hofer's homesickness, then, nostalgia is increasingly understood as a beneficial psychological tool humans use to redesign their worlds.

As this petite history illustrates, because nostalgia is attached at the hip to a bevy of other ideas (cultural and collective memory, melancholia, tradition, longing, loss, pride) and because it's studied through conflicting disciplinary lenses (medicine, politics, emotion, anthropology, media, advertising, and psychology), it's defined and redefined over and over. In response, the definition of "nostalgia" I use in this book is a bit broader than usual. For us, nostalgia is *pride and longing for lost or threatened personally or culturally experienced pasts.*

1. *Pride and longing*: Nostalgia is made up of dueling emotions: pride (a positive sense of past self/community that we build our identities upon today) and longing (a drive to recover something stable in times of flux). Where

longing is bound in loss and critique of the present, when combined with pride it can become hope, creation, and future oriented; as mother of nostalgia studies Svetlana Boym writes, "The fantasies of the past, determined by the needs of the present, have a direct impact on the realities of the future" ("Nostalgia" 8). Indeed, it's this omnitemporal aspect of nostalgia that differentiates it from a sister emotion, melancholia, which doesn't build space for new futures but mires itself in the open wound of the past. Unfortunately, as we'll see, such emotions have been used to exclude nostalgia as a "rational" asset by historians, memory theorists, and designers. But engaging human feelings leads to human designs.

2. *For lost or threatened*: Nostalgia has historically been defined as a longing for a lost past, but most recent nostalgia scholars note that nostalgics are getting younger and younger and the time between an actual event and longing for it, briefer and briefer. So, although I risk blurring nostalgia, tradition, and memory by doing so, throughout this book you'll see examples of nostalgia for things that haven't been entirely lost. Rather, nostalgia also occurs when the state of things on which one's identity is based is simply threatened. Whether it's doctors longing for a time when patients implicitly trusted their advice or the anticipatory nostalgia of gun owners who fear the loss of the Second Amendment, nostalgia is deeply protective.

3. *Personally or culturally experienced*: Early nostalgia purists like Fred Davis argue that people can't be nostalgic for events they haven't personally experienced (8). But increasingly, nostalgia is understood as a collective and generationally learned emotion. That is, as Maurice Halbwachs writes of collective memory, in nostalgia, too, "The groups I am a part [sic] at any time give me the means to reconstruct them [memories], upon condition, to be sure, that I turn toward them and adopt, at least for the moment, their way of thinking" (38). This tension between individual and collective memory is another force that differentiates nostalgia from relatives like melancholia (an individual emotion) and tradition (an intergenerational cultural process).

4. *Pasts*: Finally, and perhaps most notably for the relationship between nostalgia and inclusive design, though everyone is nostalgic for something and citizens may think that everyone longs for *their* ideal past, nostalgia is incredibly diverse and conflicting—even internally. We long for *pasts* rather than the *past*.

In light of this wide-ranging definition, throughout this book I hope readers will find themselves asking, Is this really nostalgia? Undeniably, I use the term to describe cultures that haven't often been labeled nostalgic: design clients (who long for a past when they alone controlled their business), anti-vaccination parents (who long for the medicine of their childhood and a time before autism), and even scientific experts (who long for theoretical school training when real world practice doesn't run so smoothly). In Kenneth Burke's terms, I've "casuistically stretched" the word because a theory of nostalgic design would be nothing if it couldn't be practically applied in specific milieus, and practical application always involves adapting, modifying, and stretching (*Attitudes* 230). As a result, the local contexts and cases of each chapter constantly redefine "nostalgia," dealing with it more or less directly, but always "treat[ing] the world *in terms of it*, seeing all as emanations, near or far, of its light" (*Grammar* 105).

## Can Nostalgia Really Be a Source of Inclusive Innovation?

As I was finishing this book, which seeks to recover nostalgia for inclusive technological production, something happened that challenged my central claim. President Donald Trump appeared—and was elected—on a platform driven by propagandistic nostalgia, a quest to "Make America Great Again" that doesn't seek multiple ideal pasts and futures but closes them down in favor of a vague recovery of tradition. Such agitprop is why scholars have rejected nostalgics for years. On May 5, 2016, for instance, against a backdrop of miners decked in worn coveralls and hard hats who waved "Trump Digs Coal" signs, then-candidate Trump preached from a Charleston, West Virginia, stage:

> And I'll tell you what, folks, you heard me the other night. I wasn't thinking
> even about you; I'm thinking about the miners all over this country. We're
> gonna put the miners back to work. We're gonna put the miners back to work!
> We're gonna get those mines open. Ah, coal country, what they've done. And
> how 'bout Hillary Clinton? I was watching her three or four weeks ago. See, I'm
> going to put the miners back to work, and she said, "I'm going to put the miners
> and mines out of business." . . . You're an amazing people, and we're going to
> take care of a lot of years of horrible abuse. ("Donald Trump")

But when President Trump references "years of horrible abuse," he doesn't mean a century of mine collapses, black lung, and contaminated water supplies. Nor does he trace the decline in coal to mechanization and a rise in cheaper fuels like natural gas (Kolstad). He means years of "ridiculous regulations that put you out of business" under President Obama's EPA. Trump and his crowd want to return to a pre-EPA golden age of coal. In fact, Trump lets his audience in on "a little secret. I've always been fascinated by the mines.

I always have. I don't know why. You know, I love construction. . . . And the courage of the miners and the way the miners love what they do." Embodying this childlike love of the past, Trump puts on a hard hat and pantomimes shoveling coal, an act that transforms a dangerous industry into a nostalgic plaything. In doing so, he promises to restore tradition, bring mining back, Make America Great Again. When the world becomes chaotic and treats us harshly, it's only human to long for such simple order—even if the order being shoveled is anti-scientific, authoritarian bullshit.[1]

But while Trump vowed to bring coal jobs back, his proposed 2017 budget also defunds the Appalachian Regional Commission, an organization responsible for resourcing other ventures in the region including retraining unemployed miners for new jobs. In fact, a 2017 *Reuter's* study showed that Trump's nostalgic hope for coal has caused some unemployed miners (especially in southern Pennsylvania) to reject reskilling to enter other industries (Volcovici). Similarly, Trump has cut funding to EPA studies that investigate the health and environmental effects of mining and, thereby, rupture his nostalgia. Essentially, President Trump has locked Appalachia into a nostalgic mono-economy rather than listening for other possible traditions and futures that exist there. This type of limiting nostalgia is what Boym calls "restorative nostalgia": "[R]estorative nostalgia does not think of itself as nostalgia, but rather as truth and tradition. . . . [T]he complexity of history, the variety of contradictory evidence, and the specificity of modern circumstances are thus erased, and modern history is seen as a fulfillment of ancient prophecy" (*Future* 7, 14).

Readers might ask, then, how, given such propagandistic uses, nostalgia could ever be a force for inclusive innovation. Certainly, innumerable headlines decry "Trump's Rhetoric of White Nostalgia" (*The Atlantic*); ask, "Can We Stop the Politics of Nostalgia That Have Dominated 2016?" (*Newsweek*); and argue, "Donald Trump's Budget Is Nostalgic and Deeply Destructive—And It Will Backfire" (*New Republic*). For much of its life, nostalgia's detractors have rejected it because of just such cases. Though Karl Marx disparaged the rationalization of work found in the Industrial Revolution, for instance, he also wrote judgmentally of longing: "It is better to suffer in modern bourgeois society, which by its industry creates the means for the foundation of a new society that will liberate you, than revert to a bygone society which, on the pretext of saving your classes, thrusts the entire nation back into medieval barbarism" ("Montesquieu"). In other words, at the same time Romantic authors were embracing nostalgia's radical potential, many progressives were using the label "nostalgic" to dismiss those who refused progress (Bonnett). In fact, political scientist Kimberly Smith argues that the origin of the modern sociocultural understanding of nostalgia was this type of dismissal: "Nostalgia, I contend, was invented during the eighteenth and nineteenth centuries . . . as an explanation for psychological resistance to the forces of modernization . . . that explains progressives' failure to persuade their opponents. Specifically, nostalgia accounts for the troubling persistence of those dissenting voices—conservatives, agrarians, and traditionalists of various sorts—that oppose the 'progressive' rationalization and mechanization of the means of production. The claim that such opponents are suffering from nostalgia both explains and delegitimates their political stance" (506).

Though Smith is writing about the turn of the nineteenth century, we see echoes of such rejections today. Liberal progressives make pariahs of conservatives who reason from the "backwards" traditional perspectives of religious sanctity, constitutionality, and family values. This rejection has been so naturalized in academic discourse that rhetoric instructors teach their students to avoid the "fallacy" of appealing to tradition, *argumentum ad antiquitatem*. In this context, political nostalgia has been so easily harnessed by regressive demagogues because progressives have so quickly dismissed it. But *everyone is nostalgic for something*. Several studies have proven that it's an inescapable "transideological" emotion (Hepper et al.; Skowronski et al.). Linda Hutcheon accounts: "Despite the fact that many would argue that, whether used by the right or the left, nostalgia is fundamentally conservative in its praxis[,] . . . nostalgia for an idealized community in the past has been articulated by the ecology movement as often as by fascism" (22). This doesn't mean that we have to tolerate hateful viewpoints based on blatant lies. But appeals to tradition are never going away, and by simply dismissing them, those of us who champion democracy isolate ourselves from would-be collaborators.

In response, this book attempts to introduce nostalgia as a tool for structuring conversations about inclusivity for those who seek truly human-centered designs. Returning to Appalachia, for instance, one finds organizations like Create West Virginia, a nonprofit that layers West Virginia's traditional values with innovations in order to create what Jennifer Ladino calls "counter nostalgia" that "envisions the 'home' as fractured, fragmented, complicated, and layered; to 'return' to this sort of home is to revisit a dynamic past and to invert or exploit official narratives in ways that challenge dominant histories" ("Longing" 91).

In the summer of 2016, for example, a flash flood hit eastern West Virginia, destroying thousands of homes and killing twenty-three people. In response, in addition to supporting typical disaster relief, Create West Virginia initiated two design-based tactics that each blended innovation and tradition. First, their digital media lab helped victims of the flood recover memories:

"Students and other savvy digital and social media (DIGISO) users can lend their native digital and social media skills to work with families in need to set up free file and photo sharing accounts so family pictures, memories, oral histories can finally be shared with loved ones" (Halstead, "Toward"). Such an archival process (innovative in itself) shows the emotional need for flood victims to come together with family to preserve tradition in the face of the loss of places that define their lives. But, importantly, Create West Virginia also pushed residents to rethink the design of homes in the state's valleys, where flooding is a constant threat but towns are often restored in the same way: "We love our places in West Virginia, and while it's true that we're really good at coming together for crisis after crisis, and we can make do with very little, there is an argument to be made for planning and design for resilient, durable, healthy homes and communities. . . . What if we became known for our ingenious building practices. . . . In some places, hope floats in the form of flood accommodating housing design. In others, it's on stilts, or incorporates other super cool ideas that make homes and communities more resilient" (Halstead, "Wanted").

By arguing for preserving personal tradition (family photos) and welcoming architectural innovation based in traditional West Virginian identity markers (resilience and ingenuity), Create West Virginia sparks debate about what Appalachian tradition really is. Nostalgia, thus, doesn't have to be a careless embrace of the past; it can open our minds to alternative possibilities as well. As anthropologist Brian Hoey writes of the possibilities of economic development in the state: "I speak not of a sense of place composed of essential qualities imparted by a singular history, set of practices, or a bounded, defined geography, but rather as potentially conflicting debate . . . competing and commingling around the idea of Huntington—indeed the entire state of West Virginia—and their position in the emerging economic order" (77). The nostalgic layering of numerous ideal Appalachian traditions generates inclusive innovation. This is nostalgic design.

## Why Write about Design in a Series on Composition, Literacy, and Culture?

In beginning this preface, I described some of the most common responses from colleagues when I say that I work on "nostalgic design," but I wasn't being entirely honest. Really, the first thing friends and family ask me once they start understanding the concept is "Why are you working in an English department?" You may be asking yourself a similar question: Why write about design in a book series on composition, literacy, and culture? My short answer to them and to you is that I know of no other field that teaches students to uncover and have empathy for the full messiness of humanity better than English studies, rhetoric, composition, and literacy. And, at the same time, I also know of few fields that have so poorly marketed their ability to concretely change the world for the better.

Increasingly, it's obvious that we're living in a technocracy. The big five tech companies (Facebook, Google, Amazon, Apple, and Microsoft) are more powerful and more effective at creating change than any government. But although citizens can vote for elected officials, they rarely get to vote on how these corporations shape their lives. In this context, for the humanities to transform the world, we need to train students to combine humanities theory with technological making. That is, as George Anders writes, "The more our labs and engineers innovate, the more jobs we create for people who can make the human dimension work" (5). When talking about this need with English students, I use a job ad from the design firm IDEO for a "design researcher" position: "Great design is born out of great research. Our Design Researchers lead clients and teams through a journey of human-centered research. . . . We're seeking an individual who is naturally empathetic and passionate about people. Design Researchers bring to life the voice of the people they're designing for, connecting the internal design team and client organization to the human experience."

Rhet/comp scholars already (by my observation, more so than those in many design departments) train their students in this kind of researched empathy, but we don't often teach them about jobs like this, where they can deploy those skills to better the world. In response, this book offers a route for professors and students of English alike to start thinking of themselves as designers, expert makers who shape some technology to be operated by a specific user, in a specific context, in order to "change existing situations into preferred ones" (Fuad-Luke, *Design Activism* 1–5). Of course, the subfields of computers and writing, technical communication, and the rhetoric of science and technology have contributed to this goal for decades (see Alexander and Lupton). But to push the transformation from English major to designer further, in this book I focus on (and favor in my citations) introducing readers to the field of design studies and, specifically, what I call *rhetorical design*, a subfield progressed by designers like Carl DiSalvo and Richard Buchanan that's focused on the ecologies of language, persuasion, and resistance surrounding the production and use of technology as well as on actively solving problems of power and inequity within these systems.

To help create more English majors who are designers, I give some prescriptive steps throughout the book and have included a pedagogical afterword. But I've also purposefully kept things a little messy because humans are messy things, and English majors are so great at reading and reveling in that chaos. I've tried to resist creating an easily consumable package, as graphic designer Natasha Jen critiques of the recent trend of "design thinking" (and this is the last time you will read that phrase in this book): "Design thinking packages a designer's way of working for a non-designer audience by codifying their processes into a prescriptive, step-by-step approach to creative problem solving. . . . Design has become this box where people just want to check off. And that's a problem" ("Natasha").

Ultimately, then, it's the goal of this book to start understanding nostalgia as not only a love of the past that halts progress but also as a resource for designers (whether of words or technologies) to listen carefully to the losses and longings of citizens who have been excluded from innovation. People are always nostalgic for a reason—we look back to the past when we feel lost in the present. But in looking back we're always imagining futures we're a part of. Nostalgic design, then, affords designers a chance to think outside of themselves for lost values, resources, and timelines that might make the future more human.

# I

# Identifying Nostalgic Conflicts

# Chapter 1

# Nostalgic Design

## Between Innovation and Tradition

Nostalgia, in my view, is not always retrospective; it can be prospective as well. The fantasies of the past, determined by the needs of the present, have a direct impact on the realities of the future.

**Svetlana Boym, "Nostalgia and Its Discontents"**

Do not seek the old in the new, but find something new in the old.

**Siegfried Zielinski, *Deep Time of the Media***

Revolution. *noun* rev·o·lu·tion \ˌre-və-ˈlü-shən\
1. A radical change in society
2. The regular cycle of an object through its orbit back to a point of origin

## Archiving the Moment

"Will, we care about you and the memories you share here," Facebook greets me when I log in. "We thought you'd like to look back on this post from 10 years ago." In 2015 the social network introduced On This Day, a feature that encourages users to publicly remember pictures and posts from years earlier. "Never miss a memory," the site warns; "Here's a way to rediscover things you shared or were tagged in." Like many social networking sites, my Facebook account is a technology of memory. It propels a nostalgia boom by inspiring users to revisit archived experiences that might otherwise be lost to the past, but it also persuades users to be nostalgic for the present, to see posts written about the here and now as "memories you share here." That scenic waterfall you're hiking past? It's a potential memory—take a picture before it evaporates. In doing so, Facebook fosters an affective culture driven by what social psychologist Constantine Sedikides calls "anticipatory nostalgia." Under this logic, citizens view the present as an event to be chronicled in hopes it will become a cherished memory and out of fear that without record that chance for meaning will vanish. Instagram's retro photo filters similarly trade in this addictive anticipation by vignetting, scratching, overexposing, and, thereby, digitally aging pictures taken just seconds ago. Digital weathering lends a sense of authenticity to memories of now. By housing these archives, technologies of memory acquire a patina of meaning by association, a reification of memorial labor that would be lost if you desert the sites. That is, if you quit, you don't care about all the people and experiences you've shared. But, despite popular sentiment that nostalgia is a fearful response to the new and that social networks manipulate mindless users, it would be careless to label social media users uncritical simply because they enjoy remembering. Because of the archives' publicly intimate nature—compared to private records like photo albums or home videos—we mindfully collage memories to curate an identity for the world. This account is my best me, a golden-age self I long to return to. I use it to remember a world into being. In this way, nostalgia nurtures active, personal, memorable, and, thereby, meaningful designs.

## Alienation through Innovation

Google announced its Fiber initiative in 2012 with ambitions of spreading high-speed internet across the United States. For a low start-up fee, neighborhoods are connected to an ultrafast network. Early on, only "Fiberhoods" that voted for the service could join. And if enough residents in a community preregistered, Google would make the investment, even offering free access to local schools. This campaign held the potential to wire low-income neighborhoods; internet access would be freed of income restriction. Paradoxically, Google Fiber intensified digital inequity. In Kansas City, for instance, just two days before the registration deadline, neighborhoods that preregistered and those that didn't split directly down Troost Avenue, a street that divides the city socioeconomically and racially. As Aaron Deacon, managing director of the Kansas City Digital Divide Drive, remarks, citizens who didn't vote for Fiber "focus on feeding people, finding jobs, those end-state social services. There's a little bit of a gap still in people understanding how using technology tools can achieve those end goals" (Velázquez). Perpetuating the recruitment gap, when Fiber was launched there were no Spanish-language marketing materials available for the city's sizeable Hispanic population. In failing to teach low-income Kansas City citizens how the service would benefit them, Google's pro-innovation bias asked users to replace their current concerns and culture with Google's. In this light, initially at least, Google failed to see that innovation without tradition leads to alienation. Google Fiber needed to become a nostalgic design. Though they eventually spoke with low-income users in town hall meetings, they still wanted consumers, not collaborators. After all, neighborhoods were transformed into Fiberhoods, not the reverse. Instead, Google might have considered: What are this community's technological memories, traditions, and ambitions? And how can we redesign to achieve these ideals? The goal of such nostalgic localization is the creation of technologies that are simultaneously past and future oriented and, thereby, welcome neglected citizens as their first adopters rather than just the young and rich. What if Google Fiber had *originally* been designed with the traditions of lower-income black and Latinx citizens in mind, speculating how it fit into their cherished pasts, current realities, and ideal futures? Such overlooked users should not have to wait for new technologies to trickle down to them only to discover they were designed for someone else.[1] In this way, nostalgic design affords designers a chance to think outside of Silicon Valley traditions for off-modern values, resources, and timelines that reside just outside of mainstream progress narratives but that might make the future more fully human.

## Resistant Remembering

Donna, a thirty-something roller derby skater, directs a group of high-tech digital labs at a major midwestern university. Because she was formerly a software programmer, when you pass her office now, you might think you hear the soft click of coding on a keyboard. But when you enter, rather than seeing Donna programming a web of variables and constants, you see a knitter, eyes on her monitor, while her needles weave a binary of knits and purls. From homebrewed beer to DIY house kits, Donna is a member of a generation that nostalgically turned to craft in the face of digital intangibility and ephemerality. When I ask why she thinks this trend is occurring, she theorizes, "There came a certain point where most people's jobs are about going somewhere and sitting at a desk all day. . . . [Y]our product is pixels. . . . And I kind of felt like there were people who were frustrated with that 'I came home at the end of this eight hours, and I don't have anything to show for it.' And so, knitting was a way of, like, I'm still doing something with my time, but at the end of that time there's a physical object here I can show you." Donna's job was marked by a loss of physical end products to her labor. In response, her knitting is a process of nostalgic design, a tactical drawing upon a past of feminine making—even if it isn't her own lived past—to resist cutting-edge alienation and reshape a frustrating workplace. By knitting at her high-tech job, Donna claims a nostalgic right to meaningful labor. We look back to the past when we don't feel at home in the present. But in looking back, like Donna, we're always creating futures we're a part of. Nostalgia resists, slows, and reshapes the world.

It's no surprise that when designers consider nostalgia—*pride and longing for lost or threatened personally or culturally experienced pasts*—their minds rarely leap to innovation. Whether to increase profit, skirt irrational traditions, or bolster change, philosophers of technology and design have dismissed nostalgics as narcissistically mired in idealized and artificial memories, halting progress through a "random cannibalization of all styles of the past" (Jameson, *Postmodernism* 18). In the pages of *Print* magazine, for instance, typographer Angela Riechers rejects the "misuse of the powers of graphic design" in the nostalgic interface of Churchkey Pilsner, a beer that has to be cracked with a retro churchkey can opener instead of the contemporary pop top. "Nostalgia supplies the rapture of the familiar," Riechers cautions, "rather than encouraging a venture into uncertain new design territory." Music critic Simon Reynolds similarly warns that nostalgia halts musical evolution: "[T]he place that The Future once occupied in the imagination of young music-makers has been displaced by The Past: that's where the romance lies, with the idea of things that have been lost" ("Total Recall"). Theorist of user-centered innovation Eric von Hippel argues that tech firms can learn from the hacks of the first 2.5 percent (Rogers) of technology adopters—"lead users" or "innovators"—ignoring the resistances of the last 16 percent of adopters, unceremoniously dubbed "laggards." More bluntly, a 2013 ad for the Cree LED light bulb rebukes, "The light bulbs in your house were invented by Thomas Edison in 1879. Now think about that with your 2013 brain. Do you still do the wash down by the crick while your eldest son keeps lookout for wolves? No. You don't. This is a Cree LED bulb. It lasts 25 times longer. Nostalgia is dumb" ("Cree"). At best, then, nostalgia seems to be the melancholy of the technologically illiterate, a flaw in reasoning to overcome as one learns and grows. How could it ever promote revolutionary futures?

This book investigates just that.

*Nostalgic Design* argues for using nostalgia to design more democratic, inclusive, innovative, meaningful, and human technologies. It starts from the fact that, psychologically, nostalgia is a homeostatic emotion that arises when people feel left out of the current structure of things. From survivalists who live "off the grid" in the face of new surveillance tech to refugees who turn the smallest pieces of home (a bit of cloth, a cheese grater) into heirlooms that anchor their family in time,[2] as social psychologists Clay Routledge et al. observe, "nostalgia is incited by psychological threat and serves to bolster or to restore well-being" (809). Building from this observation, this book illustrates how nostalgia can tell designers what different communities of users love about the past, miss in the present, and wish to recover in the future. What if Facebook purposefully fostered conversations between members of dissimilar traditions through On This Day? What if Google Fiber originally had been designed with lower-class black and Latinx values in mind? What if Donna's

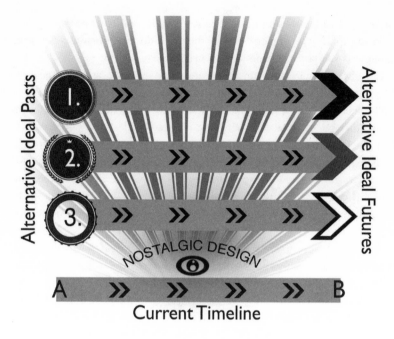

**Figure 1.1.** Nostalgic design is a set of methods that allows designers to question the inevitability of the current form of things, breaking out of their present timelines in order to explore the possibilities of parallel timelines, alternative ideal pasts, and the alternative futures that stem from them.

high-tech workplace was redesigned around traditions of feminine making? Parallel pasts and futures surround designers every day (figure 1.1).

*Nostalgic Design* offers a set of tools that helps designers reach the innovative potential of these alternative timelines. To illustrate this process, I survey the nostalgias of several U.S. technology cultures, from software programmers who knit on the job to repair activists who long to return to a time when consumers could fix a broken device themselves. Through rhetorical analyses and personal interviews, I ask each of these groups, *What are you nostalgic for, why, and to which ends?* Ultimately, we'll see that design has a nostalgic heart. That is, despite misconceptions that technology is principally future oriented, all citizens imagine good futures from what they esteem about good pasts.[3] When designers address memory and tradition, inclusive designs thrive; when nostalgic ideals are ignored, users are excluded and designs sputter out. Thus, my theses: innovation without tradition leads to alienation and, conversely, the dialogue of conflicting nostalgias leads to revolution through revolution. Designers make a technology *good* by digging into the humanity of its users— nostalgia is the perfect spade for this archaeology.

Certainly, despite a dismissal of nostalgia by advocates for technological progress, it's been pretty evident to philosophers of memory and history (Halbwachs; Nora; Assmann and Assmann) that different communities inescapably ground themselves in different collective pasts, and sometimes these ideal pasts collide. Still, few memory theorists have studied how the origin of technological inequity is so often this conflict of traditions, unheard clashes of class, race, gender, sex, age, and ability that make access to technology more difficult for some than for others. Designers Carl DiSalvo et al. label this politics "the rhetoric of design":[4] "[T]he ways in which the built environment reflects and tries to influence values and behavior and . . . the capacity of people to design artifacts or systems that promote or thwart certain perspectives and agendas" (49).

Observe, for instance, as digital media theorists Cynthia and Richard Selfe do, how the design of the computer desktop is based on a nostalgic remediation of business values (manila folders, files, desk calendars) that subtly exclude users who lack a U.S. clerical mindset. "[G]iven that these technologies have grown out of the predominately male, white, middle-class, professional cultures[,]" Selfe and Selfe write, "the virtual reality of computer interfaces represents, in part and to a visible degree, a tendency to value monoculturalism, capitalism, and phallologic thinking" (69). User localization expert Huatong Sun recounts her experience with such cultural restrictions: "But what was a file folder, why did she need to organize her files? She had no idea. As someone who was unfamiliar with American office culture, she had never used a file folder . . . Chinese culture was not as obsessed with paper trails" (3). In the design of the desktop, as in all designs, one tradition is normalized, making thinking about computing in other inventive ways difficult. But consider the possibilities revealed by reimagining the desktop through the traditions of a carpenter's workbench, a surgeon's operating table, or a chef's cutting board. Nostalgic design welcomes new old ways of viewing the world—*neostalgic redesign*. In doing so, it smashes technological determinism, the belief that "technical progress follows a unilinear course, a fixed track, from less to more advanced configurations" (Feenberg, *Between* 8).

In exploring both *nostalgia* (longing for a lost past) and *neostalgia* (longing for futures that could have been), this book also argues that the best way to recognize diverse traditions and futures in an era where power is decided by technical enterprise is through design methods that employ agonistic democracy (Mouffe)—forms of deliberative making in which stakeholders from divergent traditions design together as collaborators instead of enemies (DiSalvo, *Adversarial Design*; Björgvinsson et al.). Unfortunately, as the desktop and Google Fiber examples illustrate, technological design is usually left to engineers and scientists who haven't listened for the clash of user values that makes democracy churn. Such ignorance leads to a technocracy in which a select few voices decide how we live. Furthermore, even when the democratization of technology is theorized, many models don't provide a practical means to mediate the conflict agonistic democracy thrives on. That is, how does one plan a new park when the city council wants one thing, citizens want something else, and local business owners don't want a park at all? Designers might agree with a democratic ethic in theory but struggle to mediate between stakeholders in practice. Geoff Mulgan, CEO of the UK's National Endowment of Science, Technology, and the Arts, critiques designers for this failure to match "their skills in creativity with skills in implementation. . . . [L]ack of attention to organisational issues and cultures . . . condemns too many ideas to staying on the drawing board" (4).

In response, this book explores nostalgia as a pragmatic tool for designers—whether industrial engineers, graphic artists, UX architects, technical writers, physicians, or teachers—to innovate, mediate, and meditate within a global culture of making that is rapidly undergoing a *democratization of expertise* (Hartelius; Nichols; Gee et al.; Collins). "For a century, designers have seen themselves and have been seen as the sole incumbents and managers in the design field," writes Ezio Manzini. "Today they find themselves in a world where everybody designs" (*Design When* 1–2). Expertly trained makers can no longer create in isolation from their users. Citizens want to participate. DIY, maker culture, citizen science—nostalgic self-education on topics from home construction to medicine is at an all-time high in part because citizens feel alienated from, don't understand, and/or don't trust the science and technology they use daily. For others, doing it themselves is just plain fun. Thus, if "design" might be broadly defined as *the methods by which expert makers create some technology to be operated by a specific user, in a specific context, in order to "change existing situations into preferred ones"* (Fuad-Luke, *Design Activism* 1–5), then *good* design increasingly welcomes the diverse expertise of all citizens affected by it. That is, good design lies somewhere between outsider innovation and insider tradition. In city planning, for example, this democratization of expertise is seen in participatory charrettes, where residents are welcomed to the table (in town halls, etc.) in order to fit a new building into their preexisting neighborhood. In medicine, it surfaces in patient-centered care when, as a woman is dying from cancer, the physician considers *her* ideal notion of life, health, and death rather than doggedly chasing the most aggressive treatment

(Hutchinson; Nuland; Charon). In this new order, where user participation is not just an ethical choice but an obligation, nostalgia urges empathy by revealing and negotiating the backstories of stakeholder desire (Zhou et al.). *What are you nostalgic for, why, and to which ends?*

Ultimately, then, *nostalgic design* is a three-step process of democratic creation by which designers use nostalgia to identify inequities and assets for critical redesign, mediate between conflicting ideal pasts and futures, and design more meaningful technologies. As a scholar and practicing consultant of rhetoric, technical communication, and design research, I specifically seek the new modes of communication, collaboration, education, expertise, and production designers develop to succeed in this age. To begin my search, this introductory chapter examines the historical path of nostalgia from passive illness to critical lens. I then use this lens to provide a glimpse of three nostalgic interactions that can change the way technology affects the world and that, thereby, structure the chapters of this book:

1. *Identifying Exclusionary Designs:* Nostalgic design is a way to listen for users who feel left out of current conceptions of science and technology and harness these users' divergent perspectives to create innovative futures through inclusion. (Chapter 2)
2. *Mediating Technological Conflicts:* Nostalgic design is a platform for designers to mediate between conflicting stakeholders and decentralize their own expertise by uncovering shared logics, encouraging empathy, and concurrently critiquing the present while maintaining hope for the future. (Chapters 3, 4, and 5)
3. *Designing Meaningful Products:* Nostalgic design is a way to localize designs and urge user investment, slowing the pace of technological consumption by actively encouraging citizens to record, recall, and rethink meaningful memories of use. (Chapter 6)

Within these three moves, it's my hope that *Nostalgic Design* will intrigue readers interested in memory studies, design studies, rhetoric and deliberative democracy, technical communication, and user experience architecture. At times, therefore, I ask that you bear with me through unfamiliar (or hyper-familiar) terrain. This book, like its central concept, relies on layering disparate traditions.

## Nostalgia: From Homesickness to Critical Method

Nineteen-year-old Swiss medical student Johannes Hofer coined the word "nostalgia" in his 1688 dissertation to describe the homesickness he saw in

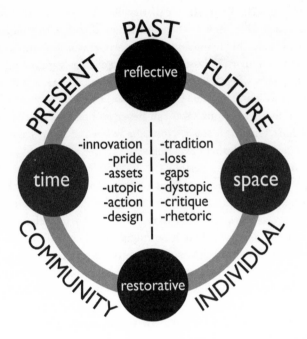

**Figure 1.2.** Nostalgia's defining tensions. On the left, one finds the creative elements of nostalgia, whereas on the right are its critical aspects. The boundary between these sides is permeable and, thereby, catalyzes nostalgia's ability as a critical production method.

mercenaries fighting abroad.[5] The term is a neologic portmanteau of the Greek *nostos* (return home) and *algos* (pain/sorrow). The root of the disease, Hofer theorized, was "the quite continuous vibration of animal spirits through those fibers of the middle brain in which impressed traces of ideas of the Fatherland still cling" (384). Though contemporary nostalgia tends to be considered a harmless longing, seventeenth-century nostalgia was more akin to modern depression, with symptoms ranging from loss of appetite to hearing voices to suicide. This deep pain of not feeling at home (still studied in refugee and military populations) was medical, real, and life altering. In its earliest days, nostalgia was also focused on spatial rather than temporal dislocation. Soldiers could potentially be cured through nostos—returning to a particular place in which they grounded their identities.

Yet, nostalgia always involves the tension between space and time, one of the many tensions that distinguish it from standard tradition or memory and, as you'll see in this book, make it a constantly moving target for would-be theorists (figure 1.2). We might recall the nostos voyage of the *Odyssey*, for example, and note that though Odysseus longs to return to Ithaca, once his adventure concludes, his home and identity are irrevocably changed by time. When he finally returns, Odysseus must slay Penelope's suitors to regain his kingdom. Yet, even when he recovers his lost home, he meets a tragic end in the *Telegony*, in which Telegonus, Odysseus's son by Circe, seeks out his father and unintentionally kills him. You can never go home again because people and places don't remain in stasis. Nostalgia is born of the permanent loss of time that is part of all human experience.

Thus, over the centuries nostalgia shifts from a medically defined homesickness, potentially cured by returning to the land of one's youth, to a culturally defined timesickness, as incurable as age. This distinction between space and time becomes particularly important with the advent of modern communication and travel. Though nostalgia would seem to be alleviated by the ability to quickly travel across space—to return home by plane, train, or Skype—it hasn't stopped. In fact, as literary theorist Svetlana Boym writes, "Somehow progress didn't cure nostalgia but exacerbated it. . . . In counterpoint to our fascination with cyberspace and the virtual global village, there is no less a global epidemic of nostalgia, an affective yearning for a community and a collective memory, a longing for continuity in a fragmented world" (*Future* xiv). Especially in our age of digital obsolescence, where technology and the cultures linked to it are constantly changing, citizens long for the seeming stability and authenticity of the past. "I'm actually quite a different person," Ödön von Horváth describes of the technological speed taking over the mindscape of the early twentieth century, "I just never get around to being him" (Rosa 317).

Nostalgia, therefore, inevitably rises with every technological and cultural revolution (F. Davis; Grainge; Boym). It reappears, for example, in nineteenth-century British, German, and American Romanticisms—often read as critical reposts to the technical advances of the Enlightenment and Industrial Revolution. Authors like William Wordsworth, the Brothers Grimm, and Washington Irving wander their childhood landscapes longing to restore losses endured with time by collecting personal and cultural folklore. In design, one sees a parallel anti-industrial push in William Morris's revival of handcrafted textiles and John Ruskin's praise of gothic architecture during the Arts and Crafts Movement. This nostalgic resistance echoes through today's craft revival (the subject of chapter 2), in which a generation that grew up on digital tech looks to physical making as a way to slow time, commune with permanence, and find meaning in knowledge-based jobs. Thus, nostalgia, as argued by Fred Davis, the first modern nostalgia critic, becomes progressively active, less a physical disease that afflicts a victim and more a critical apparatus to respond to change. It's perhaps unsurprising, then, that Constantine Sedikides et al. describe nostalgia's primary psychological function not as tentative homesickness but rather as a "resource that contributes to equilibrium in the self-system" ("Nostalgia Counteracts" 59). Nostalgia is homeostatic. When identity-disrupting events happen (moving, getting fired, signing divorce papers, having a loved one die), nostalgic reflection is a way to fight loneliness, write ourselves into a narrative of meaning, and create "self-continuity." Nostalgia is a portable safe space from which we can reach into the unknown.

As nostalgia slowly became a self-reflective tool, the motives of individual memory, collective memory, and national history catalyzed in the "memory crisis," from the French Revolution onward (Terdiman) and in the "memory boom" (Huyssen) of the 1980s. In both, cultural theorists debate the merits and failures of textbook histories, probing, "Who wants whom to remember what, and why?" (P. Burke 107). Progressive theorists accuse formal national histories of a politics of amnesia (forgetting the oppression and contributions of minority cultures) and, thereby, attempt to supplant history with the new field of memory studies, which democratizes and personalizes history.[6] From the oral narratives of Holocaust survivors to the personal archives of former slaves—memory studies unearths the alternative timelines of figure 1.1.[7] The memory boom also marks a shift in the ways memory is studied in the sciences. In the past, psychologists largely studied memory in terms of the accuracy of individual recall. But in the twentieth century, memory went social: "People's accounts of past events are treated not as a window onto the cognitive workings of memory, but as descriptions that vary according to whatever pragmatic and rhetorical work they are designed for, such that no single, decontextualized version can be taken as a reflection of the 'contents' of a person's 'memory'" (Middleton and Edwards 11). In a word, the act of remembering is always *rhetorical* (Phillips; Whittemore; Casey), designed to communicate a specific message to a specific audience for a specific purpose. We remember to redesign the world.

If we think of remembering as a rhetorical method for citizens to reach towards *eudaimonia*, and we see nostalgia, particularly, as a way to bring past ideals into the future, nostalgia becomes an excellent tool for designers to look for the diverse values of communities that have been ignored in the past. With the democratization of remembering comes the possibility of the democratization of making. Such democratization, Pierre Nora advances, defines the memory boom: "[T]his outbreak of memory is of a social nature and is linked to what might be called, by analogy with 'acceleration,' the 'democratization' of history. This takes the form of a marked emancipatory trend among peoples. . . . The explosion of minority memories of this kind has profoundly altered the respective status and the reciprocal nature of history and memory—or, to be more precise, has enhanced the very notion of 'collective memory,' hitherto little used" (440). Particularly important to understanding nostalgia, then, is that although it is terminologically about longing for a lost home, citizens long for lost pasts because they feel excluded from the present and, thereby, wish to create a future they are a part of. Hence, nostalgic design.

Still, the majority of research on nostalgic making, largely housed in media studies and advertising, has focused on critiquing (and occasionally deploying) nostalgia as an uncritical longing, a stale recycling, or a nefariously propagandistic weapon. As David Lowenthal comically lists, nostalgia has been accused of being "ersatz, vulgar, demeaning, misguided, inauthentic, sacrilegious, retrograde, reactionary, criminal, fraudulent, sinister, and morbid" (27). Because the memory crisis and boom grew in response to the amnesia of formal national histories and nostalgia is defined by its selective remembering, it is (often rightly) critiqued for perpetuating forgetting. There are reasons to be critical of nostalgia.

One of several catalysts of the democratization of memory, for instance, was Hitler's propagandistic use of German nationalist nostalgia to suggest the historical inevitability of the Third Reich. Art historian Crispin Sartwell traces the political aesthetics of Nazism (e.g., Speer's architecture and Riefenstahl's films) as they combine German romantic nationalism (Wagner, the Brothers Grimm, Herder) and nostalgic neoclassicism (Roman pillars and marble in massive proportions). "Hitler actually tried to develop a crypto-historiography," Sartwell writes. "He traced the Athenians and Spartans to German origins" (16, 25). Under this nostalgic aesthetic, policed by The Reich Chamber of Culture, there was only one nostalgic way to be German—Hitler's way. It's no surprise, then, that the Frankfurt School critical theorists that fled Germany would be anti-nostalgia.

In his *Fantasyland*, journalist Kurt Andersen traces a similar line of nostalgic anti-intellectualism flowing through America's history. Following the destruction of the Southern plantation system by the Civil War, for instance, one finds the myth of the happy slave, represented in Nate Salsbury's 1895 "Black America" traveling show, where one could find, as one *New York Times* reporter notes, "the labors that the Negroes of slavery days engaged in, and the happy, careless, life that they lived in their cabins" (119). Similarly, Andersen recounts Tennessee governor and U.S. senator Robert Love Taylor's nostalgic recollection of his youth on a plantation: "Every sunrise of summer was greeted by the laughter and songs of the darkies as they gathered in gangs and went forth in every direction to begin the labors of the day" (120). Lest we think that such feelings were limited to the turn of the twentieth century, when asked in 2017 what President Trump's Make America Great Again slogan meant to him, U.S. Senate candidate Roy Moore longed for the antebellum South: "I think it was great at the time when families were united—even though we had slavery—they cared for one another. . . . Our families were strong, our country had a direction" (Mascaro). Again, we see artificially sweetened pasts, endorsed by those in power, that pave over historical realities.

Moreover, in response to advances in new media, postmodern cultural theorists have criticized nostalgia's effect on history. Fredric Jameson describes, for example, the "nostalgia mode" of contemporary history in which recollection happens through a rose-lensed pastiche of media in order to call forth uncritical capitalist consumers. With the advance of recording technologies, history becomes "a vast collection of images, a multitudinous photographic simulacrum. . . . This mesmerizing new aesthetic mode itself emerged as an elaborated symptom of the waning of our historicity, of our lived possibility of experiencing history in some active way"—the real past is replaced by a consumerist pastness (*Postmodernism* 132, 135). And, yet, though Jameson may be right, his critique isn't new (see Plato's reaction against writing and Trithemius's distaste for the printing press), escapable, or automatically evil. And in making his argument, Jameson is ironically nostalgic for real history himself.[8]

Postmodern critic Linda Hutcheon traces this unwillingness of her colleagues to accept their own utopian nostalgias to their defining embrace of dystopian irony. She asks of postmodern architecture, for instance, "Was this postmodern recalling of the past an example of a conservative—and therefore nostalgic—escape to an idealized, simpler era of 'real' community values? (See Tafuri 1980, 52-9.) Or did it express, but through its ironic distance, a 'genuine and legitimate dissatisfaction with modernity'[?]" (Hutcheon and Valdés 18).

Importantly, then, as Kimberly K. Smith writes, nostalgia has consistently structured "progressive responses to the questions of whether and whose memory is a reliable basis for political action and what kinds of desires and harms are politically relevant" (505). Quickly dismissing nostalgia as regressive, conservative, and/or nationalist doesn't relieve us of its influences. Instead, it simply relieves critics of the responsibility of understanding an "illogical" group of constituents who aren't "progressive," and by scapegoating these nostalgics, blinds their accusers to their own nostalgic impulses. But, of course, like everyone, they too are nostalgic: for nature, for authentic culture, for slower precapitalist cycles of consumption.[9] Nostalgia, then, has been a tool of the powerful—but it has equally as often been a tool of grassroots resistance.

In contrast to these rejections of nostalgia, then, this book focuses on nostalgia's promise as a critical tool to observe and mediate multiple possible timelines. It's often been said that citizens need to know their history to know their future; I argue that designers need to know a culture's longing, pride, loss, and desire to know what's to come. To anchor this exploration, I draw upon a growing area of interdisciplinary nostalgia studies that considers the thoughtful aspects of nostalgia led by social psychologists Constantine Sedikides, Tim Wildschut, and Clay Routledge; political scientist Kimberly Smith; geographer Alastair Bonnett; eco-critic Jennifer Ladino; and designers Koert van Mensvoort and Heike Jenss. Most foundational for nostalgic design, however, is Svetlana Boym's continuum between two types of nostalgia: "Restorative nostalgia stresses *nostos* and attempts a transhistorical reconstruction of the lost home. Reflective nostalgia thrives in *algia*, the longing itself, and delays the homecoming—wistfully, ironically, desperately. Restorative nostalgia does not think of itself as nostalgia, but rather as truth and tradition. Reflective nostalgia dwells on the ambivalences of human longing and belonging and does not shy away from the contradictions of modernity. Restorative nostalgia protects absolute truth, which reflective nostalgia calls into doubt" (*The Future* xviii). To illustrate this difference, Boym describes the renovation of an Italian cathedral. Where restorative nostalgics might strip away layers of soot and superfluous additions, seeking the "original" intentions of the Renaissance architect, reflective nostalgics are "lovers of unintentional memorials of the past: ruins, eclectic constructions, fragments that carry 'age value.' Unlike total reconstructions, they allowed one to experience historicity affectively, as atmosphere, a space for reflection on the passage of time" (*Future* 15).

This distinction was illustrated in 2016, for instance, in a drive to question the historical figures after which many U.S. places are named. One of the fiercest debates was over President Woodrow Wilson's legacy at Princeton University (Hui; Martinez). His name and image adorn many campus sites, including the school of public policy and international affairs. In most textbook histories, Wilson, a former U.S. and Princeton president, is known for reawakening academic rigor in the Ivy League, his WWI reconstruction strategy, and his progressive policies from the Federal Reserve to Federal Farm and Loan. Often forgotten are Wilson's pro-segregation beliefs, expulsion of African Americans from federal office, and soft line on the Ku Klux Klan in his *A History of the American People*.

The rhetorics of nostalgia inundating this situation are deep. One group of *restorative nostalgics* advocated solely remembering the positive effects Wilson had on the campus and nation, dismissing his racism as an inescapable sign of the times. Another group sought to totally remove Wilson's name from Princeton—seeing erasure as a path towards healing. Interestingly, this faction suggested replacing Wilson with a number of black historical figures, such as Martin Luther King Jr., each with his or her own *restorative* politics. Finally, a group of *reflective nostalgics* simultaneously recognized Wilson's positive legacy while using that legacy as a means to critique the politics of amnesia involved in forgetting Wilson's racism in the first place. Artist Titus Kaphar, for example, proposes "amending" public sculptures and monuments: "I'm not saying erase it. . . . I want to make sculptures that are honest, that wrestle with the struggles of our past but speak to the diversity and advances of our present. . . . When we have a situation when we want to change a law in the American Constitution, we don't erase the other one. Along side that is an amendment. Something that says this is where we were—this is where we are, right now." What differentiates reflective nostalgia from restorative nostalgia, then, is that reflective nostalgics layer multiple traditions and futures (like layers of paint in a cathedral) rather than replacing one past ideal with another. They use the inescapability of nostalgia as a tool to open dialogues about equitable redesign.

Throughout this book I call such clashes of memory *nostalgic contact zones,* after Mary Louise Pratt's postcolonial "contact zones," "social spaces where cultures meet, clash, and grapple with each other, often in contexts of highly asymmetrical relations of power, such as colonialism, slavery, or their aftermaths as they are lived out in many parts of the world today" (34). Though nostalgia is classically viewed as a means to seek continuity with the past, thinking of nostalgia as a contact zone creates productive *dis*continuities that encourage innovative ways of thinking about the future. Ultimately, then, I don't care if nostalgia is good or bad. That's too simple. We're interested in why people feel nostalgic, how they use their pride and longing to shape the world, and what the feeling can tell us about the types of futures they want.

## Nostalgic Techno-Logics: Identifying Gaps and Assets

On December 1, 2015, Facebook CEO Mark Zuckerberg and pediatrician Priscilla Chan authored a public letter to their newborn daughter, Max. "Like all parents, we want you to grow up in a world better than ours today," Chan and Zuckerberg write. To engineer this better future, they announced the Chan Zuckerberg Initiative, through which they will give 99 percent of their Facebook shares—roughly 45 billion dollars—to redesign the world. As one might expect, a large portion of this funding has gone towards technology and technology-driven education. Zuckerberg and Chan, like numerous innovators before them, imagine technology, particularly the internet, as a democratizing force: "[S]tudents around the world will be able to use personalized learning tools over the Internet, even if they don't live near good schools. . . . [The internet] provides health information on how to avoid diseases or raise healthy children if you don't live near a doctor. It provides financial services if you don't live near a bank. It provides access to jobs and opportunities if you don't live in a good economy."

And, yet, granting universal access to technology doesn't inevitably cure social inequities. Langdon Winner critiqued this myth way back in 1986: "The political arguments of computer romantics draw upon a number of key assumptions: (1) people are bereft of information; (2) information is knowledge; (3) knowledge is power (4) increasing access to information enhances democracy and equalizes social power. . . . Alas, the idea. . . . mistakes sheer supply of information with an educated ability to gain knowledge and act effectively. (109). There's a difference between access to *information* (organized observations about the world) and an ability to apply *knowledge* (observations strategically deployed to act in context) (Tuomi). This doesn't mean that citizens who lack digital skill lack the knowledge to thrive in a digital world; it's that not all knowledge is valued equally. In a college filmmaking course, for example, a student skilled at creating popular YouTube videos might not be considered literate—despite the vast knowledge on production, virality, and distribution she can contribute (Shipka; Selfe "Students"). There are such layers of expertise everywhere; they grow in the alternative timelines of nostalgic design (figure 1.1). Good designers innovate from them.

Cynthia Selfe elaborates on the failure to see such neostalgic futures: "[B]ecause the push for technological literacy focuses on one officially sanctioned form of literacy, it encourages citizens to discount the complexities of literacy education and the importance of *multiple* literacies within our culture" (*Technology* xx). Equal access to technological things is not the same as equal access to technological literacy because technological inequity is not simply a thing-ed divide. It's a cultural, historical, socioeconomic, raced, gendered, aged, abilitied divide that sets up one official technocratic eudaimonia (often capitalist efficiency, productivity, profit) and bars others (eco-friendliness, religion, gender equality).[10] Anyone can be a scientist, engineer, or designer, this technocratic logic espouses, as long as you think like everyone else already in those fields. In this way, to democratize technology, beyond looking at access to a technology itself, designers must look to and create for the innumerable sociocultural ways of knowing technology—what we might call techno-logics—

surrounding and built into designs. There's a difference between *technological equity* and *techno-logical* equity. And by asking *What are you nostalgic for, why, and to which ends*, designers might reveal and innovate in this gap.

Given that Zuckerberg and Chan's letter is to their daughter, for instance, it's curious that they don't discuss one of the largest techno-logical gaps in the United States, the dropping number of women in science, technology, engineering, and mathematics (STEM). In 1983 women made up 37 percent of computing professionals; this number dropped to just 26 percent in 2013 (National Science Foundation). In its *Tech-Savvy: Educating Girls in the Computer Age*, the American Association of University Women (AAUW) Educational Foundation argues that girls are less likely to enter computer-centered fields than boys,[11] not because of a lack of access or ability but, rather, because girls view STEM techno-logics as male-dominated, isolating, and uncreative: "[G]irls are concerned about the passivity of their interactions with the computer as a 'tool'; they reject the violence, redundancy, and tedium of computer games; and they dislike narrowly and technically focused programming classes. Too often, these concerns are dismissed as symptoms of anxiety or incompetence that will diminish once girls 'catch up' with the technology" (ix). As usual, the emotion of not feeling at home with technology is dismissed rather than embraced as a catalyst for redesign.[12] But frustration surfaces when a technology has not been designed for a given type of user and, more importantly, the techno-logic that the frustrated user is employing.

The AAUW found, for instance, that one foundational gateway to computing that girls felt uncomfortable with was playing, coding, and hacking violent computer games with male main characters and over-sexualized portrayals of women. Girls felt gaming and, thereby, computers were not for them. "In the eyes of many of the female interviewees," literacy theorist Brigid Barron reports, "their male counterparts had 'come in programming since birth,' and had a knowledge base that far exceeded their own. . . . [E]xperience playing games was a significant pathway for a sense of competence. A lack of fit led many students to switch majors" (3). Though gaming culture has changed since the AAUW's 2000 study,[13] the target demographic for most companies is still men aged 18 to 34. In contrast, literacy gateways that target women's interests are dismissed as personal preference.

Looking at access to literacy through nostalgic contact zones encourages educators to have more diverse conversations about parallel gateways to literacy and, thereby, "provide access without people having to erase or leave behind different subjectivities" (Cope and Kalantzis 18). Currently, for example, there are numerous programs (AAUW, Scientista, WISE) that recruit women to STEM by promoting neostalgic visions of what it means to be a woman in the sciences. Each responds to the classic adage, you cannot be what you cannot see.

One such approach is pink technology (pejoratively "pink-washing"), a gateway that makes STEM literacy stereotypically "girly." Pink Legos, computer engineer Barbie—scientists can be princesses, too. There's nothing inherently wrong with pink literacy gateways; they can cultivate a sense of belonging for women in STEM, remove the stigma that STEM is unfeminine, and, at their best, promote a reflectively nostalgic feminist reappropriation of female stereotypes (see stitch 'n bitch in chapter 2). However, this approach *alone* can be restricting and infuriating. *Surprisingly*, not all women value the same feminine traditions. In December 2015, for example, IBM launched its #hackahairdryer Twitter campaign, which urged women to overcome the gender bias of STEM by taking apart a hairdryer to create a variety of science projects.[14] Though well intentioned, there was an immediate backlash by women in STEM against the stereotypes involved. Twitter user @iPeggy responds, "Yikes @IBM! I'm a girl & actually know OS Assembler language & have 'hacked' your MVS operating systems. Try again please! #HackAHair-Dryer" (Butler). @TheTrendyTechie directly attacks the restorative nostalgia of the campaign: "How to make progress in equality: start treating women like modern human beings instead of the 1950s housewife trope. #HackA-HairDryer" (Franch). Such essentialism is why nostalgia must be thought of as a contact zone, a tension of numerous right ideals. It's also why progress and tradition must be carefully negotiated, hand in hand.

Another channel for welcoming women into STEM is raising awareness of the historical and continuing importance of women scientists: a feminist historiography of science that builds a nostalgic tradition of female heroes that future scientists might join (Smith and Erb). By looking into the history of science with an eye to recovering women, one discovers revolutionaries like the first computer programmer, Ada Lovelace; radioactivity theorist Marie Curie; NASA mathematician and physicist Katherine Johnson; and the coders of ENIAC, the first U.S.-built programmable computer. Such feminist historiography is reflectively nostalgic, seeking to remember uniquely positive contributions of women that have been lost through the sexist nature of history in order to create a tradition from which women can act today. If one side of the emotion of nostalgia is loss and exclusion, the other is pride in the past upon which citizens rhetorically construct a positive identity and a space to be included.

An equally vital part of such nostalgic recovery, however, is tracking STEM literacies in places where they've been ignored in the past—asking neostalgic questions like, What technological literacy did your great-grandmother, who was a homemaker and not a trained scientist, have? In the next chapter, for example, we'll continue to meet Donna, a former programmer who sees knitting as a gateway to software programming. As Leah Buechley, designer and MIT professor, describes, "Knitting, crochet, or yarn textile crafts are very algorithmic activities. . . . There is a pattern that you follow that involves repetitions and looping and if-then. It's really an engineering discipline to turn a 1-D thing, a string, into a 3D thing" (Kraft). Thus, knitting becomes a new old way—a *neostalgic mode*—of teaching and rethinking engineering.

In the end, one of the primary reasons for bolstering techno-logical diversity is that inclusivity leads to better designs. Without female engineers, design errors have been made from early voice recognition software that couldn't identify the tones of women (Margolis and Fisher) to airbags designed for large male crash test dummies that killed children and small-statured adults (Shaver; Vinsel) to womanless senate committees writing female birth control legislation. One of the central goals of inclusion, therefore, is to transform the dominant techno-logic to benefit everyone. Currently, for example, as women are increasingly recruited to STEM, there has been a challenge to the way that Silicon Valley's new capitalism—from all-night hackathons to weekend volleyball games—excludes workers with children. What if nostalgic ideals of motherhood were designed into high-tech workplaces? By layering traditions of womanhood and workerhood, several companies (Facebook, Google, Netflix) are leading workplace reform towards better-paid maternity and paternity leave. Nostalgia encourages designers to consider what other better futures—excluded pasts as redesign assets—like this might be recovered.

## Nostalgic Deliberation: Rhetorically Mediating Traditions

And, yet, such inclusive design is easy in theory but tricky in practice. Once multiple nostalgias and the techno-logics they embody are identified as signs of struggle and assets for redesign, a designer has a critical question to face: If my goal is achieving inclusive and equitable designs, what do I do with conflicting stakeholders with dissonant nostalgic ideals? This is a defining question for the field of rhetoric, the art of designing unique texts for unique audiences with unique eudaimonia to produce unique reactions. Rhetoric is indeterminate; it thrives in alternative timelines. There are always multiple right futures and, as theories from Protagoras's sophism to Kenneth Burke's identification argue, ethical makers create from, for, and with that indeterminacy in mind. "If technology is in some fundamental sense concerned with the probable rather than the necessary—with the contingencies of practical use and action, rather than the certainties of scientific principle—then it becomes rhetorical in a startling fashion," writes designer and rhetorician Richard Buchanan ("Declaration" 6–7). "It becomes an art of deliberation about the issues of practical action, and its scientific aspect is, in a sense, only incidental." Thus, given the democratization of expertise and a parallel surge of collaborative, user-centered, and participatory design, it's increasingly the designer's job to urge and mediate arguments (Schön; Forester; Faga; Monteiro) by unearthing *stases*: shared questions, problems, and values. In such deliberations, nostalgia's ability to generate empathy, reveal tradition as foundational to expertise, open stakeholders to change, and encourage agonism is invaluable.

Take, for example, a 2011 episode of the radio program *This American Life* in which host Ira Glass interviews Erin Gufstafson, a conservative high schooler who believes "global warming is propaganda." As an experiment, Glass enlists Roberta Johnson, a climatologist and executive director of the National Earth Science Teachers Association, to persuade Gufstafson that global warming exists. Johnson lays out the best evidence she can, but in the end, the teen is not satisfied. In one of Johnson's final remarks, we see why the experiment failed: "My point is that this is really not a question of belief. This is a question of science. We look at the evidence, we use our scientific knowledge, and we come to science-based conclusions" ("Kid Politics"). Johnson is baffled that Gufstafson sees global warming as debatable.

In rhetorician Sharon Crowley's terms, Johnson speaks at Gufstafson through a *fundamentalism*, "a general imperative to assert an absolute, singular ground of authority; to ground your own identity and allegiances in this unquestionable source; to define political issues in a vocabulary of God, morality, or nature that invokes such a certain, authoritative source" (12). Note the echoes of restorative nostalgia. Though many listeners may hear Gufstafson's rejection of science as biased, more crucial for designers, Johnson speaks from a "liberal fundamentalism," a refusal to negotiate with "tradition, authority, or desire" (Crowley 15).

A similar rejection occurs when I ask writers in my technical communication courses to explain a scientific argument to nonbelievers or, alternatively, to negotiate with a client who wants a weak design. These writing students initially turn to rhetorical fallacies and hostile rebuttals that poke holes in their audience's reasoning: "Let me tell you all the ways you're wrong." Indeed, when faced with conflict, an expert's first response is often such tribalism, a restoratively nostalgic defense of her training. Holding tight to expertise as truth, she views potential collaborators as enemies in a zero-sum game (Ball et al.). Why should scientists have to teach, persuade, and collaborate with idiots? Because science doesn't exist in a political vacuum, and harsh denials don't foster productive working relationships with the citizens and legislators who control how science and technology are funded and enacted. Successful designers, then, can't ignore Aristotle's chief rhetorical edict: "Rhetoric forms enthymemes from things that seem true to people already accustomed to deliberate among themselves" (*On*, 1.2.11, 1356b). Good alliances start from what is true to stakeholders.

If designers, as Manzini describes, "today find themselves in a world where everybody designs and . . . their task tends to be to use their own initiatives to help a variegated array of social actors to design better," then (as chapters 3, 4, and 5 explore) they must study rhetorical tact in understanding, adapting to, and occasionally refusing the expertise of their stakeholders (*Design when 2*). But even refusals start from knowing an audience and locating rejections within their goals. It's in this light that nostalgia becomes an invaluable tool for mediation because it develops *empathy*, urging designers to understand the non-logos-based techno-logics of emotion, pride, loss, and tradition from which many of their collaborators' (as well as their own) ideals harken. In fact, psychologically, nostalgia primes productive alliances because feelings of nostalgia usually relate to special people during positive events. That is, as psychologists Xinyue Zhou et al. found in a series of five experiments, "nostalgia recreates the meaningful bonds one has with other persons and, in the process, fosters a renewed sense of social connectedness and secure attachment (Sedikides et al. 2008, 2009; Wildschut et al. 2006). Processes that increase social connectedness and secure attachment, in turn, provide the foundation for empathy, willingness to help others, and helping behavior (Mikulincer et al. 2001, 2005)" (Zhou et al.). Thus, nostalgic mediations start by listening to back-in-the-day stories (Forester, "Beyond"; Forester, *Deliberative Practitioner*; Winslade and Monk): *What are you nostalgic for, why, and to which ends?*

In the case of Gufstafson and Johnson, for instance, rather than vaulting straight to scientific facts, Johnson might have realized that the teenager's techno-logic was based in conservative tradition and, thereby, addressed the teenager's "moral foundations" (Haidt): environmental protection is humanity's God-directed duty as stewards of the Earth; the pollution that causes climate change is an attack on individual liberties; it is patriotic to conserve the country's resources and the tradition of the national park service (see Ladino; Feinberg and Willer; Feygina et al.). All these arguments are posed so that Gufstafson feels climate protection advances her nostalgic ideals of biblical tradition, life, liberty, and the pursuit of happiness. She doesn't have to reject her conservative ingroup identity in order to protect the environment. Nostalgic exploration reveals she already is someone who should believe in climate change. The goal, here, is not pulling the wool over an audience's

eyes but exposing layers of reflective nostalgia, common ground, stases, the
convalescence of truths (Bush and Folger).

The need for such tact reveals a key complication of design expertise: the
distinction between *epistemic technê* and *mêtis*-centric *technê*.[15] In *Nichomachean
Ethics*, Aristotle marks epistemè (ideal knowledge) as discrete from technê (ex-
perience-based craft). The field of design seems squarely situated in technê, "a
state of capacity to make, involving a true course of reasoning. All art is concerned with coming into being." (6.4.10, 1140a). Yet, designers obviously draw
upon theoretical knowledge—their training in best practices. Thus, design is
*epistemic technê*—a form of making that relies on theory. At its best, epistemic
technê is well-reasoned design, adaptive reflective nostalgia in which designers use theories as chords to improvise upon. At its worst it's what Manzini
calls "big ego design" in which, as we've seen, the designer falls defensively
into restorative nostalgia: the Eiffel Tower wouldn't have been built through
design by committee; my training and experience are the only reasonable way
to see things; it's my way or the highway!

To counter big egos, productive collaborations balance epistemic technê
with user knowledge: mêtis. In Greek mythology, Metis was Zeus's first wife,
the titan of cunning intelligence, know-how, and trickery (de Certeau; Detienne and Vernant; Dolmage). Because he fears her guile, Zeus devours Metis,
and she, thereafter, lives up in his head as wise counsel. Theorist of user-centered design Robert Johnson argues that mêtis might be thought of as the
tactical and contextual expertise of the user. In operating a design, users
learn it, hack it, adapt it, redesign it and, thereby, know it in a singular way.
Where an architect may be an expert in designing a house, for instance, the
homeowner adapts the house to their specific needs by living in it. Mêtis
makes a house a home. But where the dark side of epistemic technê is big
egos, the dark side of mêtis is a customer-is-always-right philosophy in which
professional designers simply defer to users rather than interjecting their own
skill. The strongest designs come from the agonistic collaboration of multiple
expertise—and agonism relies on conflict.

The field of design has employed a host of methods to foster such collaborations (see chapter 3), frequently based in user-centered (Norman and
Draper), human-centered (Buchanan, "Human Dignity"; LUMA Institute),
and participatory/co-design (Simonsen and Robertson) traditions. For example, defining participatory design for years to come, Pelle Ehn and Morten
Kyng's early-1980s action research in the UTOPIA project introduced new
digital technologies into a traditional newspaper production industry. Swedish computer and social scientists co-designed with printshop union workers
(Ehn; Ehn and Kyng). Through this alliance the designers melded epistemic

technê and mêtis, creating digital programs that highlighted and harnessed the expertise of workers rather than replacing it. They created an alternative future by creatively layering multiple pasts.

And, yet, contrasting rhetoric's embrace of turbulence, many user-centered and participatory design methods have strayed from their emancipatory foundations, skirting conflict because it costs time and money. Ehn, Elisabet Nilsson, and Richard Topgaard challenge, for instance, "Inventive as it may seem, this new paradigm is surprisingly traditional and managerial. The main challenge put forward is still how large corporations can harvest users' and consumers' innovations into safe and profitable mass-market products" ("Making" 3). In the index of my *Routledge International Handbook of Participatory Design*, the words "conflict," "mediation," "argument," and "debate" are conspicuously absent.[16] In contrast, to foster productive diversity, nostalgic design actively complicates ideal scenarios by situating multiple ideals in contact zones.

At roughly the same time Ehn and Kyng were working on UTOPIA, for example, Mutirão 50 (Cabannes; Faga) was a participatory housing project in Fortazela, Brazil, where millions squat illegally in *favelas*, or makeshift homes. The goal of *mutirão* (collective effort) was development through empowerment, teaching residents to build not only safer houses but also sustainable communities. There had been attempts at mutirão programs in the past, but where Mutirão 50 differed, as coordinator Yves Cabbanes explains, was that "the land should be given to the organization, existing grassroots groups are respected and there is no creation of a new one" (35). Mutirão 50 sought to innovate through tradition, empowering the mêtis of preexisting organizations and using ideals already in the favelas rather than forming new ones. To do so, Cabbanes's team carefully mediated the traditions of the state, architects, local gangs, and households in a nostalgic contact zone.

Cabbanes describes, for instance, how he responded to one clash of nostalgias—designer versus community: "You need to accept that you can be wrong even in your own field. . . . When your nice model with its tiny verandah and its expandable capacities is publicly rejected and a simpler square-shaped one proposed by a resident with no education is chosen, some young professionals would simply leave. But the community was right" (Faga 185). From a nostalgic design viewpoint, Cabbanes understands that his ideal design, based in his epistemic nostalgia of good architecture, clashed with homeowners' nostalgic notions of design, based in their mêtis of favelas. This is the democratization of expertise. Nostalgia brings a self-awareness to our place in time—seeking out the origins of our identities as experts. That is, viewing expertise as nostalgic denaturalizes it, ideally opening it to change. Indeed, as researched by van Tilburg, Sedikides, and Wildschut, because nostalgic thought processes remind citizens that they have a place in the world, they psychologically make citizens less defensive and more creative and open to new experiences: "Nostalgia instigates approach tendencies (Stephan et al., 2014) and optimism (Cheung et al., 2013) both of which reduce conservatism and diminish aversion to risk (Anderson & Galinsky, 2006; Friedman & Förster, 2000, 2002); these effects, in turn, are positively associated with openness (Hinze et al., 1997; Van Hiel & Mervielde, 2004)" ("Mnemonic Muse" 3). Such openness is crucial for collaboration.

Ultimately, what's acutely useful about nostalgia for democratic mediations, then, is how it reveals motivations for and tensions between multiple simultaneously right traditions and, thereby, multiple right futures (figure 1.1). Where previous Kuhnian models of technological progress were based on a replacement model—scientists discover something new (the world is round, revolves the sun, etc.) that replaces an older idea—this is no longer the case. Today, as argued by Cynthia Selfe and Gail Hawisher, "[L]iteracies accumulate rapidly. . . . During such periods of rapid change, humans value and practice both past and present forms of literacy simultaneously" (213–14).

## Nostalgic Designs: Meaning through Memory

So far, I've described how nostalgia enhances the *process* of design, from locating gaps and inequities to mediating conflicts. In contrast, the third stage of nostalgic design discussed in this book is planning for nostalgic products and experiences. From this perspective, nostalgic designs are creations that foster long-term emotional investment, encourage slow reflectiveness, and engage the traditions of their users. Nostalgic designs plan for, record, and evoke meaningful memories of use.

In the vignettes that preface this chapter, for instance, I described the power of Facebook and other social media as nostalgic designs that inspire the active collection of events to be reminisced over in the future. Sites like Facebook advocate for the "musealization" (Lübbe) of the self—defining one's identity upon a curated public archive and, thereby, living life in a state of anticipatory nostalgia. The sway of this triggering shouldn't be underestimated; it's a form of intimate labor that encourages investment in a design and discourages neglect. One sees this persuasive attachment in the message that appears if you try to delete your Facebook profile: "Are you sure you want to deactivate your account? [Your friend's name] will miss you. Send [your friend] a message." As behavioral designer Nir Eyal argues, by referencing a user's friends, Facebook underscores the value of "the collection of memories and experiences, in aggregate" and, therefore, prevents you from leaving (147). Of course, though Eyal appreciates the benefits of such nostalgic persuasion to a company, the ethical designer sees its pitfalls as well—overwhelming users with collection, distracting them from living in the present. Nostalgic designers must take care.

Indeed, as a "technology of memory" (Sturken; Erll; Radley; Van Dijck; Van House and Churchill), the features of Facebook (receiving likes, friending, On This Day, etc.) inspire users to remember a certain kind of memory and, thereby, be a certain type of person. Because they want to make themselves look good, users, for instance, are much more likely to publicly recall positive memories than negative ones. The site, thereby, causes the psychological effects of "Facebook envy" and "Facebook depression" (Tandoc et al.; Steers et al.). Everyone on Facebook is seemingly and constantly receiving promotions, getting married, having babies, buying houses, looking their best, and eating gourmet meals. Continually viewing others' nostalgias—their best versions of themselves—causes users to reflect negatively on their own lives.

Even more intriguing, one's nostalgic self remains after death. Facebook "memorializes" accounts when their creators die, essentially letting users write their own eulogies (Moreman and Lewis; Church; Kalan; Vealey). As one Facebook help page describes: "You can tell us in advance whether you'd like to have your account memorialized or permanently deleted from Facebook. Memorialized accounts are a place for friends and family to gather and share memories after a person has passed away. . . . The word Remembering will be shown next to the person's name on their profile[;] Depending on the privacy settings of the account, friends can share memories on the memorialized Timeline[;] Content the person shared (ex: photos, posts) stays on Facebook."

Yet, at the same time that we are becoming a culture of nostalgia, saving bits of our identity to reminisce over, there's a tension between collecting an identity and accumulating memories we wish to forget. "What shall we dream of when everything becomes visible?" theorist of speed Paul Virilio asks. "We'll dream of being blind" (Wilson). In response to this tension, citizens of the European Union implemented a legislatively defined "right to be forgotten." They can legally request that search engines remove links to information that they feel misrepresents them (European Commission; Toobin; Rosen). The tensions, politics, and disparities of power revealed when technology is examined through nostalgic contact zones highlights the troubles of such a right. On the one hand, individuals now have a direct route to removing destructive content, from faulty tax information to revenge porn. On the other hand, powerful corporations, politicians, and the like have a legal way to remove information about themselves—fraud, racism, sexism—that is critical to public decision-making.

Beyond engaging personal memories, another key quality of designs that harness the power of nostalgia—from a cherished childhood teddy bear to an antique armoire—is that they last long enough to pick up memories of use. Consumers are less likely to throw something away if they have a nostalgic attachment to it. Ideally, then, nostalgic designs age with grace and encourage a mindfulness of the lifecycle of consumption. Use becomes stewardship. Contrasting the "archival fever" (Derrida) of Facebook, for instance, design collectives Eternally Yours and SlowLab promote *slow design*, a revolutionary harnessing of nostalgia to slow the pace at which objects are consumed and, thereby, increase the rate at which they become meaningful (Fuad-Luke; Hallnäs and Redström; Strauss and Fuad-Luke; van Hinte; Grosse-Hering et al.). Creating shoes and handbags that are easily repaired, choosing materials (e.g., leather and wood) that pick up character (and memories) as they age, teaching skilled consumption like wine tasting, which values age and decay as cultural capital—"Stop, wait, think," slow design advises.

Consider making a cup of coffee. Where one user may deploy a Keurig coffeemaker to quickly produce a cup with the least thought (and most waste) possible, French press coffee is a slow design alternative. As consumers grind the beans, boil the water, and deal with the mess of leftover grounds, coffee becomes ritual, even religion. The French press slows consumption; it makes consumers mindful of and take pleasure in coffee as an experience. In many ways, slow design parallels the Japanese concept of *mono no aware*, "an empathy towards things," a wistful awareness of the decay and ephemeral beauty of the world. Mono no aware is present, for example, in the *wabi-sabi* aesthetic, which finds beauty in natural cycles of growth and decay, such as aging wood and the leisurely development of rust on metal. In slow design, things become actants in their own plays away from human users and pick up an "aura," in Walter Benjamin's terms, a unique object memory that no other design possesses. Such individuality is prized in an era of digital replicas.

Though nostalgic designs encourage users to meditate over the life cycle of their possessions, they also encourage users to reflect on their own lifecycles—seeing that designs might need to transform to help consumers themselves age with grace. Matthias Hollwich, for instance, is an architect who designs spaces with elderly occupants in mind, a concept he calls "new aging," which reminds designers: "[T]he interesting thing about 'the elderly' is that they are YOU and ME in a few years—so, in the end, we design for our own future! And, yes, architects should have long-term thinking in mind—but they should turn the issue around and use aging as inspiration." Hollwich considers what—accessibility, independence, community—the elderly nostalgically long for and how designers, through anticipatory nostalgia, can create rooms, homes, and communities now that prevent this loss later. Such an ethic of aging in place might be called *anticipatory design*—collaborating with our future selves.

Chinese *bālínghòu*, East German *ostalgie*, U.S. hip-hop's old school—a final feature of nostalgia as an inclusive design asset is its universality. Erica Hepper et al. have found similar feelings of nostalgia across eighteen countries and five continents. Such cross-cultural presence makes *nostalgic localization*—the use of a community's nostalgia to make technologies and designs fit a preexisting tradition—especially fruitful. The camping company BioLite's HomeStove, for example, is a cooking stove designed to reduce the amount of smoke inhaled from open cooking fires. In creating their stove, BioLite knew that they would be distributing to different cultures with different needs and, thereby, turned to anthropologists to localize their design. These anthropologists turned to cooking mêtis. They realized that innovation without tradition would lead to alienation and that their product would fail if it wasn't adapted. In the Indian state of Gujarat, therefore, HomeStove would have to successfully cook the staple bread *rotla* (World Design). At first, the stove cooked the bread unevenly and was rejected: "In response, BioLite is developing a cooking attachment to spread the flame even wider for rotla preparation. . . . [U]sers were pleased that the clay tawa on which the rotla was prepared fit snugly on the top cooking surface. However, BioLite decided to increase the number of supports on the surface from 3 to 6 to enable pots to fit even more securely and to accommodate a wider range of pots reflective of our diverse target customer base." HomeStove underwent a nostalgic localization by way of delayed differentiation; the stove was adapted to fit into a preexisting cultural ideal to prevent the types of nostalgic loss typical innovation creates.

In contrast, Sun explains that when altruistic designers attempt production *without* localization, designs can fail before they even begin. She describes how a group of designers attempted to build an electric well inside a small Indian village to aid women in fetching water. But the well kept getting mysteriously destroyed. "It turned out," Sun narrates, "that in an Indian village, married young women have the lowest status in a big family and they must listen to the orders of their mothers-in-law. Walking one hour to carry water was tedious and laborious; however, that was the only time in the day they could enjoy friends' company and have some time for themselves" (20). Again, the designer must be aware of nostalgic contact zones. Ideal practices (e.g., those of mothers- and daughters-in-law) often conflict within communities and are nostalgically protected.

Of course, though I value nostalgia enough to write a book about it, it's no panacea. As we'll see, nostalgic design has its pitfalls—especially when it's restorative or monolithic. To counter opinions that the company has become too corporate, for example, the coffee giant Starbucks began tailoring individual shops to fit each city it enters by employing local artists and styles. The irony of this localization is that the presence of Starbucks in a neighborhood often drives out existing local coffee shops (Thompson and Arsel). Because it hasn't started from an ethic of participatory design nor taken into account the uneven power dynamics of the nostalgic contact zone, Starbucks builds an artificial notion of the local and ends up with less localization and more gentrification and appropriation. Throughout this book we need to remember, as Boym warns, "Nostalgia can be a poetic creation, an individual mechanism of survival, a countercultural practice, a poison, a cure. It is up to us to take responsibility for our nostalgia and not let others 'prefabricate' it for us. The prepackaged 'usable past' may be of no use to us if we want to co-create our future" ("Nostalgia" 456).

In the end, then, rather than exploiting niche markets, nostalgic design ideally leads to a transformation of the dominant techno-logic. Nostalgic design, as craft theorist Glenn Adamson writes, "affords an opportunity to think otherwise" through an anarcheology of the past in which designers look for lost techno-logics and timelines that might make the future more fully human (136).

Over the course of the next five chapters, I continue to lay out the key moves of nostalgic design—identifying (chapter 2), mediating (chapters 3, 4, 5), and designing (chapter 6) within nostalgic contact zones—with the goal of illustrating how nostalgia's ability to revolutionize through revolving back can humanize all stages of the design process.

Chapter 2 explores nostalgia as a form of technological resistance and commemoration as a type of user redesign from which creators can learn. Specifically, I analyze the rise of do-it-yourself craft nostalgia in an era of digital work and ephemeral products. To do so, I explore how and why three women—Donna, Jo, and Kit—use nostalgic crafting on the job to rhetorically resist the overreach of new capitalism into their home lives, pose feminine identities in masculine workplaces, and materialize labor in jobs that primarily result in intangible products. Donna, Jo, and Kit use nostalgic mêtis to reshape their worlds. Through this analysis, I develop a method of *critical nostos*—a technique by which designers analyze nostalgic returns home for exclusions in designs and assets for redesign.

Where chapter 2 argues that designers can make their products/texts more inclusive through analyzing nostalgic resistances, chapter 3 describes how designers might mediate the conflicting nostalgias of designers, clients, and users that critical nostos reveals. To do so, I juxtapose the ways the fields of design and rhetoric imagine democratic making. On the rhetorical side, I examine how Aristotle, Kenneth Burke, Krista Ratcliffe, and Chantal Mouffe conceive of deliberative democracy. Through audience analysis, identification, listening, and agonism, each rhetorician distinctively theorizes how communicators should interact with their audiences, who should make decisions in a collective, and, thereby, what role epideictic nostalgia plays in keeping a community together. On the design side, I examine how several deliberative design theories—user-centered design, participatory design, empathic design, and agonistic design—map onto and complicate each rhetorical perspective. Ultimately, this chapter develops *rhetorical design,* a theory of deliberative production that encourages stakeholders to debate, persuade, and deliberate before, during, and after a design is created.

Chapter 4 delves into the caverns of design mediation, testing how the ideals of nostalgic design and inclusivity developed in chapter 3 succeed or fail in a highly controversial medical co-design forum: the U.S. anti-vaccination movement. Currently, numerous physicians simply refuse to see children whose parents decline vaccines (Opel et al.)—but this fundamentalist reaction is far from rhetorical, not considering its audience or why vaccine refusals occur. It doesn't resolve the problem of vaccine hesitancy. Instead, by examining the nostalgic rhetoric of anti-vaccination celebrity parents Jenny McCarthy and Jim Carrey, vaccine inventor Paul Offit, and a public hearing over the pro-vaccination California Senate Bill 277, I demonstrate how the equitable question-asking process of *nostalgic stasis theory* unearths logical narratives, destabilizes closed professional expertise, promotes empathy, and builds common ground. In doing so, I work from narrative mediation experts John Winslade and Gerald Monk's concern with "the opportunity that might be missed in the process of quickly dismissing stories as unreliable. What might be missed is the work done by stories to *construct* realities, not just to *report* on them, apparently inaccurately" (2). Ultimately, this chapter demonstrates how a nostalgic analysis of conflict can help develop rhetorical strategies for co-design between even the most polarized parties.

Chapter 5 continues to fill in gaps on how to pragmatically achieve democratic technologies by investigating how nostalgia appears and assists practicing designers in client negotiations, focusing on tactfully adapting, adopting, and refusing client expertise. I interview three designers—Lux, a freelance brand designer; Grant, a graphic designer and university instructor; and Mason, an ER doctor. Each has unique methods of interacting with good and bad clients by developing trust, running through rituals of co-education, and opening space for client co-design. When one looks carefully at Lux's, Grant's, and Mason's most meaningful collaborations, they are almost always based in a rhetoric of memory, tradition, and expertise. That is, each designer creates a transactive memory system by which they overtly illustrate the memories behind their expertise and ask clients to do the same, an ethic I call *memorial interactivity*.

Finally, chapter 6 steps back from design deliberation and communication and ponders how designers (especially at a mass scale) can create designs that collect memories and become increasingly meaningful when used—a blueprint I call *nostalgic user experience architecture*. From a favorite pair of faded blue jeans to one's Facebook account, meaningful designs record, store, and emit memories of use. But how can such memories be planned? And what are the cultural and technological implications of wielding nostalgia in this way? To answer these questions, I catalogue, rhetorically analyze, and derive best practices from designs that spark three nostalgic desires: (1) narratability (the appetite to tell stories about meaningful interactions), (2) craft (memories associated with building an object), and (3) connoisseurship (participating in consumerism that requires memorable protocols as badges of membership).

# Chapter 2

# Nostalgic Resistances

## Remembering as Critical Redesign in Everyday Workplaces

Nostalgia can project the absent ideal into the past or into the future, but mainly it's about not feeling at home in the here-and-now, a sensation of alienation.

**Simon Reynolds, *Retromania***

There came a certain point where most people's jobs are about going somewhere and sitting at a desk all day. . . . [Y]our product is pixels. . . . [T]here were people who were frustrated with that "I came home at the end of this eight hours, and I don't have anything to show for it." And, so, knitting was a way of, like, I'm still doing something with my time, but at the end of that time there's a physical object here I can show you.

**Donna, former software designer and avid knitter, *personal interview***

In 1971, after years of observing women's expertise being ignored and actively rejected in art education, Judy Chicago and Miriam Schapiro founded the first feminist college arts program. While waiting on a new space at the Cal Arts building, Chicago, Schapiro, twenty-one students, and three local fiber artists gathered in an abandoned Victorian mansion. As an inaugural manifesto, each chamber of this house was revived as an art project, using traditional handicraft to speak to high art's ignorance of feminine making. "Women had been embedded in houses for centuries and had quilted, sewed, baked, cooked, decorated and nested their creative energies away," Chicago recalls. "What would happen, we wondered, if women took those very same homemaking activities and carried them to fantasy proportions?" (104). With that question, *Womanhouse* was born. Longing for lost artistic futures, in one *neo*stalgic fantasy, Faith Wilding's "Crocheted Environment" grew from walls and ceilings, a huge web of white crochet. "Close-up, the yarn and cord, knotted in a rough pattern of bumps and gaps, resemble a wall of cells in the body," recalls *New York Times* art critic M. G. Lord. "The viewer feels enveloped in an organic space—eerily, disconcertingly in utero." The artists of *Womanhouse* nostalgically, ironically, and resistantly recovered a sullied tradition of handicraft in order to question who counts as an artist. Within this use of tradition, Glenn Adamson describes, "amateurism functioned as a rhetorical device—a reminder that the playing field was not equal—but also a means of working through the particularity of a marginal subject position" (143). Cast out pasts designed inclusive futures.

Performing a similar feat of activist nostalgia, on September 5, 1981, the Welsh group Women for Life on Earth (WLE) set upon England's Greenham Common Royal Air Force Base. They had just marched one hundred miles from Cardiff, Wales. On arrival, members delivered a letter to the base commander protesting the governmental decision to house ninety-six nuclear missiles and requesting a debate of the issue. When their appeal was ignored, WLE constructed the all-women's Greenham Common Peace Camp, which endured an astounding nineteen years. The rhetoric of the camp was built upon the traditional rights of motherhood. These women were protesting for the safety of their own children and future generations. Visually, this femininity was marked by handicrafts hung on the chain link fence circling the base. Intricately woven banners, knitted children's toys, baby clothes—peace camp occupants used their status as self-described low-tech "ordinary mums" (Anderson) to juxtapose the high-tech violence of the base. When the air force hired a bulldozer to destroy the camp's tree house, for example, it was halted by craft. The driver recounts in court, "[T]he girls got in front of the machine. They stood there and a couple walked round [the bulldozer] with woolen string, going round and round with it" (Lothian 10). Craft nostalgia was invoked to protest a society where ordinary citizens were left out of technical decisions. No one asked these women if they wanted to live near warheads. By recalling a nostalgic identity—motherhood—in which they held traditional power, the WLE built a dais from which to be heard.

More recently, from April 7 to 11, 2006, a World War II Chaffee combat tank loomed outside of Copenhagen's Nikolaj Contemporary Art Center. Slowly, this menacing war machine turned pink. Led by Danish artist Marianne Jørgensen, the feminist craft collective the Cast Off Knitters covered the tank with over four thousand knitted pink squares mailed in by international knitters to protest the Iraq war. The tank's pink jacket recalls a tea cozy made "of hundreds of patches knitted by many different people in different ways: single colored, stripes with bows or hearts, loosely knitted, closely knitted, various knitted patterns" (Jørgensen). *Pink Tank* stresses the power of individual actions—even the smallest design of a soft pink square—when gathered en masse. Craft theorists Anthea Black and Nicole Burisch depict this rhetorical muscle as analogous to rewriting history through memory: "It links remembrance of the war with our collective ability to reinterpret and affect it through public action, dissent, and dialogue" (209). Clearly, nostalgia empowers individuals to redesign the world when larger technocratic forces won't listen.

Over the last half century, there's been a surge in the consumption of crafts, from Etsy's digital bazaar to local farmers markets to the explosive growth of craft beer. Citizens have turned to the security of a completed past at a time when the technological present and future feel unknown, uncomfortable, or exclusionary. But, as these opening examples illustrate, paralleling craft *consumerism* is an uptick in *craftivism* by citizens who feel ignored by traditional forms of democracy and, therefore, literally build a better world in which they are included. Defined by Betsy Greer as simply "the use of creativity for the improvement of the world," craftivism characterizes makers who have taught "knitting lessons, sewed scarves for battered women's shelters, and knitted hats for chemotherapy patients. . . . [C]raftivism allows those who wish to voice their opinions and support their causes the chance to do just that." *Womanhouse*, the Greenham Common Peace Camp, and *Pink Tank* are all radical examples of such arts of the nostalgic contact zone, performative acts of resistant remembering used to create a better technological future by neostalgically designing with an eye towards better pasts. But what if I told you that such provocative nostalgic resistances surround you every day?

Quite a bit of attention has been paid to public political struggles of contemporary craft artists (Adamson) and activists (Buszek; Greer). Much less attention (Fields; Hackney; Dant) has been spent on the daily confrontations of contemporary crafters who don't see their making as overtly political but still use their skills to redesign the world all the same. To speak to this gap, in this chapter I explore how and why three women—Donna, Jo, and Kit—use nostalgic crafting to build comfortable spaces in new capitalist work environments. Their crafting is a commemoration of a better past (bonding with grandmothers, great aunts, and fathers) and, thereby, a force of user redesign and mêtis from which nostalgic designers can learn to create more inclusive futures. To start our journey into nostalgic design, then, the task of this chapter is fairly simple. We're going to listen to these three women's nostalgias, trusting that they're a form of expertise, and see what we can see.

## Donna

Donna is the Director of Departmental Technology Support at a large state university.[1] In her mid-thirties, she is the oldest of the three women interviewed. Donna started knitting at the onset of the current do-it-yourself (DIY) craft revival: "I taught myself how to knit . . . about 2002, 2003. I'd been out of college a couple of years and was kind of in that moment in your life where you're trying to figure out 'What am I doing?' You know, I know what I was doing professionally. I don't quite know what I'm doing as a person." To resolve this bit of existential instability, Donna turned to the "stitch 'n bitch" movement, a third-wave feminist knitting subculture that solidified around *Bust* magazine editor Debbie Stoller's 2003 *Stitch 'n Bitch* book series. In fact, a year after she began knitting, Donna formed her own stitch 'n bitch circle where young local women gathered and taught one another. Before she entered her job at the university, Donna worked as a software designer. As her prefacing quote illustrates, both at that job and in her current position, Donna knits while doing work on the computer.[2] She reads emails and lines of code with her eyes, while her hands knit away.

## Jo

Jo is a doctoral candidate in her late twenties who researches digital writing and rhetoric. To counterpoint passive, nonmaterial hobbies like reading and watching TV, she took up knitting as an undergraduate along with origami, cross-stitch, and cooking: "[O]n my mom's side of the family, people knit. My great aunt knits Christmas stockings for all of the people in her family . . . Before my great aunt was knitting, her grandmother was knitting those. . . . So, I was actually thinking, you know . . . who's gonna knit these next, right?" At the time she was interviewed, Jo was working on a "subversive" cross-stitched sampler that reads, "Fuck All Y'All" for her dad to hang in his office. She had also recently designed an ornate digital invitation for a friend's son's first birthday. An expert at digital writing, from web design to video editing, like Donna, Jo knits while in front of the computer, simultaneously doing digital work. For instance, when I first observed her knitting, Jo was concurrently reading articles for her comprehensive exams. Even when teaching, while her digital writing students complete self-guided studio work, Jo knits as she walks around the room answering questions. Unlike Donna, Jo doesn't knit as a part of a community. She prefers the feeling she gets from knitting and learning on her own.

## Kit

Finally, Kit, a professional furniture fabricator, serves as a foil to Donna's and Jo's craft hobbyist status. She is around the same age as Jo and is based in Brooklyn, New York, a locale often seen as a hub of DIY craft. But Kit is not a knitter; she crafts as a woodworker at a small studio that builds pedestals, cabinetry, and custom furniture for boutiques and art galleries: "I think it started when I was little, and I would help my dad build things because I was always his helper. So, I helped him finish our basement, and I helped him build a shed in our backyard, and I helped him put skylights in the family room." But Kit, too, is no luddite; she's created stop-motion models and video advertisements for New York businesses. At a certain point in her mid-twenties, though, Kit decided she no longer wanted to work as an executive assistant—primarily knowledge work—quit her job, and took up craft. Describing her move as part of a larger craft renaissance, Kit remembers, "Maybe the economy is shitty and people are just like me, and they were miserable doing the other jobs that they had and didn't know what else to do." Though she didn't have formal training in her new work, Kit was hired at the woodshop because of her demonstrated skill in the furniture and art she makes for friends. When referring to her creativity, Kit prefers the term "novice craftsman . . . or an apprentice because I'm learning from people. . . . Right now I call myself a creative craftsman."

Donna, Jo, and Kit each "craft"—defined here as the self-imposed choice of a labor-intensive mode of production in order to connect more deeply with the material, recipients, and memorial lineages of a design—in order to make their lives more meaningful in contexts where they are not always in control. Whether in search of nonwork identities or an escape from a "shitty" economy, they survey the past for something better. By learning to uncover the craft techno-logics and tactical nostalgia of these three crafters, I argue that designers can rhetorically analyze all sorts of similar nostalgic resistances as resources to learn about user populations. This is the first step of nostalgic design, a research method I call *critical nostos*, wherein designers analyze nostalgic user underlife for exclusions in current designs and assets for redesign. By analyzing nostalgic resistances, critical nostos guides designers in uncovering parallel and mutually symbiotic technological expertise, reading emotions as assets for redesign, and seeing communities of nostalgia and tradition as both barriers and bridges to new design possibilities. To better see what I mean by critical nostos, however, we first trek to seventeenth-century Peru.

## Critical Nostos in Techno-logical Contact Zones

Similar to our task in this chapter, in her "Arts of the Contact Zone," postcolonial literary theorist Mary Louise Pratt investigates the artful acts of resistant rhetoric that took place during the Spanish colonization of the Incan empire. To do so, Pratt introduces indigenous author Felipe Guaman Poma de Ayala's 1613 *The First New Chronicle and Good Government*, a massive four-hundred-page illustrated letter addressed to King Philip III describing the history of the Incan empire. Pratt writes: "Guaman Poma took over the official Spanish genre for his own ends. Those ends were, roughly, to construct a new picture of the world, a picture of a Christian world with Andean rather than European peoples at the center of it—Cuzco, not Jerusalem. . . .

incorporating the Amerindians into it as offspring of one of the sons of Noah.
. . . The depictions resemble European manners and customs description, but
also reproduce the meticulous detail with which knowledge in Inca society
was stored on quipus and in the oral memories of elders" (34–35). Guaman
Poma, that is, paints a neostalgic present and, therein, engages in what Pratt
labels "arts of the contact zone," acts of textual appropriation, recycling, and
parody in "social spaces where cultures meet, clash, and grapple with each
other, often in contexts of highly asymmetrical relations of power, such as
colonialism, slavery, or their aftermaths as they are lived out in many parts
of the world today" (34). Particularly fascinating for us about Guaman Poma's
transculturation is his tactful layering of Incan memory into Spanish Christian nostalgia. As he states, "I decided to write of the origins, famous acts of
the first kings . . . and descendants from the first Indian called Vari Viraco-
cha, his generation of *runa*, Vari Runa who descended from Noah after the
flood. . . . Others say he came from Adam himself" (7, 21). This is prototypical
nostalgic design. He takes what he knows the colonizers value and shows how
the Incans exemplify, even originated, that eudaimonia.

In Svetlana Boym's typology, Guaman Poma is *reflectively* nostalgic. He
neither seeks nor thinks possible the restoration of Incan or Spanish utopias;
instead, his "[r]eflection means new flexibility, not the re-establishment of
stasis. The focus here is not on the recovery of what is perceived to be an
absolute truth, but on the meditation on history and the passage of time.
. . . It reveals that longing and critical thinking are not opposed to one another" (Boym, *Future* 15). Like any good radical, Guaman Poma does not
simply reject the system that has oppressed him. A naive refusal will get him
nowhere. Rather, he speaks within the Spanish *restorative nostalgia* he finds.
He appropriates, and therein praises, Christianity by layering his people's
history into it. In doing so, he not only hopes to call up empathy in the king
through nostalgic identification; he redesigns his colonized self by claiming
and critiquing the Christian moral authority that drove colonization: "I have
not found that the Indians covet gold and silver . . . owes one hundred pesos,
tells lies, gambles, refuses to work, acts as a whore or a pimp. . . . You have
all these vices which you teach to the poor Indians" (294).

But what does this stroll through an ancient Andean text teach the contemporary designer? Examining Guaman Poma's struggle through a lens of
design should cause us to wonder, What revolutionary futures are available by
recovering forgotten, othered, and forcefully excluded pasts? In critical nostos, memory becomes a form of user expertise, mêtis, from which to learn and
redesign. Over the last half-century, designers have increasingly realized that
good tech starts from such understanding, learning from the everyday lives

of users—a standard called user-centered design. "Insight . . . does not usually come from reams of quantitative data," writes Tim Brown, CEO of the design firm IDEO. "A better starting point is to go out into the world and observe the actual experiences of commuters, skateboarders, and registered nurses as they improvise their way through their daily lives. . . . the shopkeeper who uses a hammer as a doorstop; the office worker who sticks identifying labels on the jungle of computer cables under his desk" (41).

As a method for design, critical nostos takes this observation a degree further. By identifying how users (like Guaman Poma and the crafters of this chapter) harness nostalgia to reshape their environments, designers can better understand where and why users feel excluded but also what users want, what they're good at, what they enjoy, and where they feel comfortable. Recalling that "nostalgia" is a portmanteau of the Greek *nostos* (to return home) and *algos* (pain/sorrow), *critical nostos* is a process of sociological observation by which designers learn from the ways that users innovate through returning home in memory. That is, we'll see how remembering is just as active a process of redesign as hacking a computer. And where not all users can physically redesign a product, all users *are* nostalgic, as nostalgia is global (Hepper et al.), trans-ideological (Hutcheon), and inevitable (Skowronski et al.).

## Re-Crafting Capitalism: Invoking Nostalgic Labor Rights

Take, for example, the nostalgic redesigns of nineteenth-century art critic John Ruskin. "Wherever the workman is utterly enslaved," Ruskin laments in his 1853 encomium of Gothic architecture, "the parts of the building must of course be absolutely like each other; for the perfection of his execution can only be reached by exercising him in doing one thing . . . [In contrast] if, as in Gothic work, there is perpetual change both in design and execution, the workman must have been altogether set free." Some ten years before Karl Marx's denunciation of the inhumanity of the factory system, Ruskin uses nostalgic architecture to critique the death of creativity that defines capitalism. Though nineteenth-century buildings may be beautiful in their uniformity, Ruskin observes, they're nothing compared to the individual genius of Gothic cathedrals: "[G]o forth again to gaze upon the old cathedral front, where you have smiled so often at the fantastic ignorance of the old sculptors: examine once more those ugly goblins . . . but do not mock at them, for they are signs of the life and liberty." The builder of the Industrial Revolution is a *laborer* for someone else's design, where the Gothic maker is a true *craftsman* with the freedom to revel in self-guided detail. Craft is a nostalgic right that sets the worker free.

Over a century later, the "new capitalist" creative workplaces in which Donna, Jo, and Kit find themselves are supposedly replete with tenets that similarly free workers from industrial logics. Because contemporary consumers demand originality, customization, and speed, businesses and their workers must be ready to adapt at a moment's notice. This requires creative skill. In contrast to the separation of design and labor in Ruskin's critique, "it is a principle of the new capitalism to push down control and responsibility to the lowest possible level, closest to the actual products. . . . [This] requires workers now who can learn and adapt quickly, think for themselves, take responsibility, make decisions" (Gee et al. 19). Toyota employees, for example, are encouraged to critique senior management: "Voicing contrarian opinions, exposing problems, not blindly following bosses' orders. . . . 'Pick a friendly fight'" (Takeuchi et al.). When workers have more liberty like this, goes a central tenet of new capitalist lean management, businesses work more efficiently. Employees of the creative economy are empowered again.

Describing the market catalyst of this shift, Richard Sennett writes, "Enormous pressure was put on companies to look beautiful in the eyes of the passing voyeur [or investment firm]; institutional beauty consisted in demonstrating signs of internal change and flexibility. . . . Stability seemed a sign of weakness, suggesting to the market that the firm could not innovate" (41). In this game of change, the model worker is an "expert novice"—an employee who quickly and repeatedly enters, learns, and innovates in new roles. Ideally, this flexibility empowers workers and glorifies the type of adaptive critical analysis that design and humanities educators have praised for years. Such work also addresses the whole worker (mind and body, not just laboring hands) in order to develop employees with an ardor to invest creativity long-term. This architecture of commitment is epitomized by Google's corporate campus, Googleplex, with its parks, swimming pools, volleyball courts, eighteen cafeterias, etc., all there to make workers feel more at home and, thus, more inclined to be relaxed and work creatively.

And, yet, in many ways this new capitalism is as restrictive as the old. The fun and games of Googleplex echo the paternalistic company town—one lives for, through, and with their job. In their *New York Times* exposé on the overreach of Amazon's corporate culture, for instance, Jodi Kantor and David Streitfeld report "marathon conference calls on Easter Sunday and Thanksgiving, criticism from bosses for spotty Internet access on vacation, and hours spent working at home most nights or weekends." Women like Donna, Jo, and Kit are acutely at risk: "Michelle Williamson, a 41-year-old parent of three who helped build Amazon's restaurant supply business, said her boss . . . told her that raising children would most likely prevent her from success at a higher level because of the long hours required" (Kantor and Streitfeld). Although our three crafters don't work in such hyper-restrictive climates, each faces trickledown new capitalist logics: you are where you work; you're not an individual, you are your team; adapt or die. In response, like Ruskin before them, Donna, Jo, and Kit draw upon nostalgic craft to redesign work.

The most valued skill in new capitalist workplaces, for instance, is adaptability, but as Sennett observes, mercurial work is antithetical to "the ideal of craftsmanship, that is, learning to do just one thing really well" (4). In our interviews, Donna, Jo, and Kit described their dissatisfaction with this instability, which led them to the steadiness of nostalgic craft. When asked what sparked the current craft revival, for example, Donna explains that because so many software engineers create intangible capital (digital software) as a part of an adaptable team, they produce only a small bit of an unseen final product:

> You know, I had this theory at one point. It's totally a theory. That there came a
> certain point where most people's jobs are about going somewhere and sitting at
> a desk all day. And you're typing—even if you're a graphic designer or something
> like that—your product is pixels. You very rarely see the output. And at the
> time I was learning to knit I was working in software design. So, our output
> was never printed out. It was a thing on a screen. And I kind of felt like there
> were people who were frustrated with that "I came home at the end of this eight
> hours, and I don't have anything to show for it." And, so, knitting was a way of
> like, I'm still doing something with my time, but at the end of that time there's
> a physical object here I can show you.

Donna feels a sense of loss and longing for physical output she can see, labor that can be tracked and finished, and a design created from beginning to end on her own. Meaningful work is craft. In contrast, as mechanic and former think tank employee Matthew Crawford explains, "In most work that transpires in large organizations, one's work is meaningless taken by itself. The individual feels that, alone, he is without an effect" (156). Thus, Donna styles one of the motivations for her knitting in front of the computer as a sense of nostalgic loss that surrounds collaborative digital work and the need to trouble definitions of digital product that don't display the human behind them. Do you know who coded your favorite app? Do you ever think about them? When one's labor is immaterial, one's hands can disappear, and one's work is never done. Notably, this sense of loss isn't about Donna hating digital technology. She's no technophobe. Rather, the incalculable labor promoted by digital jobs feels somehow empty. In contrast, knitting allows Donna to take pride in individual labor: "I can show you. Ok, it's two o'clock here [at one point of a scarf she's holding], and it's eight o'clock here."

Jo, whose academic labor (writing, research, and teaching) also infrequently produces tangible results, describes a similar craft exigence:

> I started doing it in college . . . I actually think it coincided with being an
> English major and not wanting to read books all the time in my spare time any
> more. Like, cause I love reading, but when you *have* to read sometimes it gets
> a little . . . you need something to do. And at some point I just wanted to not
> watch TV but actually do something that there was an end result for it. Because
> I felt like . . . all my hobbies, they didn't feel like real hobbies. I really didn't
> feel like they produced anything, basically.

Jo's need for a hobby with a tangible output rather than a consumptive pastime can, again, be read as a gap in the other forms of labor in her life. Though she loves to read, Jo's problem with reading and writing all day at her job as a full-time student, digital writing teacher, and computer lab employee, is that intellectual labor produces slow results, and the hard work behind it often isn't obvious or rewarded. Good writing, as Strunk and White advise in their infamous *The Elements of Style*, is clear and effortless.

And yet, paradoxically, though Donna and Jo find pleasure in knitting as a form of tangible labor, knitting is also a way for them to escape from work—a rhetorical signifier of a nonwork identity to counter the new capitalist bleed of work into home life. In Robert Brooke's terms, Donna and Jo participate in "underlife," "the activities individuals engage in to show that their identities are different from or more complex than the identities assigned them by organizational roles" (142). Whether in a computer lab, office, or digital writing classroom, by knitting at work for all to see, Donna and Jo's craft symbolizes they are *people* with nonwork identities. "I think it was this moment," Donna reflects, "for whatever reason in our culture when people said, 'I'm not gonna wait for someone to tell me to do something.' And that whole Gen-X kind of like, 'I'm not doing my job, my career as part of my identity. I do that for the money to further these other things I do.'" In his 2002 interviews with a local knitting circle, Corey Fields made a similar observation: "For these women, leisure was central in attempts to achieve 'balance' in life, and knitting was . . . juxtaposed against their understanding of themselves as professionals" (157). But where Fields' knitters were embarrassed to knit in public, stating, "You know, young people are not supposed to knit; that's what people think. So you don't want people to think you're a freak," Donna and Jo consciously knit for an audience of other employees and students (155). Knitting is rhetorical memory work.

In fact, beyond establishing themselves as *people* with nonwork identities, unabashedly knitting at their desks also emphasizes that Donna and Jo are *women* being creative in technical workplaces that have historically excluded them. Knitting only seems out of place, they seem to claim, because it's odd to see signs of femininity in high-tech positions. Some readers may argue that it's not their femininity that's odd but rather any sign of personal nostalgia at work. But male nostalgia floods high-tech workplaces in the form of action figures, Funko Pop, and other nostalgic desk toys. This is about being a woman. Jo, for example, intentionally knits in front of her digital writing class to highlight this discontinuity: "Sometimes I do make a point of knitting in class while they're working, you know. Oh, yeah, they find it very, very funny. Especially in my classes . . . about digital identity, digital age, stuff like that. We throw those terms around, and they are like, 'You're knitting?' And I'm like, 'Yeah, I'm knitting . . . ' Because they think of it as arts and crafts, doing cross-stitch, purposeless, unimportant."

What's intriguing about the crafters' specific nostalgic responses to the economy of workplace overreach, then, is how, like the feminist crafters who began this chapter, Donna and Jo might be seen as posing an ironically essentialist female identity to claim a nostalgic right for women in the workplace as well as time away from work. By implying that the opposite of work is tradition, life, and hobby and, thereby, that a way to counterpoint work is by engaging in a feminine form of nonprofessional labor, Donna and Jo reflectively experiment with gendered memory. Using crafts as ritualistic objects to remember with, they ironically posit that knitting is more "authentically" feminine than new capitalist labor. In doing so they engage in Ladino's "counter-nostalgia," in which "to 'return' to this sort of home is to revisit a dynamic past and to invert or exploit official narratives in ways that challenge dominant histories" ("Longing" 91). Like Guaman Poma claiming the power of Christianity, they redesign oppressive memory structures (women belong at home) to claim a traditional right to time away from work (traditional women don't answer email at home). Diana Fuss theorizes such counter-nostalgic gender essentialism as the difference between the "fall into" "real" essentialism and those who "deploy" or "risk" tactically "nominal" essentialism to further feminist goals (20). We've similarly theorized this tactical use of memory as the difference between restorative and reflective nostalgia. Where the technologies of new capitalism create a moral universe in which workers feel guilty for time away from work (you must answer email at all hours), Donna and Jo's nostalgic craft constructs a moral universe in which there is more to life: "I'm not doing my job, my career, as part of my identity."

## Critical Nostos: Uncovering Repertoires of Expertise

"When I say that innovation is being democratized," Eric von Hippel begins his *Democratizing Innovation*, "I mean that users of products and services—both firms and individual consumers—are increasingly able to innovate for themselves" (1). Von Hippel focuses primarily on the innovations of an advanced set of "lead users," who aren't your typical operators of design but rather are the 2.5 percent (Rogers) of field-specific extreme experts who embrace technologies first. But he "pathologizes" non-users (Selwyn), those who reject technology. What's missed in a tight focus on high-tech gurus is those users like Donna and Jo, who hack technologies but aren't invariably snug on the cutting edge.[3] By observing Donna's and Jo's nostalgic responses to a new capitalist ennui, we've found a need to design a workplace that connects the everyday digital worker to the calculable products of her labor, that sets boundaries between work and home, that welcomes women, and that allows some tasks to be completed on one's own to promote proud craftsmanship. Discounting such resistant remembering builds a world in which the only admirable user innovation is one that progresses things as they are. That is, I agree with designers Victor Papanek and James Hennessey, that in response to technical problems, "there is the capitalist approach (make it bigger), the technocratic one (make it better), the 'revolutionary' solution (portray the problem as an example of an exploitative system) and the pre-industrial romantic fallacy (don't use it; maybe it will go away by itself.) We propose a fifth alternative response: Let's invent a different answer" (27).

To investigate this fifth way, critical nostos actively redesigns by layering new and old expertise. In doing so, it parallels Judith Irvine and Susan Gal's "fractal recursivity," a model of linguistic variation that poses that the same tensions by which communities differentiate themselves *externally* (digital vs. tangible labor, for instance) are those most pondered *internally*: "[Like] fractals in geometry . . . the myriad oppositions that can create identity may be reproduced repeatedly, either within each side of a dichotomy or outside of it" (38). Donna and Jo don't simply reject digital technology, for instance. Externally, digital work is how they distinguish their jobs from other careers. They are expert digital knowledge workers, teachers, and artists. But, internally, to maintain happiness in their jobs, each crafter balances the values behind digital work with craft. They compose their working identities semiotically by composing crafts. They are not trapped in a backward-looking melancholy but instead move forward through an omnitemporal critical nostalgia. These are the arts of the nostalgic contact zone.

Critical nostos suggests, therefore, that designers scout the mêtis of users who are simultaneously cutting and trailing edge innovators, those who love technology but also use nostalgia and tradition to reshape it. Literacy scholars Bill Cope and Mary Kalantzis argue this point in educational theory: "Learning is not a matter of 'development' in which you leave your old selves behind; leaving behind lifeworlds which would otherwise have been framed by education as more or less inadequate to the task of modern life. Rather, learning is a matter of repertoire" (124). Indeed, an adaptable repertoire of expertise leads to what Tim Brown calls "divergent thinking." Where von Hippel's lead users are industry experts who may think in similar ways to the original designers of the products they are hacking (Kristensson et al.), Donna's and Jo's repertoire of lead and low expertise allows them to think outside the box. Design innovation comes from users and experts who reuse, recombine, and creatively juxtapose from their entire repertoire of expertise.

One of the first lessons critical nostos teaches the contemporary designer, therefore, is to look for resources not only in the high-tech hacks of lead users but also in the underlife of other users—knitters, grandmothers, children, etc. (see Emilson et al.). Nostalgia reveals extreme expertise in seemingly non-extreme people: revolution through revolving back.

## Crafting Emotions: It Feels Good to Do It Yourself

Still, given its association with illogical inexpertise, pride, and longing, one can understand why nostalgia has been steadily overlooked as such a revolutionary design asset. Like craft's relationship to high art in the opening vignettes, nostalgia is othered relative to memory because of its emotional moors. Emotion, especially technological emotion, is branded as naive and, historically, as "feminized weakness" (Niesche and Haase 1). It's something to be banished through learning (Sachs and Blackmore). Literacy historian David Barton describes this common correlation between emotion and illiteracy, for instance, when in response to "inner-city riots in Britain in 1991 . . . a leading British politician referred to a situation where there was 'not a high level of literacy so people were excitable and likely to be led astray'" (11). Even Donald Norman, a designer celebrated for his regard of the psychology of emotion writes, "One way of overcoming the fear of the new is making it look like the old" (*Design* 159). Norman's advice is a great nostalgia-centric idiom, but it's more a formula for persuasion than understanding. It doesn't help us answer *why* Donna, Jo, and Kit enjoy craft. In contrast, critical nostos examines emotion as a logic that can inform designers if we just pause to ask, *What are you nostalgic for, why, and to which ends?*

Each of the three crafters, for example, repeatedly describes negative affective reactions—"frustrated" (Donna); "frustrated me" (Jo); "miserable doing the other jobs" (Kit)—as what cued them that new capitalist labor wasn't working. They resolved these feelings by turning back to pride in a stable familial past, pursuing work and identities that other family members (grandmothers, great aunts, and fathers) enjoyed. Though sentiment is often seen as a liability in technology studies, nostalgia is a platform by which Donna, Jo, and Kit transform a vague negative *affect* like frustration into the answerable *emotion* of loss. When I use the term "affect," I mean, as Brian Massumi describes, the "prepersonal" state of being affected (xvi). Affect is emotion before interpretation, a bodily response, the feeling of sadness before it is attributed to a cause. In contrast, "emotion" is what affect becomes once it is reflected upon and given a social life. Emotion is the rhetorical presentation of affect to oneself and the world, involving the interpretation/appraisal of what affect means: "I am sad because . . ." To build comfortable workplaces, Donna, Jo, and Kit transform affect to emotion. In converting frustration into information, they also engage in a cybernetic feedback loop of nostalgic redesign.

Cybernetics, the study of regulatory systems in organisms and technologies, is usually thought of in terms of "feedback loops." In *Steps to an Ecology of the Mind*, for example, Gregory Bateson describes the cybernetic loop of a blind man using a cane to navigate his environment. If the touch of the cane signals that a curb is nearing, the man adjusts to that feedback and steps higher as not to trip: "[T]he street, the stick, the man; the street, the stick, and so on, round and round" (465). Bateson uses the phrase "the difference which makes a difference" to describe how the cybernetic loop highlights what one needs to pay attention and adapt to in a specific context, the curb in his example. Within Bateson's loop, Donna's, Jo's, and Kit's affective experiences (frustration, discomfort, etc.) act as their "cane" to highlight the information that has caused their unease. The workplace, the emotion, the women, round and round. In order to resolve the emotional gap, Donna, Jo, and Kit look to what Andreas Huyssen calls "temporal anchors," stable traditions on which to dock themselves and revise their lives (7). Negative affects initiate a nostalgic search of the past for something better and an eventual attainment of nostalgic equilibrium. "A noxious stimulus or aversive psychological/physiological state will have a negative influence on an outcome (e.g., function)," report Constantine Sedikides et al., "but it will also trigger nostalgia. Nostalgia, in turn, will alleviate this negative influence. Accordingly, the negative direct influence of the noxious stimulus is attenuated or counteracted by its positive indirect influence via nostalgia" ("To" 233). This loop—*difference* → *clash* → *affect* → *emotion* → *search of the past* → *adaptation*—is one that nostalgic designers can use to make technologies more inclusive (Stacey and Tether).[4] In the case of nostalgia, the *difference* → *clash* → *affect* sequence is bound in loss and critique, whereas *search* and *adaptation* are bound in pride, hope, and redesign.

Perhaps the clearest affective feedback loop in Donna's, Jo's, and Kit's stories appears in the feelings of loss emanating from the lack of tangible products completed in their work, a desire for individual agency, and a corresponding nostalgic pride in self-sufficient familial pasts. As described above, new capitalist workplaces usually require creating as a part of adaptable teams. But constant teamwork leads to a lack of ownership and craftsmanship. Crawford writes of this loss, "The rise of 'teamwork' has made it difficult to trace individual responsibility, and opened the way for new and uncanny modes of manipulation" (9). In contrast, Kit reflects upon the origins of her love for making:

> I think it started when I was little, and I would help my dad build things because I was always his helper. So, I helped him finish our basement, and I helped him build a shed in our backyard, and I helped him put skylights in the family room and, like, anything that needed fixing or building I would help my dad do it. And I really liked understanding how to build things. I remember when we were finishing the basement, and we were starting out the first wall. I had a moment when I was like, "Oh my god! I know how to build a room now! Oh my god!"

Kit's story stresses the self-sufficient creative pleasure she gets from DIY and the revelation of knowing how to do something on her own. This joy is why, she described to me, she shifted from working as an executive assistant to her job at the furniture studio. Compared to vague new capitalist collaboration, in craftsmanship one takes pride in the personal generative power of creating something from nothing. Kit gains extra pride in anchoring herself into a stable nostalgic narrative. She ties herself to a nostalgic story of DIY, almost from birth. Kit's identity is, and always has been, DIY.

Like Kit, Jo feels pride in the fact that she is "self taught in all of these, all of crafting. And I just, basically, would search online, and look at pictures, and watch YouTube videos. . . . So, no one ever taught me how to do any crafting. And I kind of like it that way because part of it is problem-solving, like figuring out how to do this." Even though she earlier explained how knitting is part of a familial tradition inherited from her great aunt and grandmother, these women serve more as patron saints of craft than teachers: "Even my grandma, who also knits on my dad's side, and then my aunt, who also does a lot of crafting, they never taught me explicitly how to do these things." Intriguingly, Jo told me she also identifies with a tradition of DIY making flowing through the men in her family:

> First my dad's an engineer, his brother is also an engineer. . . . So, I do come from a family of people who like to figure things out. . . . My dad's dad, he was

a plumber . . . he was super, super smart, but he just didn't have the opportunity to pursue further schooling. . . . So, he was blue collar, but he was always interested in new things and learning new technologies. . . . He actually adopted, very early on, a home computer. . . . I think the troubleshooting, I don't know, press it and see what happens thing came directly from my dad. . . . I enjoy the figuring out part. So, I don't tend to ask that many questions.

Jo uses nostalgia to layer what might be stereotypically called *high* (computers and engineering) and *low* (knitting) technical skills as well as the contradictory pleasures of self-sufficiency and familial connection therein. Nostalgia, because of its tensions of loss and pride, past and future, self and community, is often internally contradictory in this way. But it's these points of contradiction and overlap—nostalgic contact zones—that are so fruitful for designers. For example, in making the comparison between what she loves in both craft and computers, Jo surprised herself in our interview: "[It's] a connection I haven't made, but absolutely. Because a big part of how I approach new technology is to just press buttons and see what happens." Jo identifies an overlap of values across her craft and digital memories to determine the best way she learns any technology.

Kit performs a similar emotional plot, connecting memories of early DIY with her father to the pleasure she gets from making experimental art projects: "Well, it's really rewarding to conceive of something, and then actually build it with your hands. . . . That's been the most rewarding thing about working in an actual workshop now. . . . especially with Teddy's [a miniature stop motion movie set based on a real world bar], that was definitely an exercise in resourcefulness. . . . tons and tons of trial and error. . . . I don't usually Google 'how to do this.'" Ultimately, by exploring nostalgic tensions (DIY vs. familial connection, masculine and feminine technological traditions), Kit and Jo discover which learning styles work for them (experimentation, self-sufficiency, trial and error) and which don't (instructions, asking for help, great amounts of caution).

Of course, running in tandem with Jo's and Kit's DIY nostalgia is the pleasure of non-work stress relief in simply doing something well. Jo, for example, observes, "I also do it for stress relief. . . . It's definitely a soothing practice. Because it's methodical, because it's repetitive, and all those things. It's sort of, it's very relaxing. . . . And I will do it to have quiet meditative time where I'm just not thinking about my work." Numerous books (*Mindful Knitting*, *Zen and the Art of Knitting*, *The Knitting Sutra*) have focused on the repetitive, challenging, and meditative state of mind knitters enter into. Psychologist Mihaly Csikszentmihalyi calls this ritualistic emotional state "flow." A mixture of arousal and control, flow is an internally motivated (autotelic) affect in which the user feels in the zone, completely rapt by an activity, loses a sense of time, and focuses intensely. Csikszentmihalyi describes how the pleasure of flow, like Donna's and Jo's workplace crafting, stems from a sense of control: "[O]ptimal experiences add up to a sense of mastery—or perhaps better, a sense of *participation* in determining the content of life" (4). Donna describes impressing passersby with her flow when trying to meet a knitting deadline: "And it was mindless, it was eight rows of six stitches. . . . I was walking down Main Street with the yarn in my backpack and just knitting away. And people sitting in parked cars were just freaking out about, What is this woman doing?!"

So, where I've been arguing that nostalgia is ripe with critique of the present, nostalgic activities are also particularly good catalysts of flow because they are safe, known spaces and, thereby, allow users to more easily shut down the self-critical aspects of their minds that prevent flow. Sedikides, Wildschut, and Baden describe, for instance, that "nostalgic engagement can be therapeutic. . . . This can be achieved by reveling in past Thanksgiving dinners, school fares . . . or by collecting old baseball cards" (207). Indeed, there's been a generational revival of traditionally childish activities—coloring books, for instance—that evoke this calm but creative state. Several psychologists have also studied how the stability of such nostalgic flow leads to more creative, welcoming, and happy people. Wijnand van Tilburg et al., for example, asked 175 participants to recall a nostalgic memory and then compose stories that featured a cat, princess, or race car, or began with the sentence "One cold winter evening, a man and a woman were alarmed by a sound coming from a nearby house . . ." (2). Compared to a control group, the nostalgic writers scored higher on a linguistic creativity scale. As the authors explain, nostalgia is an approach-oriented emotion, leading test subjects to seek out new answers: "Nostalgia led to higher levels of openness, which in turn contributed to creativity" (6).

## Critical Nostos: Emotional Cues for Redesign

Increasingly, designers have recognized that emotion is an asset for production. Numerous neuro- and computer scientists studying artificial intelligence (Picard; Damasio; Cytowic; Clynes) have argued, as Rosalind Picard states, "Emotions play an essential role in rational decision making, perception, learning, and a variety of other cognitive functions" (x). Without emotion's link to the limbic system, and thus memory, decision-making is irrational. We can't trace the causality of when things have gone right or wrong and why (Picard 6). Putting these observations into practice, in a special issue of *The International Journal of Design*, Pieter M. A. Desmet and Paul Hekkert delineate two basic goals of mixing emotion and design: "The first was that not being aware of these effects can generate unexpected and unwanted user responses. . . . [T]he second was to stimulate intended user responses" (2). Interface designers, for instance, seek to prevent frustration at slow-loading computers by adding feedback mechanisms like spinning beach balls and hourglasses that say the computer is working. In contrast, car designers spark pleasurable emotion by making cars colorful, loud, and fast. Both approaches, as Richard Buchanan describes, assume that the "problem for design is to put an audience of users into a frame of mind so that when they use a product they are persuaded that it is emotionally desirable and valuable in their lives" ("Declaration" 16). Yet, although these two avenues have been utilized in emancipatory ways,[5] in both instances makers are still attempting to incite affect rather than learning from users' rhetorical activation of preexisting critical emotions to reshape their environments. Users are treated as things to be manipulated rather than experts with mêtis.

In contrast, critical nostos follows usability researcher Elizabeth Sanders in reading emotion as a means to understand users. Sanders classically describes how design research is built through three routes of data collection: say, do, and make. Designers frequently listen to what users *say* in interviews, watch what users *do* through ethnography, and co-*make* with users through participatory design. Much less frequently, however, Sanders writes, "[u]nderstanding how people feel gives us the ability to empathize with them. This way of knowing provides tacit knowledge, i.e., knowledge that can't readily be expressed in words (Polanyi, 1983)" (3). Thus, strong designers not only evoke and prevent emotions, they ask, Why are you feeling this and what can we learn from your feelings?

One key observation that emotion provided Jo and Kit, for instance, was which learning method worked best for them: DIY. The enjoyment of flow that came from DIY signaled DIY was a strong method of learning. Though flow has been studied in design research as an emotional state to incite in users (Cho and Kim), for us, flow states aren't just an end. Designers should be considering how flow is used to self-medicate pain in other areas. That is, designers don't often ask, Why are my users actively seeking out flow states? How is flow being wielded? Flow is a part of an emotional feedback loop. For Donna, Jo, and Kit, flow counterpoints overwork, intangible products, and feelings of inauthenticity in a context where adaptability and teamwork rather than long-term individual craft labor is required. Workplace designers might use such a feedback loop to understand that Donna's and Jo's use of flow stems from their other work lacking meditative expert labor. Ultimately, the second lesson critical nostos teaches inclusive designers, then, is that the emotional work users perform means something and is worth investigating not only to sell a product but also as a way to generate inclusive futures.

## "My Grandma Taught Me": Tactical Remembering in Communities of Nostalgia

"Nostalgia," Fred Davis describes, is "one of the means . . . we employ in the never ending work of constructing, maintaining, and reconstructing our identities" (31). Throughout this chapter, we've seen this identity work in the rhetorical nature of Donna's, Jo's, and Kit's technological memories. Each crafter uses specific memories in response to specific situations towards specific ends. Early in our interview, for example, Donna described how she was called to knitting at a time of existential instability and transition: "I taught myself how to knit, it was probably about 2002, 2003. I'd been out of college a couple of years and was kind of in that moment in your life where you're trying to figure out, 'what am I doing?' You know, I know what I was doing professionally. I don't quite know what I'm doing as a person." In order to define a nonwork identity for herself, Donna (like Jo and Kit) turned to familial tradition and the nostalgic craft of her grandmother:[6] "My grandmother always sewed for us, and so she made a lot of my clothes growing up. And so, after I learned how to knit I made her this sweater vest one year for Christmas. And the entire family, we were all crying. Because she was just so touched by that." What's particularly fascinating about Donna's selection of her grandmother's craft as a tradition she wants to join, however, is that she not only revels in memories of her grandmother in order to connect to her family, she also does so to join a nonfamilial community of nostalgia.

In other words, as father of collective memory Maurice Halbwachs writes, "The groups I am a part [sic] at any time give me the means to reconstruct them [memories], upon condition, to be sure, that I turn toward them and adopt, at least for the moment, their way of thinking" (38). In Donna's case, the stitch 'n bitch culture of young feminist knitters that she identifies with hails one's grandmother as a badge of membership. To join, you must remember your grandmother in a specific way. In her foundational *Stitch 'n Bitch: The Knitter's Handbook*, for example, Debbie Stoller sets this standard in her opening lines: "My grandmother sits, straight-backed, in the living-room, her feet firmly planted on the floor in front of her. As always, her hands are in motion—constantly in motion—as her knitting needles go back and forth" (3). Part of this rhetorical selection branches from stitch 'n bitch's third-wave feminist roots. Where second-wave feminist advice like Betty Friedan's *Feminist Mystique* argues that women should cast off the shackles of cooking, cleaning, and knitting, third-wave feminism asks, as Stoller writes, "Why couldn't we all—men and women alike—take the same kind of pride in the work our mothers had always done as we did the work of our fathers?" (7). Stitch 'n bitch remembers in a certain way, then, in order to reshape the meaning of womanhood.

In remembering as a community of nostalgia with shared loss and pride, however, stitch 'n bitch members also move away from connecting to lived history and towards an imagined collective "grandmother." In doing so, they create what my colleague (and wife) Krista Kurlinkus and I call a *nostalgic other*, the transformation of real people and history into a lost archetype—never truly reachable—from which to rhetorically construct an identity. The nostalgic other is simultaneously an icon to reach towards and a voice that is refused. Certain populations get trapped in the stereotypes of nostalgic otherhood. In the United States, for example, indigenous nations and Appalachians are often looked upon as cultural signifiers of a lost authentic America while simultaneously rejected as hopelessly backward. Nostalgic otherhood is how one can claim that an Indian sports mascot is celebrating native traditions while at the same time maligning indigenous human rights protests (see Dakota Access Pipeline). Nostalgic others are completed objects of the past to be used as symbols, rather than living human beings. When conflicts between such real humans and ideal archetypes are ignored, oppressive restorative nostalgia emerges. But when this conflict is unpacked, as in critical nostos, reflective nostalgia and collaboration blooms.

One of the most fascinating discrepancies between Donna's stitch 'n bitch nostalgic other and the real women on whom it is based surfaces in Donna's description of the changing craft economies of the knitting revival. The phrase "stitch 'n bitch" comes from post–World War II knitting circles in which women joined together to knit and discuss their lives. Stoller drew upon the power of this women-only space as a third-wave feminist tool. What hasn't often been discussed in descriptions of stitch 'n bitch, however, is how in reviving knitting, the stitch 'n bitch movement simultaneously transformed (and occasionally excluded) the very women it idealized.[7] In stating that there's been a knitting "revival," there's an assumption that knitting stopped. But knitting never died, and many old-school "stitching bitches" were earning a comparatively small living at their own yarn stores. When new knitters arrived in the early 2000s, the older generations sometimes felt threatened. Donna describes:

> I can remember, you know, printing out a pattern from knitty.com, a free pattern, and walking into a yarn store with it and knowing I would get a different response at different stores. Stores were really threatened by that. Because, "Oh, you have this free source for patterns. We have them [for sale]." . . .

[T]hey were very, very threatened by it, and they would try to kind of steer you to something else. Well, those patterns that they were selling in the stores had not yet caught up. They may have been "classic" designs, but there was a whole lot of awful, you know? So, there's one store in particular in Midwest City that probably, maybe eight years ago, I would say, I would still have gotten some pushback. . . . But they now have a computer in their store, where you can print patterns. And so they completely changed their tune because I think they started to realize that this wasn't threatening, this was bringing new customers in.

As a modern movement, stitch 'n bitch transformed the tradition it sought to nostalgically take part in by demanding new technologies: free digital patterns, better knitting needles, higher-quality yarns. Though at first the yarn storeowners resisted these changes, by embracing new technologies, the waning fiber arts industry was revived. Importantly, there was an ethical commitment to these storeowners ("let's help our grandmas") that led to collaboration and transformation. They listened to the nostalgic other. In this way, stitch 'n bitch engages in reflective nostalgic *sensitivity* ("attentiveness and curiosity, tactfulness and tolerance for the pleasures of others") rather than *sentimentality* ("ready-made postures" of unaware longing) (Boym, *Future* 338). Had this ethic not been in place, young knitters might have simply gone elsewhere, dismissing the nostalgic other they simultaneously praised. The layering of nostalgia and high technology saved a culture that could have been lost. These points of nostalgic intersection and transition—nostalgic contact zones—are key for inclusive designers to study as they illustrate how old and new communities can come together under one design.

Similar to encountering the old-school crafters that ruptured her imagined stitch 'n bitch nostalgic other, Donna told me how several years ago she won a 1920s sock-making machine at a craft fair auction. Reviewing the tattered box of documents and mechanical parts, Donna discovered something (figure 2.1). Though she had assumed it was for personal use, the device's original owner used it to produce socks for a company: "And, you . . . got this machine, and they sent you the wool, and you churned out these socks, and sent them back to the company . . . sort of this cottage industry. And then the Depression hit. And I have the letters where they're telling her, 'Slow down; we can't pay you.' . . . And, so, there was kind of this element of making money at that point, which I never had realized. And mechanization of what had once been handwork." Encountering memorial ruptures like the old-school craft store owners and this sock-making maven is requisite to the critical reflection and instability that is part of critical nostos.

CHAS. T. KURTZ, FRED C. WEIHENMAYER, Receivers

## GEARHART KNITTING MACHINE CO.
(INCORPORATED)

MANUFACTURERS OF

GEARHART STANDARD HOME KNITTING MACHINES.
AND
*Allwear* WOOLEN HOSIERY
KNOWN THE WORLD OVER

EGM

CLEARFIELD, PA.

# 50830

September 23, 1925

Mrs. Margaret Hepp,
New Riegel, Ohio.

Dear Knitter:

        As you were informed in our last letter, our
production of heavy weight hose is large and we now plan to
manufacture various weights. You are one of the group of
knitters we have selected to work upon the new light weight
hose we plan to make, and though there has been some delay
in obtaining the new yarns, we hope to have them in hand shortly.

        Unfortunately, we have been advised by Counsel that
certain changes must be made in the methods of conducting this
business; that no more yarn can be sent out on consignment
and that the present consignment accounts must be closed.

        Acting under permission of the Court, we plan to
pay amounts due Knitters, but we have been advised not to
pay any knitter until his or her consignment account is
closed. In view of this condition, and of your having been
selected to knit our new product, we request you not to knit
any more heavy weight hose, but to return all hose and unused
yarn in your possession at once.

        When your consignment account is closed, we plan
to mail you your checks for knitting wages and to send you an
initial supply of five pounds or less of yarn at the nominal
price of $2.00 per pound, with which to continue your knitting
for us. This is a very low price, as you will appreciate, but
we do this to be of as much service as possible, and make it as
easy for you as we can.

        We fully realize that you have been greatly in-
convenienced by all that has happened, and wish to assure you
that we are doing everything possible to protect your interests,
but we must have your full co-operation in order to succeed.
Please, therefore, give us this co-operation by sending in your
yarn and hosiery AT ONCE so that we will be able, in turn, to
help you.

                        Very sincerely yours,

                        GEARHART KNITTING MACHINE CO.

R-31
                                Chas. T. Kurtz,
Enc. Shipping Label               Fred. C. Weihenmayer,
                                        Receivers.

**Figure 2.1.** A section of one of the letters that Donna found in her sock-making kit that ruptured her stitch 'n bitch nostalgia.

Like Donna, Kit, too, remembers rhetorically to join a community. Though she describes her workplace as diverse, Kit says her field is male dominated: "I think there still is a big difference between the number of men and women. Like, there aren't as many women, especially in construction and woodworking." Thus, although she briefly mentioned her mother's crafting, when talking about her job, Kit steadily invoked masculine traditions and what literacy theorist Deborah Brandt terms male "literacy sponsors": "agents, local or distant, concrete or abstract, who enable, support, teach, model, as well as recruit, regulate, suppress, or withhold literacy—and gain advantage by it in some way" ("Sponsors" 167). During our interview, for instance, Kit recalled her first memories of making: "I think it started when I was little, and I would help my dad build things because I was always his helper." Kit identifies memories of her father, apprenticeship, and remodeling their home as the inauguration of her love of craft.

I argue that Kit makes this memorial selection purposefully to write herself into a male-dominated work tradition. After all, she calls herself a "creative crafts*man*." In David Middleton and Derek Edwards' words, Kit is "telling the right kind of story, at the right time, to the right person, about what went on, or did not go on" ("Introduction" 9). Like Donna and her grandmother, Kit wears her father as a badge of belonging. Thus, in contrast to Donna, Kit participates in a masculine community of nostalgia:

> I was helping Clancy at [a local trade school nonprofit], and I was listening to the orientation speech. . . . He was saying that . . . woodworking is a tribal skill, because it is passed down from a master to an apprentice, and that really stuck with me, because there is no other way you can actually learn most of these things. You can read books, and you can watch videos on YouTube . . . but it's about doing it, and usually it's about doing it over and over and over again until you kind of understand the material you're working with. There's no substitute for that experience.

Kit's description of woodworking as a tribal/trade-based skill illustrates how collective memory is hackable. Though the tradition Kit invokes here (trade guilds) wasn't historically accessible to women (see Federici), Kit writes herself into it. She does this hacking not only by invoking memories of her apprenticeship ("I was his helper") and valuing craft technology but also by illustrating that she shares the same techno-logics (DIY, learning through doing) that the trade tradition values. Collective memory serves as a gateway to community literacy.

## Critical Nostos: Layering Communities of Memory

We don't remember away from the specific communities in which we exist. Friends, family, religions, and workplaces encourage us to build memories across some key ceremonies (birthdays, holidays, weddings) and not others. Individuals do not remember by themselves; individuals in groups do. As we'll see throughout this book, an often-ignored fact of this observation, however, is that participation in one community of memory sometimes prevents or grants access to others. Memories act as bridges and walls. James Gee, Glynda Hull, and Colin Lankshear discuss this boundary as it appears in law school: "For some, being inducted into law school social practices [formalistic language study, intense competition, 'adversarial dialogue' with authority figures] means learning behaviors at odds with their other social practices [culturally contextual language, cooperation, innate respect for elders] that are constitutive of their other social identities. People like me don't do things like that; I'm not that kind of person. And yet law school summons me to do just that; to be precisely that kind of person" (*New Work Order* 11–12). Jack Bratich and Heidi Brush depict a similar conflict of identity in business settings:

> In a *Boston Globe* column called "Miss Conduct," a concerned reader offered the following conundrum: "I recently attended a professional conference and during a couple of sessions noticed several women in the audience knitting as they listened to the presentations. It seemed a little rude, as it was clear they were not giving their full attention to the discussions. Am I being unreasonable?" Miss Conduct rules that the knitters were indeed being "terribly rude." *The Globe* coverage appeared on Etherknitter, a blog devoted to knitters. . . . Anna writes, "I've been dying to knit in law school lectures btw but I know it would NOT be looked on kindly. *sigh*." Martha warns, "I do think . . . that working women might need to consider how professional they look knitting at an industry conference. While I think we all agree that knitting helps us pay attention." (236–37)

That these women could not knit at a conference because craft is deemed out of place, despite the fact that they learn better when doing so, is disturbing.

Fortunately, though belonging to one community of memory might make access to other worldviews uncomfortable, it can also be a bridge. Donna, for example, discussed craft's link to problem-solving and, intriguingly, to programming: "The other thing I like to say about knitting . . . it's nothing more than ones and zeros. Because every single thing you do in knitting, no matter how fancy it is, is a knit stitch or the reverse, which is a purl stitch. So, if you knit a stitch; you call that a one. You flip it over that little hump there is the purl. And so that's what I've always said is a zero." In this remediation

**Figure 2.2.** Mathematician Daina Taimina with her non-Euclidean crocheted organisms. Photo: Tom Wynne.

of digital lexis upon knitting, Donna hints that knitting expertise, especially the breakdown of complex processes into easily-chartable steps, might be an unexplored literacy gateway into math, coding, and new media work.

Latvian mathematician Daina Taimina takes this connection and runs. Since the nineteenth century, mathematicians have known that the abstract concept of non-Euclidean hyperbolic space was theoretically possible, but modeling such space seemed unachievable. It was not until 1997 that Taimina realized, "Well, you know, I *can* make models of this space using crochet. . . . And the funny thing is that hyperbolic geometry is not only *not* impossible, but organisms in the marine world have been utilizing these structures for hundreds of millions of years" (Buszek 279). By rethinking geometry through the nostalgic lens of crochet, Taimina made a breakthrough (figure 2.2). The only way to model hyperbolic geometry is through crochet, a fact missed for over a century because women have been systematically excluded from mathematics.

Building upon how strikingly similar Taimina's non-Euclidean creations are to coral and anemones, Margaret and Christine Wertheim created *The Crochet Coral Reef* project. In *The Crochet Coral Reef*, the Wertheims invite women from around the world to follow Taimina's non-Euclidean crochet code in order to make and submit their own corals to a traveling art exposition. The reef has two goals. First, it brings attention to global warming and the death of reefs it causes. But, second, the reef spreads the love of advanced mathematics to a community of women who may not have been interested or welcomed in the past. Ultimately, then, viewing mathematics through a neostalgic lens not only invites an entire new group of women into mathematics, it invites a new tradition of mathematical thinking that revolutionized the field. Critical nostos teaches designers to seek out nostalgic contact zones and the polysemous identities created within them—knitter and mathematician, knitter and computer programmer, woman and craftsman—as revolutionary assets for design that transform communities. This is the power of nostalgic design.

## The Ethics of Nostalgic Ideation

In this chapter I've introduced critical nostos, a method of ideation that can aid designers in gathering the critical returns home of users. In critical nostos, designers learn from reminiscence as mêtis. Though I've focused on one small subsection of crafters and one type of nostalgia, critical nostos applies to all communities, from old-school hip hop fans to scientists. Design researcher D. J. Huppatz, for instance, describes a similar resistant wave of nostalgic design in anticipation of Hong Kong's transition to the Chinese Communist regime: "In the lead up to the 1997 handover, the nostalgia of Chan's or Shanghai Tang's designer goods helped construct a particular Hong Kong identity that was opposed to the conformity of communist China. . . . [N]ot only were their references specifically local, but these techniques also were key design techniques in 1920s and 1930s Shanghai design and advertising. . . . In the anxious years preceding the mainland's reclamation of the city, Hong Kong thus is identified with the particular historical narratives of South China's port cities and their connection to global trade and capitalism" (27).

And yet, critical nostos as a method must be anchored by ethics. In developing nostalgia as a resource for redesign, designers can't be a kid in a candy store, scooping up others' memories indiscriminately. In her "Gone Digital: Aboriginal Remix and the Cultural Commons," for instance, Kimberly Christen describes her work helping the Waramungu aboriginal people digitally record familial and cultural memories. The Waramungu are highly protective of their cultural heritage because of years of colonial oppression and appropriation. Only recently have many familial memories, photographs, artifacts, etc., been recovered from Australian museums and government archives. Once recovered, such "objects of legacy," as Zeynep Turan labels them, "encode continuity between and across generations. They become cultural objects that provide a connection to a trauma experienced by one's ancestors" (176). Thus, Christen observes, "Elders and knowledge owners who restrict and grant permission provide a framework for younger generations and others to produce cultural products as well as preserve older ones. 'Creators of the past' are not necessarily restrictive or hoarders of power. Their influence is not always oppressive, it can be liberating as well" (333). Restricting memories is protection—fighting to avoid erasure and to maintain cultural identity. By guarding their objects of legacy, the Waramungu elders get to decide who is a member of their community of memory and who is not, who holds sway over them and who does not.[8]

Thus, there are reasons why tradition, nostalgia, and memory are not simply free game for designers. In craft, such appropriation can turn into what Anthea Black and Nicole Burisch call "craftwashing"—slapping the label "craft" on any object to increase its cultural cachet and price. Donna describes: "My roommate and I have been laughing that Crate and Barrel . . . were billing it as an 'artisan cheese plate.' . . . It was a big piece of slate. Well, then we had a windstorm and a piece of slate came off my neighbor's roof, so we were like, 'Oh, look at that, there's an artisan cheese plate on our patio.' . . . There's this kind of co-opting of that word 'artisan.'" Craft becomes an inauthentic signifier, emptied of its meaning. The final lesson of critical nostos, then, is that designers must interrogate their personal drives to use nostalgia, considering, how, why, and to whose benefit they harness memories. Just as the stitch 'n bitchers valued and sought to design *with* the craft store owners, nostalgic designers must seek out direct collaboration with communities of nostalgia. To plan for this collaboration, in the next chapter I champion not only an ethic of involving users directly in design (participatory design) but also an ethic of actively inciting and mediating argument, disagreement, and dissent among collaborators, a tactic I call *rhetorical design*.

# II

# Mediating Nostalgia

# Chapter 3

# Nostalgic Deliberations

What I Mean When I Say "Democratizing Technology"

Making some forms of communicative action possible or easy and others difficult or impossible. . . . Rhetoric and technology share this dynamic and its twin dangers because they are both arts of design: they are both in the business of balancing innovation with tradition, of initiating change and then compensating for it. If rhetoric is the art that adjusts ideas to people and people to ideas, we might characterize technology as the art that accommodates the material world to people and people to the material world.

**Carolyn Miller, "Foreword," *Rhetorics and Technologies***

There is a genuine call for innovation through user-centered design, and even a belief that innovation is getting democratized. At the same time, inventive as it may seem, this new paradigm is surprisingly traditional and managerial. The main challenge put forward is still how large corporations can harvest users' and consumers' innovations into safe and profitable mass-market products.

**Pelle Ehn, Elisabet Nilsson, and Richard Topgaard,**
***Making Futures: Marginal Notes on Innovation, Design, and Democracy***

The subtitle of this book promises that I'll teach you how to democratize technology. The most basic definition of "democracy" is the rule of the people; so, to democratize technology is to govern the design of technology by listening to the citizens affected by it. But what does this type of making actually take? Lying in wait are negotiations of expertise and power, public participation and its problems, debate and persuasion, consensus and dissensus, continuous redesign, and, usually, excluding citizens who don't agree with the majority vote. Maybe I should have chosen an easier subtitle. Chapter 2 approached democracy by arguing that designers can make their projects more inclusive by using critical nostos to detect design inequities and the nostalgic repertoires citizens use to answer those inequities every day. But techno-logical disparity doesn't always readily identify itself, it's not obvious what creators should do with ideological clashes once they're unearthed, and craving inclusivity isn't the same as democratically planning for it. From deciding who gets to participate in deliberation to mediating several equally rewarding futures, as the next three chapters explore, democratic design—collective decision-making across techno-logical diversity—isn't easy.

In fact, in 1984, as memorably described by Langdon Winner, an enclave of tomato farmers actually sued the University of California over the hazards of democratic design. Professors Jack Hanna and Cody Lorenzen had been developing the mechanical tomato harvester since World War II, when a decrease in labor and a rise in demand for tomatoes caused an industry-wide panic (Rasmussen). The UC Davis Department of Agricultural Engineering responded by cultivating a new harvester that produced a greater yield, for less money, more efficiently, with fewer hands. It was perfection. Hanna even crafted vf-145, a breed of tough (if flavorless) tomato that stood up to mechanical handling. In 1964 only 3.8 percent of California's tomatoes were reaped by the machine. By 1965, that number leapt to 24.7 percent and by 1970, 99.9 percent (Friedland and Barton 35). Conversely, approximately fifty thousand workers harvested tomatoes in 1964; by 1972 the number of pickers dropped to about eighteen thousand (Friedland and Barton 37). Mechanization, as it so often does, was liquidating the workforce. But what really led to the Californian Agrarian Action Project's 1984 lawsuit was a concentration of growers. The machines were so expensive and required such huge tracts of land to justify their investment that only the largest farms could afford them and, thus, survive. The number of growers fell from 4,000 in 1964 to just 597 in 1973 (Friedland and Barton 38). The mechanical tomato harvester decimated small competition. So, small competition sued. The trial ended up being about what it means to pursue scientific and technological innovation in a democracy.

Following a techno-logic that equates unfettered technical advance with cultural progress, in court the university argued that democratic design means academic freedom: "We have a university that's one of the greatest research universities in the world. . . . If we told researchers what to do, we'd be second-rate," and "[California agriculture] has been a tremendous success in terms of productivity, and in large part that is due to the work of the university" (Curtis). The farmers battled back that the university's techno-logic violated its land grant mission by prizing efficiency over the lives injured by the state-sponsored system. If a small number of corporate farms were benefiting from the university's research, those corporations, not taxpayers, should foot the bill. The benefits of university research should be democratically distributed. Ultimately, then, the farmers didn't seek remuneration but, rather, "a court order directing the university to assess the social consequences of mechanization studies before they begin" (Curtis).[1] The farmers essentially argued that design needs to be rhetorical. For technology to be democratic, they felt, stakeholders must debate, persuade, and deliberate before, during, and after designs roll out.

One increasingly common response to such calls is *participatory design*, an inclusive set of practices that welcomes stakeholders (users, clients, designers, engineers, et. al) into co-creation. The participatory ethic was initially sparked by dehumanizing scientific management like Taylorism and, later, the social injustices of city planning projects like Robert Moses' New York expressways, St. Louis's Pruitt-Igoe housing projects, and parallel urban development across the globe (Emilson). As these social engineering projects displaced working-class neighborhoods with no real input from their residents, citizens began to realize: "So far as decisions affecting our daily lives are concerned, political democracy is largely overshadowed by the enormous power wielded by the masters of technical systems: corporate and military leaders, and professional associations of groups such as physicians and engineers. They have far more to do with control over patterns of urban growth, the design of dwellings and transportation systems, the selection of innovations, our experience as employees, patients, and consumers, than all the governmental institutions of our society put together" (Feenberg, "Democratic").

Responding to a distrust of such technocracy, participatory design encourages designers (experts at theory and production) and users (experts of use and context) to create together. As mentioned in chapter 1, perhaps the most notable early venture to benefit from this alliance was the Swedish UTOPIA project, 1981–1986 (Ehn; Bødker et al.). At the time, computers were inundating traditional Scandinavian industries. Much like the tomato farmers, workers felt at a loss as they watched their jobs being automated, their traditions ignored, and their coworkers fired. In response to union pressure, UTOPIA used action-research to ask, How can we add computers to the newspaper production process by collaborating with and learning from our workers rather than replacing them? The Nordic Graphic Union banded with a cadre of sociologists, computer scientists, and designers to draw upon the tradesmen's knowledge of typesetting, page make-up, etc. Together, they built a digital platform that fostered worker talent rather than deskilling employees. From its roots, then, participatory design (also "co-operative" or "Scandinavian" design) has been driven by a commitment to empowering citizens through deliberative action. This, surely, is the heart of democratic design.

And, yet, participatory design doesn't inevitably glide so slickly. Over the years it has sometimes substituted its democratic sheen for a dull managerial agenda that paints users as inert resources for profit (Ehn et al.; Emilson; Spinuzzi, "Lost"). In the early 1990s, for example, planner Ken Reardon had to shake off this miasma to take a participatory approach in rejuvenating a historic Manhattan street market. Initially, Reardon's team came to the project thinking that because large supermarkets were threatening the local bazaar, the success of these competitors might be drawn on for inspiration: "We were going in to Wegmanize this street market. What's the perfect visit to Wegmans [an east-coast supermarket chain]? You're in and out in fifteen minutes and you don't talk to anybody" (Forester, "Beyond" 300). Reardon's team surveyed locals, and their hypothesis seemed validated. Fortunately, Reardon also directly interviewed residents about the market. Compared to the etic (designer-driven) survey, the emic (user-driven) interviews revealed that citizens valued a different shopping tradition altogether. They held a protective nostalgia for community and conversation over speed and isolation. "We were studying the wrong species of institution," Reardon describes. "We collected the surveys, we had all the statistics . . . but it just didn't mean a goddam thing to the people we were working with. . . . The fact that there were closed-ended questions in the instruments shut people down so that they gave closed-answer-like responses. . . . We did not spend any time doing participant observation at the site, and we didn't do much informal interviewing" (300). Even for expert designers, democratic deliberation takes work. Reardon's team took surveys, compiled statistics, and attempted to welcome participation but still nearly failed because their initial methods didn't provoke discussion, critique, or empathy. Like the design of the tomato harvester, they lacked a rhetorically provocative force.

Though participatory design is a step towards democratizing technology, then, some instantiations miss the mark because they lack incitement, a plan for mediating conflict, or a measure for deciding who gets to participate and how each voice should be weighed. The success of participatory design depends on divergent thinking and debate—hearing and understanding multiple logics from multiple stakeholders. Likewise, the success of nostalgic design relies on mediating multiple conflicting nostalgic pasts and neostalgic futures. But without a strong rhetorical backbone, productive debate isn't assured, and our hopes of democratic design are dead in the water. To address this dilemma, in this chapter I compare several models of *rhetorical design*, a relatively new field of production that coalesces rhetoricians' and designers' theories of working with citizens towards inclusive futures.

So, where's nostalgia in all of this? Though nostalgia may seem tangential to this mission, as we'll see, rhetorical deliberation has rarely been theorized without it. Nostalgia is crucial to deliberative action because it advises designers, rhetoricians, users, and audiences to consider, *Who are we?* That is, nostalgic design asks the two central questions of deliberative democracy:

Who *are* we—what are our values, histories, and collective identities? And *who* are we—who gets a say in decision-making?

## The Origins of Rhetorical Design

Rhetorical design is a relatively overlooked movement in the fields of both design and rhetoric that examines the ecologies of language, persuasion, and resistance surrounding the production and use of technology and that seeks to solve problems of power and inequity within these systems. Though many forebears precede him (e.g., Bonsiepe; McKeon; Krippendorf), designer Richard Buchanan is the founder of this terrain.[2] Buchanan's 1985 *Design Issues* article "Declaration by Design: Rhetoric, Argument, and Demonstration in Design Practice" cultivates the field by arguing that design is a rhetorical problem (5). Like rhetoric, design persuades its audiences to form a specific opinion about the past (forensic rhetoric), present (epideictic rhetoric), or future (deliberative rhetoric). But rather than deploying language, Buchanan suggests designs persuade through use. As depicted in chapter 1, for instance, the design of Facebook persuades users to think other people's lives are incredible because Facebook's interface is created to inspire positive posts. Buchanan argues that *all* designs make such arguments about how we should live. Even the design of the light bulb not only allows humans to see at night but also argues that we should stay up later. Buchanan, thus, imagines "the designer as a speaker who fashions a world, however small or large, and invites others to share in it[,] . . . [and] an audience of users who may be persuaded to adopt new ways and means to achieve objectives in their lives" ("Declaration" 8). Here, Buchanan introduces the two central parties of rhetorical design: the user audience (an audience who is persuaded through use) and the rhetorical designer (a designer who sees his creations as arguments).

Perhaps more significant to rhetorical design than the fact that technologies persuade user audiences, however, is that in viewing designs as arguments, the rhetorical designer realizes that the invention of new technologies is not an inevitable progression from less to more advanced forms. Technology is not deterministic. And, because it's indeterminate, Buchanan observes, it requires the deliberation of multiple stakeholders: "If technology is in some fundamental sense concerned with the probable rather than the necessary—with the contingencies of practical use and action, rather than the certainties of scientific principle—then it becomes rhetorical in a startling fashion. It becomes an art of deliberation about the issues of practical action" ("Declaration" 6–7). Thus, design, like rhetoric, is "a discipline fundamentally concerned with matters that admit of alternative resolutions" (Buchanan, "Rhetoric" 25). Rhetorical designers deliberate over and select one solution among many potentially good solutions. This choice among equal futures is what Horst Rittel and Melvin Webber call "the wicked problem of design." Wicked problems don't have a single definition, a single solution, a clear stopping point, and yet still hold those who seek their answers responsible. By introducing this focus on indeterminacy, choice, deliberation, and responsibility, rhetorical design inevitably disrupts professional expertise. Neither the designers of the tomato harvester nor those of the street market, for instance, have a special claim on defining agricultural or shopping eudaimonia for all citizens. Rhetorical design obliges democratic design.

Buchanan further outlines that, like rhetoric, design is "architectonic," an art of connecting other arts. What this means is that in rhetorical design "the subject matter of design is not given. It is created through the activities of invention and planning, or through whatever other methodology or procedures a designer finds helpful in characterizing his or her work" ("Rhetoric" 24). But although this statement hints that rhetorical design is a process of creating as much as it's an argument made through technology, Buchanan rarely ventures what rhetorical design looks like as a method. Similarly, from Langdon Winner and Andrew Feenberg's democratic philosophies of technology to the deep sociohistorical analyses of rhetoricians of technology like Adam Banks, academics have been great at theorizing *why* technology should be democratic and inclusive but have less frequently focused on *how* to reach that goal (see Ehn et al.; DiSalvo, "Design"; Friess, "The Sword"). It's this focus on technique that differentiates rhetorical design from sister fields like the rhetoric of science and technology and that structures this chapter. If deliberative democracy is government by conversation, then rhetorical design is the conversation that leads to inclusive technologies.

Ultimately, Buchanan advises: "Rhetorical and philosophical studies of the pluralism of design thinking would be a significant contribution to further development of design and to its understanding among people outside the field" ("Design" 197). Responding to this call, in this chapter I explore how four popular theories of deliberative rhetoric—Aristotle's audience analysis, Kenneth Burke's "identification," Krista Ratcliffe's "rhetorical listening," and Chantal Mouffe's "agonism"—map onto four contemporary models of deliberative design—user-centered design, participatory design, empathic design, and agonistic design. The resulting four schemes of rhetorical design aren't meant to be representative of either vast field; they're not even representative of the full complexity of each author. Rather, each is matched, blurring design and rhetoric, to uncover the gaps, resources, and shared points of analysis that help explain just exactly what it takes to democratize technology.

## Aristotle, Audience Analysis, and User-Centered Design

Formalized western rhetoric "begins" with Aristotle.[3] And knowing one's audience is the heart of Aristotelian rhetoric, so much so that the Greek philosopher claims, "Of the three elements in speech-making—speaker, subject, and person addressed—it is the last one, the hearer, that determines the speech's end and object" (1.3.1, 1385b). In this light, though the extent to which Aristotle actually welcomes his deliberative audience (the Athenian *ekklēsia*) as an active and worthy contributor to design is contested,[4] in theory, Aristotle designs with them through audience analysis and constructing enthymemes: "Since the persuasive is persuasive to someone . . . and since no art examines the particular . . . but for persons of a certain sort . . . neither does rhetoric theorize about each opinion—what may seem so to Socrates or Hippias—but about what seems true to people of a certain sort. . . . Rhetoric [forms enthymemes] from things [that seem true] to people already accustomed to deliberate among themselves. . . . And we debate about things that seem to be capable of admitting two possibilities" (1.2.11–12, 1356b).

Aristotle wrangles several audience-centric paradigms in this defining passage. Orators don't address individuals but rather grouped audiences (the young, the old, the rich, etc.). Speakers need to know what is reasonable to these different groups who already have unique forms of deliberation and different conceptions of the world. And rhetoric is a wicked problem, a form of *phronesis* that comes into play when two equally probable choices are debated. For deliberative rhetoric, the goal of all this analysis is to persuade an audience "to do or not do something" (1.3.3, 1358b). In Aristotelian rhetoric, therefore, the speaker often begins by reaffirming a worldview the audience already knows (*eikota, koine, topos*, etc.) and proceeds by making enthymematic connections from there. Though speaking of judicial rather than deliberative oratory, Thomas Schmitz describes, "The citation of these unwritten rules emphasized that both the speaker and the jurors shared common ground, that their whole outlook on the world and on human behavior was similar" (32). For example, the tomato harvester's inventors might begin a deliberative argument with the *doxa* that "everyone knows that the more tomatoes we harvest the more money we'll make and the more people we'll feed." The rhetorician learns this first premise from her audience: relevant prior experiences, memories, and traditions must be attended to if a speaker wants to succeed.

Within Aristotelian rhetoric, then, nostalgia cozily resides inside this need to understand an audience's worldview. The enthymeme's reliance on commonplaces, probability, and plausibility for its premises (and the collective memories, myths, and nostalgias such notions are derived from) is one such mode of understanding. But more than uncovering values, nostalgic rhetoric solidifies them. Lawrence Prelli describes, for instance, that the epideictic rhetoric of ceremonies, eulogies, and other popular occasions is key to democracy: "Aristotle's epideictic is oratory of paramount civic importance since it commands members of a community to join together in thoughtful acknowledgment, celebration, and commemoration of that which is best in human experience" (3). Though epideictic rhetoric is ostensibly about urging actions in the present, then, its content is often nostalgic—reviewing who we were so that we can maintain that identity into the future. Epideictic rhetoric, that is, generates communities of nostalgia. In the United States, for example, one sees this constitutive force in references to the "founding fathers" and U.S. Constitution as if both predicted the future we stand in today. Thus, nostalgic rhetoric answers the question, Who *are* we? It's in this light that Chaim Perelman and Lucie Olbrechts-Tyteca further describe that "Epidictic oratory has significance and importance for argumentation, because it strengthens the disposition toward action by increasing adherence to the values it lauds" (50). Where deliberative rhetoric reaches towards future actions, epideictic rhetoric reaffirms and intensifies community values—"Win one for the Gipper!" "Make America Great Again!"—to make sure citizens have motivation to actually take action. Indeed, several recent psychological studies prove this provocative force. Xinyue Zhou et al., for example, found that the feelings of social connection and empathy produced by nostalgic reflection increases the likelihood that citizens will donate time and money to charity. But what does any of this have to do with design?

To match a notion of design with Aristotelian rhetoric, we begin with the central tenet of user-centered design: products need to be created for specific communities of users based on what those users deem the technological good. User-centered design (UCD), as advanced by Donald Norman and Stephen Draper in 1986, is a form of creation that puts the user, their context, and their goals at the center of design rather than a designer's *epistemic technê*. UCD, Norman describes, is grounded by the fact that design errors occur because designers have failed to adequately research users in context: "[When] the machine does the wrong thing, its operators are blamed. . . . It is time to reverse the situation. . . . It is the machine and its design that are at fault. It is the duty of machines and those who design them to understand people. It is not our duty to understand the arbitrary, meaningless dictates of machines" (*Design* 6). In *The Design of Everyday Things*, for example, Norman infamously describes a situation that I'm sure has embarrassed many of us in the past, a set of doors, artistically fabricated, that he can't open because the handles don't make sense: "I push doors that are meant to be pulled, pull doors that should be pushed, and walk into doors that neither pull nor push, but slide" (2). To resolve such problems, a classic sociological method of user-centered design is the user ethnography in which a designer enters a technical system and observes and interviews users about how a design succeeds or fails. Ethnography reveals how users see the world; it discovers premises for the arguments of design. Another typical UCD tool that results from such ethnographies (Blomquist and Arvola; Friess, "Personas") is the user persona—a short biography of a statistically imagined user (name, gender, age, skills, education, flaws, likes and dislikes, etc.) paired with a photo and scenario of use so that the designer keeps a specific person in mind when making. User-centered design, like Aristotelian audience analysis, reveals the memories and experiences of users so that a new design (an argument through use) can enter the activity system with the least trouble possible.

But, as we saw in Ken Reardon's street market, user-centered design is not necessarily participatory.[5] Where participatory design is about designing *with* users, user-centered design is often about designing *for* users. It's possible to have passive user-centered methods of data collection like surveys that don't really put user needs and emancipation at the forefront. In response, proponents of "*human*-centered design," like Julka Almquist and Julia Lupton, critique, "User studies ultimately construe the human subject of design as a predictable bundle of reflexes and impulses that can be torqued, tuned, and tweaked in order to do the bidding—and the buying—prescribed by a consumer-savvy cabal of designers, engineers, and marketers" (3). That is, in user-centered design, designers treat people first and foremost as "users" rather than experts (Satchell and Dourish). There's a similar objectification of user audiences in Aristotle's definition of rhetoric: "The faculty of observing in any given case the available means of persuasion" (1.2.1, 1355a). People are passive and complete things (*dociles auditores*) to be persuaded. "Aristotle's audience may make judgments," writes Arabella Lyon, "but they do not make counter arguments" (33). User audiences don't contribute anything new; they aren't collaborators, let alone co-designers. UCD focuses on how people interact with technical systems but not necessarily on how people reshape or live outside of those systems. The lessons and resistances we learned from Donna, Jo, and Kit in chapter 2, for instance, are nowhere to be found.

An Aristotelian form of rhetorical design, therefore, has several shortcomings. First, it's centered on stereotypical character types (the *male* hot-tempered youth, balanced middle-agers, and wary elderly of *Ars Rhetorica*). We see this stereotyping creeping into the user persona, which takes ethnographic data and generalizes it (Nielsen et al.; Clemmensen; Sharrock and Anderson). Such essentialism causes problems, to say the least. In 2011, for example, Bic came out with Bic for Her, a pen "specifically designed to fit a woman's hand." Its only major design changes were a thinner barrel and pastel color palette. The product was widely criticized in hilarious Amazon reviews, which took up the voice of its stereotypical female user persona:

> I have asked my husband if I am allowed these, he says that my weekly allowance for lady things is sufficient, and that "if there is any writing to be done I will do it thank you." I realized of course that he is right as in all things, and this is an unobtainable dream and I will stick to my pink crayons (Jjo54321).

> My mother, a hard-working woman who raised twelve kids single-handedly whilst doing all the ironing (as nature intended), was furtively abashed by her illiteracy. . . . [T]his product has definitely helped start the ball rolling. We tried to give her men's pens but she used to rip the cartridges out and drink the ink. Typical woman . . . (jonny)

Such gaffs are a result of a data-oriented (rather than participatory) design process. "The user mentality," Almquist and Lupton write, "excludes meaning and improvisation in favor of targeted functions and knowledges based on ignorance" (9). Indeed, with ignorance rather than expertise at the forefront, sometimes UCD slips into "user-friendly design." For better or worse, user-friendly designs are technologies purposefully crafted to be simple with a user's illiteracy in mind (R. Johnson 125). The point-and-shoot camera, for instance, is prototypical user-friendliness. Though the camera is easy to use, powerful composing options (focus, zoom, film developing choices) are removed because they are presumed too complex for the average user. Designers imagine an ignorant user rather than a sophisticated one who needs information delivered in relation to their mêtis. User-centered design, thus, often takes a deficit rather than an assets-based approach to technology: "The rhetorician has nothing to learn *from* the audience, she only learns *about* the audience" (Porter 18).

Like weak versions of user-centered design, Aristotelian rhetoric can leave little room for conflicting opinions within audience types. For Aristotle, the *polis* is privileged above the individual: "The man who is isolated, or has no need to share because he is already self-sufficient, is no part of the city, and must therefore be either a beast or a god" (*Politics* 1.2.1253a). Aristotle doesn't describe deep-seated conflicts over common knowledge nor a means for mediating such conflicts because though his audience types may differ from one another, there's no internal debate over what's foundationally good within those groups. Premises for enthymemes are pre-agreed upon and audience types are easily pandered to. For Aristotle, the goal of nostalgically praising the past in epideictic rhetoric is making sure such consensus about what's good exists (Prelli; Rosenfield).

## Burke, Identification, and Participatory Design

Twentieth-century rhetorician Kenneth Burke's neo-Aristotelian theories of "identification" and "consubstantiality" resemble Aristotle's rhetoric in their focus on audience analysis and, thus, that "[y]ou persuade a man only insofar as you can talk his language by speech, gesture . . . attitude, idea, identifying your ways with his" (*Rhetoric* 55). But where Aristotle assumes a preexisting common ground in each polis (all he really has to do is target an eternal stereotype), Burke begins from *division*, the futility of pure togetherness. "Rhetoric," Burke envisions, "is concerned with the state of Babel after the Fall" (*Rhetoric* 23). In Burke's democracy, therefore, it's much harder to answer that central deliberative question, Who *are* we? In his post-Babel world, there's no assumption of shared logics nor that values are even uniform within any single citizen. Burke's complex audience is perhaps best seen in his metaphor of the parlor:

> Imagine that you enter a parlor. You come late. When you arrive, others have long preceded you, and they are engaged in a heated discussion, a discussion too heated for them to pause and tell you exactly what it is about. In fact, the discussion had already begun long before any of them got there, so that no one present is qualified to retrace for you all the steps that had gone before. You listen for a while, until you decide that you have caught the tenor of the argument; then you put in your oar. Someone answers; you answer him; another comes to your defense; another aligns himself against you, to either the embarrassment or gratification of your opponent, depending upon the quality of your ally's assistance. However, the discussion is interminable. The hour grows late, you must depart. And you do depart, with the discussion still vigorously in progress. (*Philosophy* 110–11)

This audience learns, adapts, and, most importantly, contributes to the design of conversation.

Yet, though Burke appreciates difference, ambiguity, and change, his rhetoric is still largely concerned with acting-together, returning to an ideal Aristotelian state of community, and halting wickedness: "For substance, in the old philosophies was an act; and a way of life is an acting-together; and in acting together, men have common sensations, concepts, images, ideas, attitudes that make them consubstantial" (*Rhetoric* 21). To reach this state of "consubstantiality," Burke's most powerful rhetorical move is "identification": "[A] speaker persuades an audience by the use of stylistic identifications; his

act of persuasion may be for the purpose of causing the audience to identify
with the speaker's interests" (*Rhetoric* 46). Burke's identification is what we
might call soft persuasion; it's often argued that it's not even persuasion at
all because of how indirect it is. Humans naturally want to be in a community, so rhetors use identification to take advantage of this need: here's how
we are like one another; here's how my argument fits into your worldview.
What's particularly intriguing about Burke's identification and consubstantiality today is that they're increasingly backed up by neuroscience. Brain
imaging scans have shown, for example, that "mental representations of the
concepts of the *self* and of *close others* emerge from the same brain circuitry.
Activating either of those concepts can lead to neuronal *cross-excitement* of the
other concept and the consequent blurring of identities" (Cialdini 176–77).
Consubstantiality is real. We believe people who are like us because we believe ourselves. Ultimately, acting together, which definitionally focuses on
action—doing something—is the *telos* of Burke's rhetoric, "the use of language
as a symbolic means of inducing cooperation in beings that by nature respond
to symbols" (*Rhetoric* 43). But as much as acting together is induced through
identification, it's also created by excluding, even "scapegoating," those who
are not consubstantial (Burke, *Rhetoric* 20–21; *Philosophy* 191–220). For Burke,
identity is as much about what we are as it is about what we are not.

Paradoxically, however, Burke's recognition of division and exclusion from
decision-making is one of his major strengths for deliberation. Through exclusion in the name of action, Burke begins to direct us towards a pragmatic
*decision-making we*: the *who*, who gets a say. "Democratic logics always entail
drawing a frontier between 'us' and 'them,'" Chantal Mouffe describes of the
necessity of such exclusion. "Those who belong to the 'demos' and those who
are outside it. This is the condition for the very exercise of democratic rights"
(4). In the wake of the atomic bomb, for instance, Burke writes that scientists
need to distinguish themselves from the military: "To speak merely in praise
of science, without explicitly dissociating oneself from its reactionary implications, is to identify oneself with these reactionary implications by default"
(*Rhetoric* 27). Scientists should control science and exclude warmongers. Aristotle has the luxury of not delineating a decision-making we (it's assumed his
audience consists of free, male, militarily-trained citizens). Burke, however,
has a larger, more diverse citizenship and must theorize exclusion. In order to
democratically take action, some voters' opinions and values are always going
to be left out.

Where Aristotle relies on examining nostalgic commonplaces to learn
about his audience, one of the unique ways in which the Burkean rhetorician
knows his audience (and, thereby, makes himself consubstantial with it) is

the survey of *god terms*, words by which a community's worldview might be divined. "In any term we can posit a world," Burkes observes, "in the sense that we can treat the world *in terms of it*, seeing all as emanations, near or far, of its light. Such reduction to a simplicity being technically reduction to a summarizing title of 'God term,' . . . we must forthwith ask ourselves what complexities are subsumed beneath it" (*Grammar* 105). God terms are intricate value systems condensed into a single representative word. In the tomato harvester saga, for instance, the University of California poses "progress" and "academic freedom" as its defining god terms. In Chapter 2 we observed the complex and contradictory values "subsumed beneath" the term "craft." Building on Burke, I argue that such god terms might be productively viewed as *god memories*, for god terms (as a form of epideictic rhetoric) are always deterministically advanced on some nostalgic power of the past. Where else do god terms reside but in the collective memory of a community? "The groups I am a part [sic] at any time give me the means to reconstruct them [memories]," Halbwachs writes, "upon condition, to be sure, that I turn toward them and adopt, at least for the moment, their way of thinking" (38). Someone has benefited from thinking in restoratively nostalgic terms of "progress," "academic freedom," or "craft" and, thus, those complex histories were condensed into mnemonic touchstones upon which to construct a community.

Given Burke's action-driven rhetoric, a Burkean design method might encourage one design, briefly debated, then created, because rhetorical action for Burke stems from an almost Hegelian synthesis of multiple interests into a consubstantiality. In technical communication and design, such participatory synthesis is seen in practices like A/B testing, in which two or three versions of the same product (versions of a website, for instance) are simultaneously released. Designers then observe which design (A or B) works best for users. But, as Burke's critics point out, one design for everyone means that some audiences are left behind (Ratcliffe; McKenzie). In A/B testing, those users who prefer the losing design aren't considered, nor, typically, are the reasons why the losing product failed. Only the benefits of the winning design are studied (Pratt and Nunes 181).

A more nuanced design parallel to Burkean rhetoric can be found in the consubstantialities created in Robert Jungk and Norbert Müellert's *Zukunftswerkstätten*, future workshops (FW), a widespread German participatory method framed to get conflicting stakeholders to come together to critique the present, design ideal futures, and shape a course of action. The FW has five steps that mediate conflicting opinions while resulting in concrete actions (Lauttamäki; Vidal; Apel; Dator). It's prototypical participatory design.

1. *Preparation*: Before the future workshop starts, the designer locates a general problem that needs to be redesigned, prepares questions, invites and introduces participants (Jungk and Müellert recommend no more than 15 to 20), and gives rules for participation. Collaborators are either carefully selected by the designer or come together through a wide invitation. But a variety of perspectives (Burke's "Babel after the Fall") is vital. Of particular importance in forming a decision-making we, however, is the designer's awareness of the power structures of the invited participants (Emilson and Hillgren). Are bosses and their employees present? How might statements be made anonymous? Planning ways to destabilize unequal hierarchies and creating safe spaces to participate is vital.

2. *Critique*: In the critique phase, participants are encouraged to talk about what they believe has caused the problem—typically using sticky notes and a white board. The first stage of critique harnesses divergent thinking; as many causes as possible are listed. In the second stage, sticky notes are organized, categorized, and prioritized. Notably, the goal of critique is quantity and categorization rather than solutions or evaluations. And participants are not allowed to criticize one another's statements.

3. *Fantasy*: The fantasy stage is the method's true substance. Participants imagine ideal (as distinct from possible) futures. The goal is to develop utopias. The design mediator's role, thereby, is encouraging unconventional solutions and unrestricted thinking while limiting criticism. The guiding question: What would we do if we had no constraints?

4. *Balancing and Implementation*: In this fourth step, the ideas of the fantasy phase are evaluated in terms of implementation and reality. How can we actually achieve our ideals? Where do they overlap and where do they conflict? The mediator and participants are charged with finding links between individual utopias. Utopias are assessed in terms of possibility, and plans of action are developed that generate these utopias. Some ideas are accepted; others, rejected.

5. *Follow-Up*: This final phase takes place after the plan of action has begun. At regular intervals stakeholders reconvene to evaluate whether the plan is working and where tweaks and pivots are needed.

To teach the power of the future workshop in writing courses, I've occasionally asked students to redesign the English major in light of national declines in student numbers. Students attempt to balance training in literature; high theory; cultural studies; rhetoric, composition, and literacy; and job preparation. The first three phases of the workshop generally go pretty well. Students easily critique the major and develop numerous utopias. Developing actionable plans in step four, however, is always more difficult. Some students don't like that their fantasy was not chosen or synthesized. And futures often conflict. Unsurprisingly, the career goals of technical writing and Victorian literature students aren't always the same. Like the average citizen involved in a future workshop, students also don't often know the administrative, financial, and legal restrictions on their plans. To overcome this problem, I send groups out to interview "'intermediaries' that could spot ideas and translate dreams into a language that could be accepted by bureaucracy" (department chairs, deans, professors) or ask students to focus on what they have the assets to do themselves (action through clubs, etc.) (Emilson and Hillgren 71).

If democratic design looks like anything, it seems like it would be the future workshop. And compared to the more passive Aristotelian user-centered design, future workshops are certainly more participatory, but are they actually democratic? Part of where the future workshop, like Burkean rhetoric, falls short is that though it recognizes conflict, it urges identification and passivity. It requires, for instance, that participants don't argue with one another. Moreover, it recognizes but doesn't really plan for inequalities and differences in power. Asking an employee to publicly collaborate with a boss, for example, can be pretty dodgy. This is the utopic, unemotional, reason-centric, consensus-achieving deliberation of philosophers like Habermas (see Hauser and Benoit-Barne). Like Burkean rhetoric, the FW is also about developing a single plan of action. But what happens to the other critiques and fantasies that arise along the way? What happens to my students who feel left out in class? They generally lose interest unless I urge them to keep critiquing. *Ideally*, such outsider criticism is what keeps the feedback loop of deliberative democracy churning. Every few years (or months, or days, with the increasing speed of production) a new design is voted on and a new group of outsiders and insiders is formed. In his description of god terms, for example, Burke suggests we deal with the wickedness of rhetorical design by making the best consubstantiality we can and then, from that temporary stability, critique ourselves and become even better: "The very strength in the affirming of a given term may better enable men to make a world that departs from it. For the affirming of the term as their god-term enables men to go far afield without sensing a loss of orientation . . . the stability of the new order they have built in the name of the old order gives them the strength to abandon their old god-term and adopt another" (*Grammar* 54).

What Burke doesn't theorize, however, is that the same minorities are often left out of decision-making again and again. It would be a mistake to discount these excluded citizens. As we saw in the last chapter (and will see in the next), they rarely sit on their hands waiting for their turn. Rather, from knitting at work to bootlegging whiskey, omitted users seek their own solutions through unofficial channels. They are bricoleurs, hackers, tacticians. Good designers actively look for these differences. But Burkean rhetoric doesn't have a clear mechanism for this search. Typical future workshops, similarly, don't save those answers cast off in the balancing and implementation step. They should. "What happened to the unnecessary differences?" Krista Ratcliffe critiques of this gap. "A corollary question is: Who defines and who decides what is necessary and unnecessary. . . . In most cases, the answer is: the 'I' with the power" (59).

## Ratcliffe, Listening, and Empathic Design

In many ways, Ratcliffe's "rhetorical listening"—"a code of cross-cultural conduct[,] . . . a stance of openness"—is the ideal rejoinder to the exclusion of Burke's consubstantiality (17). Rhetorical listening is an ethic of individual responsibility and empathy that leads designers to create using the differences that Burke leaves behind by listening for consistently excluded voices. That is, where Burke's rhetoric is about coming together through identification, comparison, and demonstrating how we are like one another, Ratcliffe's rhetoric involves understanding how each individual is simultaneously similar and different, what we can learn from those differences, and innovation through juxtaposition.

The critical empathy of rhetorical listening entails four moves (26–33). First, Ratcliffe promotes an understanding of the other side rather than persuasion. She argues that though understanding can't escape intent, the rhetorician can choose a stance of "strategic idealism" in which "conscious identification among people . . . is based on a desire for an intersubjective receptivity, not mastery, and on a simultaneous recognition of similarities and difference, not merely one or the other" (27–28). That is, Ratcliffe picks up Burke's cast off differences. One cannot understand someone else without understanding how one is both similar to and different from that other. We don't always need to be consubstantial because coming together can be coercive. Differences mustn't be ignored in favor of persuasive action. Audiences aren't passive things to be manipulated. Second, by "holding oneself accountable," Ratcliffe speculates that "[A]ll people necessarily have a stake in each other's quality of life" (32). Citizens have a responsibility to be aware of their privileges. This stance disrupts "our excuses of not being personally accountable *at present* for existing cultural situations that originate *in the past*" (32). Third, through "building identifications off of similarities and difference," Ratcliffe balances Burkean and postmodern identification. Burke's identification is too focused on quick consensus, Ratcliffe argues. There are benefits to knowing how and why we are *not* like one another. Thus, where Burke's identification relies on metaphor and the seamless joining of substance (consubstantiality), Ratcliffe characterizes identification as metonymic, stressing borders. In metonymic identification (like contact zones), though audience members might temporarily join together for action, the individual is not lost in the whole. The rhetorician has a responsibility to read boundaries. Finally, rhetorical listening involves "seeking out the logic of an other." Ideas that one disagrees with come from alternative systems of logic rather than illiteracy. "By focusing on claims and cultural logics," Ratcliffe theorizes, "listeners may still disagree with each other's claims, but they may better appreciate that the other person is not simply wrong but rather functioning from within a different logic" (33). If you feel like you've seen these four points earlier in this book, that's because you have—rhetorical listening has been deeply influential to nostalgic design, and this final tenet, "seeking out the logic of an other," is foundational to how I understand ignored techno-logics and listening to nostalgia in critical nostos.

Indeed, within rhetorical listening, one powerful link to nostalgia is Ratcliffe's "accountability." Ethical creators look to the past and understand how their privilege, power, and way of thinking are historically situated. In the next two chapters I'll argue how good rhetorical designers question the sources of their expertise using this type of accountability, a form of self-aware professional knowledge I call *reflectively nostalgic expertise*. To urge this type of reflection, Ratcliffe develops a tactic she calls "eavesdropping," "a means for investigating history, whiteness, and rhetoric[,] . . . a mode of historiography, or thinking about history, that shifts our emphasis from origins to usage, foregrounding how we may circle through history even as history circles through us" (103). Similar to how I've theorized the need to appreciate not only that nostalgia is rhetorically constructed but also that it is *used to do things*, Ratcliffe's eavesdropping reminds rhetorical designers that because we use memories to act in the present, we are responsible for the hegemonies contained within those memories. Eavesdropping, for example, can be used to cast a critical eye on the remediation and digitization of old technologies. As Selfe and Selfe ask, When the computer desktop metaphor remediates the old desktop and file system, what workplace politics get transferred on as well? If rhetorical designers choose to remediate some nostalgic past into the present, they must probe the realities of that past, its attendant hegemonies, and the memories that are forgotten in every nostalgia. Nostalgic designers don't use the past without being liable for it.

Because of Ratcliffe's focus on metonymic borders, listening for different logics, and questioning expert privilege, a Ratcliffean model of design is akin to "empathic design" (Koskinen et al.; Postma et al.; Mattelmäki and Battarbee), a form of democratic making in which creators attempt to understand the cognitive, emotional, and behavioral (Gagnon and Côté) states and contexts of their users in order to create better experiences. If empathy is the attempt to understand and share others' experiences without actually living them, then empathic design is a means to bring users and designers into a co-understanding through the recognition of difference. In empathic design, often "the designer has to go through some degree of role immersion, and an attempt to seriously keep her data-inspired imagination in check with empirical data" (Koskinen et al. 47). To redesign hospital experiences, for instance, a designer might spend the night on a gurney, a process known as empathic modeling.

Similarly, design student Deborah Adler engaged empathic design to create a better version of the prescription pill bottle ("Clear"). One night, Adler's grandmother, Helen, took her grandfather's pills by accident (both grandparents have the initials H. Adler). In response, Adler created the "Clear RX" bottle (formerly found at Target). In her redesign, Adler sought out the design features she took for granted as an able-bodied, clear-sighted designer (small print, text that curves around a bottle, random numbers) but that hindered her grandparents. She listened for difference. Adler's new bottle was designed as a wedge that must be balanced on its cap. The name of the patient and medicine is in large print at the top of the wedge, so that when someone picks the bottle up (especially someone with poor eyesight), that information is the first thing they see. The system even has unique color-coded rings for each family member to distinguish whose prescription is whose without having to read the small print that is on most pill bottles.

Ratcliffe's argument that rhetoricians need to seek different perspectives to question their own privileges is also found in *metaphorical design* (Casakin; Saffer; Blackwell; Madsen), an empathic method in which designers take up different metaphorical lenses in order to see design contexts in a new light and "conceptualize one domain in terms of the other" (Lakoff and Johnson 8). "Metaphors constitute an uncommon juxtaposition of the familiar and the unusual," writes designer Hernan Pablo Casakin.

The app developer Heroku, for example, is celebrated for using such uncommon juxtaposition at its 2014 Waza developer conference (figure 3.1). At the gathering, Heroku COO Oren Teich juxtaposed numerous forms of nostalgic crafting—bookbinding, origami, and quilting—with higher-tech making like Arduino programming in order to take his developers out of their every-

**Figure 3.1.** Software engineer and printmaking lead Marissa Marquez (center) teaches a group of conference attendees how to create woodcut linotypes. Also pictured (right of center) is the creative director of Waza, Todd Matthews. Photo: Todd Matthews.

day mindset and consider their app designs in a new light. "Why do we care about crafts?" Teich asks. "Because I want you to be thinking not just about 'how do I write the best line of code,' but 'how do I open myself up to world of what's possible.' . . . If you're just working with what you know, you have a very narrow view of the world, but if you can look at origami or printmaking, you're going to be a better programmer" (Mitroff). Understanding the world through someone else's nostalgic metaphors allows designers to step out of their own techno-logic and, hopefully, critique it.

A final form of empathic design is found in Bill Gaver, Tony Dunne, and Elena Pacenti's "cultural probes," fill-in-the-blank packages given to users to learn about cultures completely foreign to the designer. In the original instance of cultural probes, for example, Gaver, Dunne, and Pacenti sought to "increase the presence of the elderly in their local communities" (22). Inside the packages they provided were a variety of context-sketching interactions, designed to engage their elderly users in individualized making. There were postcards that participants mailed back to the researchers with handwritten responses to prompts such as "Tell us about your favorite device" and "Please tell us a piece of advice or insight that is important to you." There were local maps that participants were asked to mark, designating places they go to meet people, to daydream, and would like to go but can't (23). There were even disposable cameras that participants used to take pictures of designs that were boring, desirable, and home defining. One can see how probes engage these elderly users as experts and break with the essentialism of Aristotelian design. The designers focus on individuals. "We tried to reject stereotypes of older people as 'needy' or 'nice,'" the authors describe (25). Compared to the passive, problem-centered interactions of user-centered design and future workshops, the data from probes is a more holistic and empowering tour of the use context.

Still, this model may be too "human-centered" and individual. Community and consensus are relatively (even purposefully) absent. There hasn't been much research, for example, on what actually happens to the conflicting data collected from cultural probes (Boehner et al.). Gaver, Dunne, and Pacenti write that the goal of probes is not data—it's speculative design: "inspiration, not information" (25). But though they are empathic, cultural probes aren't necessarily empowering. The designer decides what activities stakeholders take part in and then decides how to translate those findings (Dindler et al.; Hulkko et al.; Paulos and Jenkins).

Similarly, though Ratcliffe[6] argues for a concept of identification that balances modern community and postmodern difference and rejects "relativist empathy,"[7] she privileges difference, borders, metonyms, negotiating "troubled identifications," and personal responsibility. This focus on individual difference over community action can make collective decisions pretty difficult. In the tomato harvester design, for example, should *everyone* (farmer, consumer, politician, scientist, citizen) have an equal voice in deliberation or only those most affected or most expert? Who gets to vote? How can a collective decision be made? How is responsibility shared? The Burkean telos of collective action is purposefully missing.

Moreover, just as the proponents of human-centered design (HCD) critique UCD for focusing on users as mere components of technical systems, Donald Norman critiques HCD (and, thereby, empathic design) for overvaluing user opinions:

> One basic philosophy of HCD is to listen to users, to take their complaints
> and critiques seriously. Yes, listening to customers is always wise, but acceding
> to their requests can lead to overly complex designs. Several major software
> companies, proud of their human-centered philosophy, suffer from this problem.
> Their software gets more complex and less understandable with each revision.
> Activity-Centered philosophy tends to guard against this error because the focus
> is upon the Activity, not the Human. As a result, there is a cohesive, well-

articulated design model. If a user suggestion fails to fit within this design model, it should be discarded. Alas, all too many companies, proud of listening to their users, would put it in. ("Human")

Where I suggested Aristotelian design might consider only passive notions of the user, faulty versions of empathic design discount collaboration in the other direction. In this flawed model, the designer gives the user everything she wants, despite what the designer's expertise advises. This silencing of designer expertise, what Ezio Manzini calls "participation-ism," is one of the inherent pitfalls of contemporary participatory rhetoric and design ("Design Culture" 57). A customer-is-always-right perspective, as the stories of chapters 4 and 5 will illustrate, is rarely ideal. Rhetorical design relies on a careful balance of designer and user expertise.

## Mouffe, Agonism, and Agonistic Design

To achieve this balance, philosopher Chantal Mouffe's agonistic rhetoric dwells somewhere between Burke's consubstantiality and Ratcliffe's individual responsibility.[8] In *The Democratic Paradox*, Mouffe argues that the problems of deliberation in many contemporary democracies stem from the gap between *democratic* and *liberal* traditions. The community-centric democratic tradition (see Aristotle and Burke) strives for the betterment of the polis through collective decisions by the people. Through core values of equality and popular sovereignty, democracy puts the polis first and the individual second. On the other hand, in the liberal tradition individual liberties and human rights come first (see Ratcliffe).[9] Difference and freedom are privileged. In contemporary *neo*liberalism, however, Mouffe critiques that in order to find some action-driving consensus among diverse individual freedoms, public ethics and private morality are artificially separated (Condit; MacIntyre; Farrell).

In the isolation of private values (conflicting traditions of religion, family, sexuality, etc.) and public scientifically rational ethics, contemporary liberalism transforms itself into a fundamentalism and, thereby, sequesters anyone that reasons from morals. Kimberly Smith, as mentioned in chapter 1, argues that nostalgia itself, rather than being truly ancient, arose in the nineteenth century to be rhetorically used in this way by progressives to account "for the troubling persistence of those dissenting voices—conservatives, agrarians, and traditionalists of various sorts—that oppose the 'progressive' rationalization and mechanization" (506). This fundamentalist stratagem of keeping private values out of public deliberation shuts down debate and makes harnessing diverse repertoires of mêtis (which are largely based on private values) impossible. It's futile to separate private values and public interests in a democracy.

Those who claim to do so are often just saying that *their* values should be the ones publicly recognized as logical. As we'll see in the next chapter, such exclusion tends to create a political polarization between, for instance, science and religion, which can lead to religious citizens feeling excluded from decision-making and, thereby, rejecting or creating their own versions of science.

In contrast to exclusive democratic and liberal models, Mouffe imagines a *liberal democracy*: "By constantly challenging the relations of inclusion-exclusion implied by the political constitution of 'the people' . . . the liberal discourse of universal human rights plays an important role in maintaining the democratic contestation. On the other side, it is only thanks to the democratic logics of equivalence that frontiers can be created and a demos established without which no real exercise of rights could be possible" (10). Liberalism, in other words, deciphers the riddle of the stagnant outsider in Burke's consubstantiality, whereas, democracy answers the hitch of the relative lack of collective action in empathic design. Democracy needs rich conflict to survive.

To initiate this balance, Mouffe theorizes *agonistic rhetoric*, which, similar to Ratcliffe's listening, suggests that the *them* of us vs. them arguments must "no longer [be] perceived as an enemy to be destroyed, but an 'adversary' . . . which does not entail condoning ideas that we oppose . . . but treating those who defend them as legitimate opponents. . . . Each of them propose its own interpretation of the 'common good' and tries to implement a different form of hegemony" (102–04). This last statement on hegemony is especially important because it embraces the fact that even in idyllic pluralism or community there is power. The goal of the agonistic democracy is not to extinguish power nor find permanent consensus but to take temporary actions that an interim decision-making we can agree upon and to maintain debate so that when citizens select a design it will be open to change. "We have to accept that every consensus exists as a temporary result of a provisional hegemony," Mouffe writes, "and that it always entails some form of exclusion. The ideas that power could be dissolved through a rational debate . . . are illusions which can endanger democratic institutions" (104–05).

Within Mouffe's agonistic rhetoric, nostalgia winds through her juxtaposition of the liberal and democratic we. According to Mouffe, to answer the question, *Who* are we? both liberal and democratic governments have a nostalgic notion of a pre-lapsarian community in mind, an ideal public to which they seek to return. Where the liberal nostalgic we is all of humanity (an almost pre-societal we of non-closure),[10] the democratic we is a nostalgic polis (a small group of people who know one another and quickly make decisions). Both of these collectives are shaken by the realities of contemporary democracy. The democratic side is disturbed that once a nation gets too big, truly democratic decisions are slow, ill-informed, and sacrificed through mechanisms like representative voting. In contrast, liberalism embraces a vast we, but, in doing so, forgoes the possibility of the individual rights it fights for. "If the people are to rule," Mouffe argues, "it is necessary to determine who belongs to the people. Without any criterion to determine who are the bearers of democratic rights, the will of the people could never take shape" (44–45). It's the agonistic nostalgic contact zone between these two types of nostalgic we that drives democracy. The democratic desire for exclusivity allows for decision and action while the liberal desire for inclusivity is a platform from which to critique those decisions and fight for more inclusive redesigns.

An amalgam of the design styles described thus far, Mouffian agonistic design might seek quick and critical choice (like Burke) but try to reincorporate those techno-logics not included in later designs (like Ratcliffe) through constant debate.[11] Fortunately, I don't have to imagine this theory from scratch because designer Carl DiSalvo has been developing it for the past decade as "adversarial design." Adversarial design, DiSalvo explains, "is a kind of cultural production that does the work of agonism through the conceptualization and making of products and services and our experiences with them" (*Adversarial Design* 2). The goal of an adversarial design (which for DiSalvo is a thing rather than a process) is to provoke thought through conflict and spark debates about possible futures. DiSalvo argues that most theories of "design for democracy" have focused on designing for *politics* (clear laws, voting mechanisms, etc. that make democratic consensus easier) rather than designing for the *political* (opening and encouraging public debate over designs) ("Design"). In contrast, adversarial designs are odd creations that spark conversations and debates about the question, Who *are* we?

Such agonism is found, for example, in Dunne and Raby's "critical design," in which designers create "speculative design proposals to challenge narrow assumptions, preconceptions and givens about the role products play in everyday life. . . . Its opposite is affirmative design: design that reinforces the status quo" (Raby). The designers' "Evidence Dolls" (figure 3.2), for instance, ask, How will dating change once DNA analysis is easily accessible and undesirable genes are quickly identifiable? Raby explains: "The project consists of one hundred specially designed dolls used to provoke discussion amongst a group of young single women. . . . A black indelible marker allows women to note down interesting characteristics of their lover. Hair, toenail clippings, saliva, and sperm can be collected and stored in the penis drawer. Four single women told us about their lovers . . . and speculated on the implications of DNA on dating in the future." The Evidence Doll is designed to incite conversations about designer babies, screening for genetic "defects,"

**Figure 3.2.** Anthony Dunne and Fiona Raby's "Evidence Dolls." Photo: Kristof Vrancken / Z33.

and even DNA theft. It takes ideals about dating and procreation and uses a possible future to call those ideals into question. Thus, the women who interacted with the dolls began to critically engage the contact zone between dating nostalgias and the future of DNA sequencing. "I think claiming a child from one of the lovers would be a bit disconcerting," one woman states, "but if that lover had died it might be comforting. . . . If he was a really close, close friend and you brought him back as one of your children." Another participant reflects, "I quite like that idea that men can be the test tube for women, women can be empowered in some sense." Designer Preben Mogensen calls this type of designerly conversation starting "provotyping" (a portmanteau of "provoke" and "prototype"). In provotyping, designers act as provocateurs seeking to "help the practitioners experience what is wrong with the present before making decisions about the future" (16).

Ultimately, DiSalvo, Dunne and Raby, and Mogensen contribute to rhetorical design by illustrating how designers might provoke their users to reconsider their lives by becoming aware of the arguments of the things around them. That is, rhetorical designs hail critical user audiences that can actively participate in democracy. In the rest of this book, I call this purposeful awakening *informed dissent* (as opposed to informed consent), the critical training of user audiences to disagree with designers and become partners in agonism. When fostering informed dissent, the designer shows what complications and changes a community might encounter if it selects a certain design—specifically juxtaposing the new possibilities with the cherished traditions of a community. As John Forester describes in *The Deliberative Practitioner,* "The challenge of democratic deliberation is not to avoid, transcend, or displace conflict but to deal with practical difference in and through conflictual settings" (84).

Because agonism is foundational to nostalgic contact zones, I also see some of nostalgic design's drawbacks in it. The deepest of these pits is its utter devotion to conflict. Agonistic design doesn't want pure resolution because resolution gums up the feedback loop of democracy. Resolution doesn't promote redesign. Mouffe disdains centrist politics and promotes polarized political parties for this reason. But, as we've seen in recent U.S. politics, one of the dangers of this style of democracy is how quickly it becomes mired in fundamentalisms, antagonism, and duality. DiSalvo, for example, describes the adversarial software *Agonistics: A Language Game.* The goal of the game is to have a debate. Winners are those players whose ideas are discussed the most. "One way to have your idea referenced by others," DiSalvo explains, "is to take a controversial position, thereby provoking response" (*Adversarial Design* 5). This idea that controversy wins democracy (though increasingly true) is frightening. Thus, like the metaphor of the contact zone, agonistic design might too quickly promote cleanly opposed parties that sensationalize one another. Technology is never an either-or choice. Multiple traditions co-exist simultaneously.

The constant conflict of agonistic design can also simply be agonizing. For example, as mentioned in chapter 2, Jeff Bezos, CEO of Amazon, takes an agonistic approach to Amazon's organizational design. He urges employees to constantly review and critique one another: "Of all of his management notions, perhaps the most distinctive is his belief that harmony is often overvalued in the workplace—that it can stifle honest critique and encourage polite praise for flawed ideas. Instead, Amazonians are instructed to 'disagree and commit.'" Employees working in this system quickly burn out: "Ms. Willet's co-workers strafed her through the Anytime Feedback Tool, the widget in the company directory that allows employees to send praise or criticism about colleagues to management. . . . Because team members are ranked, and those at the bottom eliminated. . . . [M]any workers called it a river of intrigue and scheming. They described making quiet pacts with colleagues to bury the same person at once, or to praise one another lavishly. Many others, along with Ms. Willet, described feeling sabotaged by negative comments" (Kantor and Streitfeld).

But there's a more central critique of agonistic design—a critique of democratic design in general. Why should the inexpert, uninformed, and misinformed public have a say in technological decision-making at all? Walter Lippmann, for instance, infamously argues in his *Public Opinion* that when ignorant citizens insist on having a say in deliberative forums, those uninformed ideals constrain, manipulate, and replace the knowledge of experts. Indeed, such manipulation is exactly what happens in Amazon's feedback tool. The next two chapters approach this concern in detail, but for now, my retort is that the rhetorical designer's and user audience's expertise aren't the same nor should they be approached as such. There's a difference between the epistemic technê of designers and the mêtis of users. Listening to the conflicts of these experts in nostalgic contact zones is less about valuing all opinions equally than it is about valuing them for different purposes, considering: What competing publics have these conflicts come from? What can we learn from them? And how can we form a new decision-making we? We shouldn't be okay with experts and nonexperts simply agreeing to disagree or a passive moral relativism where all facts are true. We really do need to listen to experts. But the examples of this chapter—tomato farmers working with crop scientists, trade unions working with computer programmers, prescription bottle designers listening to the elderly—illustrate that it's not only possible for "nonexpert" citizens to co-design with experts, it's prudent. This, in the end, is what the democratic design of technology looks like.

## Conclusions: Rhetorical Design and Democracy

So, what have we gained from touring democratic deliberation on the twin rails of rhetoric and design? To start, we've seen how design methods—from user ethnographies to future workshops—show what it takes for democratic deliberation to work as a small-scale vernacular practice. All of our design methods illustrate that contrary to Aristotle's polis, the publics involved in democratic deliberation aren't static or predetermined. Rather, they rise in response to opportunities for action and are constantly changing. In conjunction, our rhetorical theories have shown that the deliberative design of technologies (despite many technical experts' objections) will never be a purely rational decision. Because design is inescapably rhetorical, it will always involve negotiations of emotion, trust, tradition, persuasion, exclusion, empathy, and the like. In this way, rhetoric highlights what makes design human and design grounds rhetorical theory in the human world. Each of the models of rhetorical design described in this chapter poses a different view on how to capture and/or bring about the construction of these uniquely human deliberations:

## Aristotelian User-Centered Design: Analysis

- *Benefits*: Minimizes a designer's subjectivity through direct observations and interviews of users. Can provide useful qualitative and quantitative data on user groups.
- *Drawbacks*: Focuses too closely on etic data rather than the wide variety of alternative design solutions and needs that could be provided by a fuller understanding of users away from the immediate context of technological use. Can fall into a stereotypical understanding of user groups. Avoids mediating between conflicting user groups.
- *Lessons*: Theories of rhetorical design need to understand how to read a user audience, including and beyond their place in a technical system.

## Burkean Participatory Design: Action

- *Benefits:* Pragmatically focuses on action. Defines the necessity of limiting the decision-making we. Argues (though does not theorize how) citizens cast out of the consubstantiality must be redesigned for at some point.
- *Drawbacks:* Excludes the same minorities from the consubstantiality again and again. These minorities are often the most innovative users.
- *Lessons:* Theories of rhetorical design need to understand that not everyone's voice will be incorporated into final design decisions but also need a mechanism to reincorporate those voices repeatedly excluded.

## Ratcliffean Empathic Design: Empathy

- *Benefits:* Recognizes simultaneously right design traditions and futures based in different cultural logics. A privileging of outsider identities and a deconstruction of the designer's own power. Urges questioning professional expertise as a nostalgic narrative of power. An ethical responsibility for the other.
- *Drawbacks:* Focuses on individuals and broader contexts of use, making it difficult to leap from user understandings to a single action/design. No theory for ethically balancing user mêtis and designer epistemic technê—user difference is privileged.
- *Lessons:* Theories of rhetorical design need to seek out minority user voices to be inclusive but also need a pragmatic means of mediating stakeholder expertise in collective actions.

## Mouffean Agonistic Design: Argument

- *Benefits*: Understands the impossibility of true consensus and the necessity of constant deliberation and argument before, during, and after design decisions in order to motivate reincorporating minorities necessarily ejected from the decision-making we in favor of action. Welcomes all human discourse including and beyond purely rational decisions.
- *Drawbacks*: Has a devotion to conflict and abhorrence of consensus that causes a rise of sensationalist values in debate.
- *Lessons:* Theories of rhetorical design incorporate spaces for noisy users: users who argue, solve problems, contribute knowledge, etc. They train critical user audiences that become agonistic adversaries in deliberation: *informed dissent.*

Analysis, action, empathy, and argument—at one end of this spectrum of rhetorical design we have Aristotle and Burke, who seek action-packed consensus through persuasion and identification. On the other we have Ratcliffe, who listens for individuality to challenge hegemony and welcome difference. In between is Mouffe, who encourages the clashes between these two other bands. Importantly, though I've critiqued each model, all four are indelibly true.[12] Because democracy always takes on unique forms given unique combinations of problems, stakeholders, and resources, it's fairly pointless to imagine it abstractly. Good rhetorical designers will calculate when to ply each method to bring about collective action.

It's in this focus on acting collectively in communities that are never chastely rational that we return to nostalgia. To understand the foundation of publics and, therefore, how and why they act in deliberations, rhetorical designers must understand different communities' traditions, enthymemes, god terms and memories, and values. Whether it's making the best design or the best argument, rhetorical designers must imagine and balance the deliberative issue from multiple publics' views simultaneously.

In doing so, we also come back to that question, *Who are we?* The nostalgic contact zones revealed by this community-centric question focus designers on the tension between innovation and tradition, permanence and change, or as Preben Mogensen writes: "One can focus on tradition or transcendence, but the question is always that of tradition *and* transcendence—we are always to some degree bound in our tradition and, at the same time, have to transcend the present in order to solve our problems" (2). Though nostalgia hasn't been the key player in this chapter that it is in others, then, it's vital to understand how its tensions define where all publics have been, where they are, and where they are going. Without understanding and constantly rebalancing nostalgia's constitutive force, as we'll see in the next chapter, citizens get frozen in unmoving debates and refuse to co-design together. To escape such locks of incommensurability, democratic design must involve forming new communities of nostalgia. In the next chapter, I test how this rebalancing works in an incredibly arduous negotiation of tradition and transcendence between scientists, physicians, worried parents, celebrities, state legislators, and autistic citizens—the U.S. anti-vaccination movement.

# Chapter 4

# Nostalgic Mediations

Asking the Right Questions in Vaccine Communication

Mommy instinct . . . I know my kid . . . I know what's going on in his body, so this is what makes sense to me. . . . My science is named Evan, and he's at home.

**Jenny McCarthy, anti-vaccination advocate, *The Oprah Winfrey Show***

The media likes controversy. It's not a controversy—only one side is supported by science.

**Dr. Paul Offit, vaccine scientist and advocate, "Vaccine Disputes"**

Our concern is with the opportunity that might be missed in the process of quickly dismissing stories as unreliable. What might be missed is the work done by stories to construct realities, not just to report on them, apparently inaccurately.

**John Winslade and Gerald Monk, *Practicing Narrative Mediation***

For over a millennium smallpox plagued civilizations from China to Egypt to England, killing billions and leaving untold more blind and scarred for life.[1] Combatting the disease seemed hopeless, and little was done beyond bloodletting, herbal tinctures, and prayer.[2] It wasn't until the late eighteenth century that Englishman Edward Jenner made a world-altering observation: milkmaids exposed to the less-deadly cowpox seemed immune to smallpox's ravages. Of course, this fact had been known by farmers for decades if anyone had bothered to listen. But in May of 1796 Jenner formally tested the hypothesis. He injected eight-year-old James Phipps with cowpox, freshly harvested from the lesions of local milkmaid Sarah Nelmes. After Phipps recovered, Jenner injected the boy with lethal smallpox. No disease developed, and the "vaccine"—from the Latin *vacca*, cow—was born.

Almost immediately, the first anti-vaccination movement surfaced. Though the vaccine was incredibly effective, it bred fear by violating traditions of medicine, nature, and religion. Some citizens, for instance, saw smallpox as divine judgment, citing Job 2:7, "So went Satan forth from the presence of the Lord

**Figure 4.1.** Satirist James Gillray's 1802 "The Cow-Pock—or—the Wonderful Effects of the New Inoculation!" featuring Dr. Jenner vaccinating frightened citizens.

and smote Job with boils, from the sole of his foot, unto his crown" (Mnookin 25). Others were confused about how contracting one disease could thwart another. In an 1802 cartoon (figure 4.1), satirist James Gillray illustrates anxiety about this unnaturalness by depicting citizens growing cow-shaped lesions and horns. A new technology, as they so often do, instilled fear of the future because it didn't engage a graspable past. Though the vaccine may have served the greater good, in terms of chapter 3, its designer didn't understand it as an argument; it wasn't rhetorical; it didn't engage with its user audience. Innovation without tradition led to alienation.

Over the centuries, anti-vaccination sentiment wanes and waxes, surfacing in response to advances in medicine, perpetuated by an anxiety of the unknown, and (like so many technology-hesitant cultures) always chasing god memories of "nature" and "self-determination." Its most recent manifestation, for instance, began in England in response to a 1998 study by gastroenterologist Andrew Wakefield.[3] Wakefield's co-authored *Lancet* paper distorted patient histories to erroneously link the measles, mumps, and rubella (MMR) vaccine; bowel disease; and autism. This article was soon retracted, invalidated, proven fraudulent. Wakefield even lost his medical license. But, reacting to media coverage and uncertainty on autism's true origins, anti-vaccination sentiment thrives.[4]

The belief usually spreads by one of two paths. On the first, a friend, family member, or television show warns a (typically white, college-educated, upper-middle-class) new parent about vaccinations.[5] The parent Googles "Are vaccines safe?" and finds captivating personal anti-vaccination stories. On the other track, the parent of an autistic child, facing a doctor without a clear answer, Googles "What causes autism?" and finds a similar set of narratives. Both types of parents are nostalgic for hope, control, and protection in the face of the "chaos" of autism, and the anti-vaccination community offers it. Remember, nostalgia's primary psychological function is the homeostatic search for stable identities and communities in times of change. Thus, in parts of Oregon, New York, and California, childhood vaccination rates have plummeted, triggering spates of disease not seen for years. In December 2014, for example, 145 Americans contracted measles spread by 40 visitors to Disneyland. Of 110 infected Californians, 45 percent were unvaccinated (Zipprich et al.). Today, 85 percent of healthcare providers have encountered a parent who refuses to vaccinate (Healy and Pickering).

For their part, physicians are enraged by the trend, wondering why scientific expertise is no longer simply trusted. They argue that vaccination is a public health, not private, issue and that patients should just listen to their doctors. Paul Offit, vaccine scientist and the face of *anti-* anti-vaccination, for example, describes, "The media likes controversy. It's not a controversy—only one side is supported by science. It's like screaming into the wind on some level" (Coombes 1530). Yet, physicians and scientists who deploy such "science says you're wrong" arguments *are* "screaming into the wind" but not for the reason they think. Like the anti-vaccination movement's nostalgia for nature, liberty, and a time before autism, vaccine advocates argue (or refuse to argue) through their own restorative nostalgia, longing for a time when science was Truth. Such responses are about as far from rhetorical design as you can get.

This chapter explores the mediating powers of nostalgia in an era where technical design is increasingly democratic and democracy, increasingly incommensurable. In it, I argue that rather than refusing anti-vaccination parents, medical communicators, representing many creators struggling in science and technology-hesitant climates, can become nostalgic designers who engage in rhetorical design. Where in answering the worry, "Is your technology safe?" a typical scientist might simply reply, "Yes, here's some evidence," the nostalgic designer opens a forum for informed dissent, considering: Why are you asking this question? Why do I simply want to reply, Yes? How and why do our concepts of good design differ? And what are we each nostalgic for, why, and to which ends? Such questions move scientific arguments away from questions of fact and towards questions of identity and commonality. Ideally, they lead to co-design as a form of mediation and community building. In other words, though science has disproven most anti-vaccine claims (and, therefore, anti-vaccination is a "manufactured scientific controversy," in Leah Ceccarelli's terms, because there is no real debate among scientists), scientific redesign is not the point, here. For science and design to work in this era where citizens long for simpler knowable pasts, science *communication* and *expertise* must rhetorically adapt to fit different user audience realities. For, whatever one's opinion, the fact we begin from is that anti-vaccination activists are users of a design they feel has failed them. They've nostalgically turned to a pre-vaccine past out of fear of a technology that's been falsely associated with autism. And falling vaccination rates verify that vaccine safety most certainly is a controversy that must be addressed. Therefore, though most readers might disagree with vaccine-hesitant parents, just as we studied the nostalgic crafters of chapter 2, we can learn from these excluded users' reminiscences as mêtis.

To test nostalgia's mediating powers and seek out this mêtis, in this chapter I analyze the rhetoric of three vaccine controversy texts: a segment of a 2004 *Larry King Live* interview with anti-vaccination celebrity parents Jenny McCarthy and Jim Carrey; a 2011 interview with Paul Offit; and the proceedings of a 2015 California State Senate Committee on SB 277, a bill requiring children attending school to be vaccinated. In doing so, I cultivate *nostalgic stasis*, a technique of using nostalgia to generate questions that initiate informed dissent and agonistic redesign, a search for technological identities and platforms for persuasion and, most significantly, empathy, common ground, community, and hope.

## The Rise of Participatory Medicine

At first glance, though, applying the deliberative methods of chapter 3 to the high stakes of medicine might seem disturbing. Is this really a democratic design milieu? What expertise beyond a list of symptoms can a patient contribute? What if a patient's participation endangers herself or others? Don't well-trained doctors know best? Rhetorician William Covino calls such questions "arresting magic," language that simplifies the world so that the speaker's epistemic technê appears to be the only way to live. We've called this magic "fundamentalist rhetoric," "technological determinism," "big ego design," and "restorative nostalgia." But as we've seen, design, rhetoric, and expertise are always indeterminate. The nostalgic designer uses contact zones and critical nostos to transform arresting magic into *generative magic*, "a (re)sorcery of spells for *generating* multiple perspectives" (Covino 9). There's a long tradition in medicine, for instance, that ruptures doctor-is-always-right nostalgia and awakens medical expertise to its place in time.

At the dawn of "biomedicine" (medicine employing the study of biology like the vaccine, germ theory, and pasteurization) there were numerous healthcare traditions to choose from: surgeons, barbers, midwives, apothecaries, homeopaths, et al. Nineteenth-century healthcare was indeterminate. Biomedicine was new and (as seen in early vaccine fears) not really trusted. In order to compete for patients, biomedical practitioners deployed what Barbara Ehrenreich and Deirdre English label "heroic medicine." Bleeding, vomiting, and sweating were biologically unnecessary but powerfully rhetorical acts that calmed patients' fears of the new by engaging the highly visual Gallenic tradition. In this way, early biomedicine was user centered and adapted for patient traditions even if it wasn't participatory.

A century later, one might see 1979 as the dawn of the modern user-centered healthcare moment. Responding to a crisis of confidence triggered by one hundred years of violations of biomedical ethics (e.g., Nazi experiments in the 1940s, birth defects from thalidomide in the '50s, the Tuskegee syphilis experiment from the '30s to the '70s), in 1979 the National Commission for the Protection of Human Subjects of Biomedical and Behavioral Research prepared *The Belmont Report*. The report empowers research subjects through informed consent, clear appraisals of risk, and equitable subject pools. Deploying the ethics of *The Belmont Report* in practice, the 1991 Patient Self Determination Act (PSDA) requires every Medicaid- and Medicare-receiving facility to inform patients of their right to specify advanced directives such as do not resuscitate (DNR) orders. Patients are increasingly empowered to participate in medical decision-making. Still, this style of medicine is pretty user centered instead of participatory. Users choose within but don't reshape the system. Though *The Belmont Report* urges informed consent, for instance, "consent" is limited to approval, not input or redesign.

*The Belmont Report* and PSDA are the biomedically sanctioned side of user-centered medicine. But accompanying these ratified moves has been a long line of patient-determined *participatory* happenings. Concurrent with *The Belmont Report*, for example, feminist movements of the 1960s and '70s urged women to trust themselves, including a right to birth control (Griswold v. Connecticut; Eisenstadt v. Baird), midwives, abortions, and other choices that support traditional feminine mêtis (see *Our Bodies, Ourselves*). Serving capitalist rather than emancipatory intents, the 1980s saw the dawn of the direct-to-consumer advertising of drugs, which similarly urged patients to participate in their healthcare by requesting specific medications. And, of course, the '90s saw the Oprah-frication of medical expertise. Blurring fantasy and fiction, Oprah welcomed as scientific experts Dr. Oz (a real M.D. who pushed quack elixirs, homeopathy, and psychics) and *The Secret* author Rhonda Byrne (who encouraged viewers to heal themselves through the power of positive thinking). Today, WebMD and millions of online medical forums further counterpoint physician expertise. Perhaps most transforming, given a rise in immeasurable chronic conditions such as migraines, fatigue, and fibromyalgia, patients increasingly turn to non-biomedical therapies from chiropractic to acupuncture. Though such practices often fail randomized controlled trials, they help patients by way of the social, psychological, and empathic interactions that biomedicine—because of an impetus of speed and thrift—no longer provides (Derkatch; Kaptchuck and Eisenberg). Healthcare dialogue, debate, and choice are on an upswing. Medicine, once again, is indeterminate.

Despite administrative calls for efficiency, then, biomedicine has responded to this indeterminacy by creating its own alternative future: *participatory medical design*. I use the phrase *participatory medicine* in this chapter rather than parallel terms like "patient-centered," "whole-person" (Hutchinson), "biopsychosocial" (Engel), "integrative," and "narrative" (Charon; Schleifer and Vannatta) medicine because I'm interested in how the democratization of medical expertise fits into the larger participatory design setting of this book. Increasingly, patients expect individualized healthcare and to be respected as experts about their own bodies. Thus, the central transformation of participatory medicine is "shared decision-making," in which "the patient's task is to tell the doctor his or her health beliefs, and the doctor's task is to enable this to happen. The doctor must also convey his or her (professionally informed) health beliefs to the patient. The intention is to form a therapeutic alliance" (Marinker 747–48). But, as you might guess, what this statement from physician Marshall Marinker minimizes are conflicts between patient and physician expertise. "The notion of medical expertise today highlights the tension between those whose knowledge is based on science and those who understand illness through personal, lived experience," writes E. Johanna Hartelius (42). In such wicked settings, nostalgic designers start by defining shared questions.

## Nostalgic Stasis: A Method for Defining Shared Questions

Chapters 2 and 3 focused largely on reflective nostalgia, the critical layering of multiple pasts to redesign the present. In contrast, this chapter seeks to mediate and find productive discontinuities in *restorative* nostalgias. Restorative nostalgia, as Svetlana Boym theorizes, is the nostalgia of fundamentalists who reject the mutable nature of the past and, thereby, anyone that reasons from non-sanctioned traditions. Where actual customs (medicine, government, religion) constantly change, restorative nostalgics isolate a moment in history that benefits them, cherish it as a god memory, and challenge, Why adapt if it's worked in the past? This freeze halts collaboration, agonism, the search for parallel pasts and futures in nostalgic contact zones, and, thereby, democratic design.

One rhetorical method for disrupting such restorative thinking is *stasis theory*, "cooperative and organized question-asking practices [that] calm complex interdisciplinary . . . disputations" (Shea and Mozafari 20). Stasis is the permanence that leads to change, the construction of an arena for deliberation, a method of argumentative invention, and a system of mediation. Classically, as a heuristic of argument, ancient rhetoricians (Hermagoras; Cicero; Hermogenes) used stasis to plot how a debate might unfold. Stasis predicted points and counterpoints by answering four questions: fact (Did it happen?), definition (What happened? Was it a crime?), quality (What is the character of the act? Was the crime justified?), and policy/jurisdiction (What should we do? Who should try this case?). In contrast, in contemporary mediation (Gross; Brizee; Shea and Mozafari) stasis is the ability to stabilize complex debates by finding agreed-upon questions. Stasis ensures that each party is talking about the same thing and, in doing so, forms a new community. In health deliberations, for example, the stasis *What medical eudaimonia are we trying to achieve?* must be carefully mediated given differences between what Ronald Schleifer and Jerry Vannatta call medicine's "chief complaint" (a medical description of the disease) and "chief concern" (patients' fears about how illness might transform their lives).[6]

Stasis theory also decentralizes expertise by finding questions that all parties can expertly answer. Epistemic technê and mêtis collaborate in an agonistic Q&A. In rhetorician Thomas Goodnight's typology, questions must be framed in a way that deliberators from personal (the average citizen arguing among friends), technical (scientists debating with colleagues), and public (legislators deliberating about a bill) spheres can all participate in the conversation using their own lines of logic and expertise. As we'll see, increasingly these spheres are indistinct. Thus, all stakeholders must be able to answer stasis questions with some skill; otherwise stases become *asystatic freezes*, topics that halt mediation because one party holds sway over the other (Pullman). Asystatic freezes often arise as accusations or unfairly reframing an opponent's argument. Why don't anti-vaccination parents listen to the facts? is asystatic. *How does each party understand the risks of vaccination?* is static. In this way, stasis seeks to form a new decision-making we in which all parties are included in deliberation.

Our lens of nostalgia adds many jetties to stasis, but its strongest offerings are a focus on emotion, assets, and hope. Where other reconciliation methods reject emotion as prohibitive to rational consensus, nostalgia's twin emotions of loss and pride are productive stases in themselves because they individualize, contextualize, and humanize technological decisions. The nostalgic designer and user audience ask, *Why are we feeling loss, anxiety, chaos, anger, and fear?* Emotion is treated as a rational asset for redesign. Moreover, where traditional mediation theories (e.g., future workshops) begin by focusing on the problem, erecting a negative past that must be overcome, nostalgic stasis simultaneously asks: *What has been lost?* And, *What do you cherish in the past that can be used to redesign the future?* This localizing tension of loss and prideful hope is nostalgia's gift to mediation. In fact, mediation experts John Winslade and Gerald Monk actively seek out this tension in a method they call "double-listening": "In mediation we are, on the one hand, particularly interested in the conflict-saturated relationship narrative in which people are stuck. And we are, on the other hand, also interested in the alternative relationship story out of which people would prefer to relate to each other, if they could" (8). It's through these bookends of loss and pride that I, again, support my search for new communities in each case by asking, *Who are we?*

- Who *Are* We? What restorative and emotionally charged god memories does each side use to progress their argument? What has caused this loss? What hope can be recovered from these nostalgias to redesign the future?
- *Who* Are We? Who does each side think should and should not make decisions about designs? What counts as expertise? Where can common ground be found? How can a more inclusive public, where all stakeholders possess expertise, be formed?

## Redesigning for an Excluded User Audience: What and Why Are Our Stories?

At the heart of the anti-vaccination movement is the parental story, a cautionary narrative of illness shared by parents as proof that vaccines have injured their child. These stories are anecdote filled, passionate, and highly identifiable—everything that typical scientific and medical texts are not. Such stories follow a specific arc that initiates parents into a community of nostalgia and loss: I took my child to the doctor to get vaccinated; I watched my child's personality change; the doctor said the illness wasn't caused by vaccines but didn't have an explanation; I know it was the vaccine, but the doctor won't listen; I felt so alone; I'm so happy I found this community of like-minded parents to give me a feeling of control. Thus, anti-vaccination stories set up a contact zone in which the mêtis of the parent (personal observation) juxtaposes, even scapegoats, biomedical authority (scientific research). They also portray a nostalgic hope for returning to a "normal" time before autism through pseudoscientific cures.

Crucially, one reason parents share their stories is because doctors have not given them a sympathetic ear, an explanation, a community to join, or hope. Rather, physicians refuse parental experience, what Jenny McCarthy calls "mommy instinct," as nonscientific. But, as Winslade and Monk write of such refusals, "Our concern is with the opportunity that might be missed in the process of quickly dismissing stories as unreliable. What might be missed is the work done by stories to *construct* realities, not just to *report* on them, apparently inaccurately" (2). Keeping such listening in mind, our first stases appear: *What are vaccine stories? Why are people telling them? How do they redesign the world? What hope might be revealed within them?* And, generally, *What are they nostalgic for, why, and to which ends?*

## Unpacking Parental Nostalgia: Why Tell Vaccine Stories?

For example, anti-vaccination celebrities Jenny McCarthy and then-boyfriend Jim Carrey's 2009 interview on *Larry King Live* about their son Evan's autism is prototypical of anti-vaccination parental anecdotes.[7] In this account, McCarthy's son, Evan, soon after being vaccinated, developed autistic characteristics. Though her doctor didn't have an answer, McCarthy's observations ("mommy instinct") and online research told her the MMR vaccine caused Evan's change. McCarthy "typed in autism on Google" and identified a diet regimen that "undiagnosed" Evan ("Jenny McCarthy's").

One way to spark communication redesign from McCarthy and Carrey's story is listening for the god memories the parents associate with the past and future in order to find "what complexities are subsumed beneath" them (Burke, *Grammar* 105). Like Burke's rhetorician, the nostalgic designer unpacks memories, not to debunk nostalgia but, rather, to help opposing sides understand one another's techno-logics so that collective decisions can be made. A running god memory throughout McCarthy and Carrey's story, for example, is the 1989 vaccine schedule:

MCCARTHY: Go back to the 1989 schedule, when shots were only ten, and the MMR was on that list. I don't know what happened in 1990; there was no plague that was killing children that we had to triple the amount of vaccines.

CARREY: What happened back in 1989 that warranted twenty-six more vaccines?

MCCARTHY: Greed. . . . This is what I'm saying. First of all, autism is treatable and preventable.

CARREY: I have seen this with my own eyes.

MCCARTHY: The vaccine schedule is too bloated right now—thirty-six shots right now. Back in 1989, the shot schedule was ten shots given.

CARREY: Ten shots given.

KING: When I was a kid, what did we get, three? . . . .

MCCARTHY: Space out the vaccines, delay them till after one, clean out the toxins that are in them; we don't need that many. ("Jenny McCarthy's")

For the celebrity parents, 1989 represents a simpler, more natural, unspoiled time before autism, before corporate greed muddled healthcare and overloaded children's immune systems. The date is restoratively nostalgic, however, in that the celebrities don't investigate reasons beyond avarice for changing the schedule, such as deaths from chicken pox. Moreover, McCarthy and Carrey's claim that the number of vaccines has gone up isn't really scientifically accurate. Though the schedule has gone from three vaccines to fourteen since 1980, the number of antigens (substances that cause immune reactions) has gone down from 3,041 to 177 (Children's). And, yet, what I'm doing here—my immediate urge to dissect McCarthy and Carrey's argument—it's wrong. It won't work. I'm not looking for mêtis, new community, or collaborators. I'm screaming into the wind because I'm focusing too closely on what the parents are nostalgic for rather than why they are nostalgic and to which ends.

The goal of examining god memories shouldn't be to hurl more facts at anti-vax parents. One should be wary of countering emotion with data. Especially, here, the citation of statistics just continues to discount the parental story and cyclically encourage feelings of exclusion. Our goal is to grant both parties expertise and create a space for co-redesign and community. By mapping god memories, we seek empathic redesign. A better response to McCarthy and Carrey's story, then, is to ask: *Where and why has nostalgic loss been felt? And what do each party's god memories mean?*

In the above excerpt, for example, god memories are intriguing because Larry King inadvertently challenges McCarthy and Carrey by asking, "When I was a kid, what did we get, three?" King's memory of three vaccines during his 1940s childhood when a polio epidemic loomed creates a nostalgic contact zone. It breaks the firm contrast between doctors and anti-vax parents and, in doing so, draws attention to the fact that fewer shots doesn't always mean healthier children. This introduction of new parties is a key move of nostalgic stasis because it breaks unproductive expertise dichotomies. There are more than two ways to view vaccination. In response, McCarthy and Carrey redraw themselves. They are not anti-vaccination, they claim. They are nostalgic for the 1989 *vaccine* schedule, after all. Recalling that nostalgia always involves loss and pride, then, let's reverse our stasis: *What nostalgic past do you hope to recover?*

Such a question might be answered through *nostalgia-typing*, a breed of neo-stalgic design in which a technology-hesitant group designs an ideal future based on an ideal past. An alternative timeline is imagined as a resource for redesign. What would McCarthy and Carrey's ideal future look like based on their 1989 nostalgia? The goal, here, is to welcome an excluded population into co-design by drawing on nostalgia as expertise and asking, *What do you feel you've lost?* Ideally, parties discover that their values overlap in places and, thereby, form a new community of nostalgia. Importantly, such co-design ascribes parents expertise on creating ideal futures but not on how to reach those futures. A model parental future might be one where autism is better supported, for instance, but how to achieve that future is medicine's expertise. Parents are granted métis, power, and hope but not a forum to unproduc-tively argue, "Stop vaccines!" In this way nostalgia-typing shifts the locus of community from anti-vaccination to pro-autistic rights, which all parties can gather around.

As a method of mediation, nostalgic stasis regularly shifts between hope and loss. So, let's return to the stasis *Where and why has nostalgic loss been felt?* Anti-vaccination parental stories paint illness and autism as unnatural losses of control. As McCarthy describes, Evan was fine one day and having seizures the next: "Boom! Soul, gone from his eyes" ("Jenny McCarthy"). There was nothing she nor her doctor could do. One might wonder where nostalgia possi-bly resides in such traumatic stories. But it's there, within the imagined ideal of normality, once predicted by expecting parents, now seemingly impossible because the vaccine (really autism) has "spoiled" it (Goffman). Illness shatters anticipatory nostalgia, and it ousts parents from a group of "normal" peers. It's isolating. In response, anti-vaccination parents use stories to order their lives, find community, and seek a control they once had. Thus, in Tom Hutchinson and James Brawer's terms, these parents tell stories to seek a Hippocratic cure (to return to some nostalgic imagined normality) rather than Asklepian heal-ing (to accept that their life has changed and move into the future) (31–43). Loss, longing, and the stories that perpetuate them are shared because change is not accepted. Like all nostalgics, anti-vaccine parents do not feel at home in the present, so they look back to a time when they did.

Unfortunately, the restorative search for a cure (rather than a reflective search for healing) creates parental guilt and a constant quest for answers. It prevents hope in the future. Retelling the story again and again as a badge of memorial membership in the anti-vaccination community perpetuates the idea that there was only one way for this family to have a good life—a non-autistic way. Mountain Mama, for example, is the author of a viral anti-vaccination story shared across Facebook and Twitter. "I'm pretty sure that I will never forgive myself," Mountain Momma writes, "for my transgressions are embodied in a beautiful seven-year-old who tells me daily that I am 'the best Mom in the universe.' I know the truth." Mountain Mama tells her story as a form of penance. It's a way to warn others, punish herself, and control her life through narrative order. Sadly, in retelling this story she also dismisses the potential happiness of her child, who praises her as "the best Mom in the universe."

In this light, by asking, *What are our vaccine stories?* we also discover the failure of medicine to offer a future-oriented healing narrative; as Mihaly Csikszentmihalyi describes, "One of the major functions of every culture has been to shield its members from chaos, to reassure them of their importance and ultimate success" (11). Currently, there's no scientific cure for autism, so biomedical expertise seems to offer no shield. To defend against the chaos of illness, parents turn to pre-autistic nostalgia. When designing medical communication, therefore, physicians must better address the isolating chaos of illness by granting narrative expertise and offering community.[8] That sense of community is especially crucial because when they are ejected from a community of normal parents, parents with autistic children scramble to find another ingroup identity, even if that means embracing an entirely new understanding of facts. As communication scientist Dannagal Young suggests: "Thinking in terms of evolutionary psychology for a moment, if we are factually wrong about something, but we are part of a group of people, we will survive. But if we are correct about something, but we're completely alone, we'll probably die. So, our bodies and our brains prioritize group identity, having that solidarity and that allegiance, over any sense of need for accuracy" ("Breaking"). In response, doctors as nostalgic designers might shift from the defensive, "Why don't you believe this scientific fact?" to, *What's your story? How can I help you move through this loss? How can I help you heal and create a new order?*

## Anti-Vaccination's Decision-Making We

To answer these questions, the second phase of nostalgic stasis is seeking each party's decision-making we and, ideally, forming a new community identity. In McCarthy and Carrey's interview it's clear the celebrities trust parents over doctors. "We want to empower parents to educate themselves," McCarthy describes. "Do we need to have the chicken pox [vaccine]? Do we have to have a hepatitis B shot on the second day of life?" Many physicians would agree with McCarthy on empowering parents (though not on the answers to her questions). Really, it's impossible to practice medical diagnosis without the patient's (or parents') narrative of illness. Parental expertise isn't the same as physician expertise, but these modes of knowledge don't have to be antagonistic. When they are, such as when anti-vaccination parents feel ignored, exclusion and isolation surface. For instance, if parents feel ignored, they start doing their own research and take medicine as a personal rather than a social responsibility. Such "individualizing" moral foundations (Graham et al.) perpetuate parental guilt (it's my fault I let my son be vaccinated) and encourage parents to value personal health and safety above community health (I don't care if my son spreads illnesses going unvaccinated; I care about my personal responsibility to him).

In describing their parental decision-making we, McCarthy and Carrey also define a not-we:

> CARREY: The AAP is financed by the drug companies. Medical schools are financed by the drug companies. . . . This is a huge business. Vaccines are the largest growing division of the pharmaceutical industry. $13 billion.
>
> MCCARTHY: They control medical schools. I mean these doctors are not learning about prevention or vitamins or diet.

Unfortunately, in painting all medical science as corrupt, the celebrities write their opponents out of collaboration, and, thereby, freeze deliberation. Svetlana Boym describes this restorative transformation: "'We' (the conspiracy theorists) for whatever reason feel insecure in the modern world and find a scapegoat for our misfortunes. . . . We project our dislike onto them and begin to believe that they dislike us and wish to persecute us" (*Future* 43). Again, however, we need to resist the urge just to say, here's proof that the AAP is not controlled by the pharmaceutical industry. We can say that, but it's not the strongest engine for redesign. Rather, nostalgic designers double-listen for hope and community in loss: *Was there ever a time when you trusted doctors? When contemporary biomedicine worked for you? How can we redesign towards that nostalgia?* McCarthy and Carrey's 1989 god memory contains an assumed nostalgia for a time when doctors and parents collaborated. Again, we might nostalgia-type, encouraging anti-vaccination parents to redesign what good medical interactions look like from this memory.

Ultimately, then, the nostalgic designer pursues redesigned futures from ideal pasts. In technology-hesitant environments, such futures often involve *nostalgic others*: idealized (often historic) groups that did not, seemingly, undergo the loss the nostalgic did but that also aren't given a forum to represent themselves. In McCarthy and Carrey's story (here, embodied by colleague J. B. Handley) this nostalgic other is other first-world countries. "We looked at thirty other countries where vaccines were introduced since 1990," Handley observes, ". . . . twenty-seven countries chose not to vaccinate for the chicken pox. The vaccine has been out for fifteen years. What are these other countries choosing to do that we're not?" ("Jenny McCarthy's"). The nostalgic designer explores how and why this other is being used: *What do you want that this other country has—fewer vaccines, less autism, something else?*

Many European countries, for example, have different methods of diagnosis that lead to lower recorded levels of autism. Concretely discussing the question, *Why has this nostalgic other not adopted our standards?* is also important. But the principal move that finding a nostalgic other makes available (like Larry King's memory, above) is breaking an expertise dichotomy and creating a new community. Anti-vaccination debates (like all technological debates) tend to center around two parties (pro- and anti-technology), in this case, scientists and parents. What might happen if this third party, the nostalgic other, represented themselves? Rather than debugging anti-vaccination claims, the goal of inviting this third party is including an outsider perspective with solutions beyond vaccinate/don't vaccinate. Third ways are always possible.

## *Storytelling to Heal and Form New Communities of Memory*

I've discussed the ability of anti-vaccination stories to make parents feel they are being heard when a doctor doesn't develop a space for patients to participate and heal. That is, as Winslade and Monk write, "The foremost healthcare need by patients and their families is the desire to be listened to and respected. . . . [W]hen patients' and families' concerns are ignored, anxiety, fear, and distress quickly escalate" (247). Anti-vaccination stories control the chaos of autism and form a protective community when medicine has not listened. Currently, one communication design the CDC uses to respond to such stories is its own celebrity advocates. Actress Sarah Michelle Geller, for instance, has advocated for the pertussis vaccine, and 2016 presidential candidate Hillary Clinton tweeted from a grandmotherly ethos: "The science is clear: The earth is round, the sky is blue, and #vaccineswork. Let's protect all our kids. #GrandmothersKnowBest." But though pro-vaccine texts adapt to anti-vaccination ethos, they don't seek healing. They promote what political scientist Robert Putnam calls "bonding" rather than "bridging" social capital: "Bridging social capital draws people in, and embraces diversity, making links between different people and groups. Bonding social capital, on the other hand, is more exclusive, tying together people who are already similar, or have interests in common" (Gauntlett 139). Pro-vaccine messages often seek consent to a restoratively nostalgic set of scientific values rather than forming a new community. In this way, they don't respond to McCarthy's call that "you have a choice of listening to the medical community, which offers no hope, or you can listen to our community, which offers hope," ("Jenny McCarthy's"). To find a new model of hope and community, we again turn to a third party, a group rarely invited into vaccine debates: autistic citizens themselves.

The Autistic Self Advocacy Network ("nothing about us without us"), for example, is a civil rights group run by citizens with autism. It condemns autism groups that are driven by anti-vaccination and pseudoscientific cures (e.g., Autism Speaks). "Some organizations rely on fear and pity as fundraising tactics," the ASAN website states. "When the message of autism awareness becomes one of stigma, dehumanization, and public hysteria rather than one of civil rights, inclusion, and support, we face a grave threat to our efforts to be recognized as full and equal citizens in our communities." Rather, ASAN endorses narratives of healing through the acceptance of autistic identity and *neurological diversity*, "which promotes social acceptance of neurological difference as part of the broad landscape of human diversity and seeks to bring about a world in which Autistic people enjoy the same access, rights, and opportunities as all other citizens" (Autistic). Neurological diversity offers healing to families who thought there was only one way forward—and anticipatory nostalgia, community, and hope are restored.

In the Larry King interview, for instance, a 14-year-old nonverbal autistic blogger, Carly Fleischmann, has one of her blog posts read: "My name is Carly Fleischmann. I am 14. For as long as I can remember I have had autism. I overheard Jenny say that her son commented that he felt like Dory from Nemo because he didn't remember things when he was autistic. However, I have a great memory for many things. I also know many autistic kids that are exactly the same way. Parents know what I'm talking about, kids that can tell you the name of every subway line. . . . Doctors would like to tell you that we have a hard time processing information. Its not really true, our brains are wired differently. . . ." Fleichmann offers a third way. She seems to disagree that autism is the hopeless loss that McCarthy describes, but she also doesn't identify with the medical descriptions of autism.

Of course, autism stories are not all happy. It's reductive to focus solely on the hopeful narratives of the "shiny autistic," "a term used in the Autistic community to denote an individual who is held up as an example of 'what autistics should be'" (Heilker). Like all human stories, autism narratives contain hope, failure, trauma, and survival. The goal of listening to autistic citizens' stories is not to use humans as tools (the nostalgic other); rather, it's informed dissent, welcoming autistic citizens as co-designers, adding needed complexity to a formerly two-sided debate. What would autistic citizens' nostalgia-types look like? By including autistic citizens, a new set of experts is welcomed, and a new community is formed. The stories of autistic citizens like Fleischmann offer a new timeline in which autism is not a disorder but an identity. Autistic rhetorician Melanie Yergeau describes this nostalgic transformation: "Coming to autism rhetorically recasts items such as 'difficulty smiling'—from pitiful disease symptom into autistic discourse convention, from a neurological screw-up into an autistic confluence of structure and style" (Heilker and Yergeau 489).

## Redesigning Medical Expertise: What's at Risk? Can Expertise Be Shared?

So far, I've analyzed "nonexpert" healthcare nostalgia in search of critique, hope, and redesign. But technical experts, contrary to popular belief, are nostalgic, too. Indeed, expertise itself is a form of nostalgia, always longing to re-create the successes of one's theoretical school training in real-world scenarios where perfect replication is impossible. Like all nostalgia, then, professional expertise can be restorative or reflective. Unfortunately, in response to anti-vaccination parents challenging their ideals, the medical profession has usually held tight to the notion that science is the only source of curing and, thereby, further alienated parents who want their stories heard. But innovation, inclusivity, and healing don't come from shouting, "I'm right!"

To find stases for redesign within scientific nostalgia, we move to a 2011 interview with Dr. Paul Offit, a professor of pediatrics at the University of Pennsylvania, chief of the Division of Infectious Diseases and director of the Vaccine Education Center at the Children's Hospital of Philadelphia, and one of anti-vaccination's most vocal opponents.[9] In this *Medscape One-on-One* interview with Dr. Eli Adashi of Brown University's medical school, Offit describes his motives and methods for combatting anti-vaccination. Though Offit seems to share pro-vaccination stories to protect scientific rationalism, below the wake he is full of an anger that twins anti-vaccination fury. Within this shared emotion, we find a second stasis. Offit is angry about the risk of vaccine-preventable illnesses. Yet, he fails to engage personal models of risk, triggering parental anger. Physician and parental emotion, therefore, might be brought together through the deceptively simple question, *What's at risk in using and refusing vaccines?*

## Offit's Nostalgias: Science, Risk, and Emotional Othering

Offit begins his interview by answering this question on nostalgic footings. His narrative is ripe with god memories and loss. "I think we're at a tipping point," Offit warns, "[W]e have a whooping cough outbreak in California that's bigger than anything we've seen since 1947. . . . [W]e're starting to see these vaccine preventable diseases, these once historic diseases, come back" (Paul). Offit's terms "vaccine preventable" and "historic" diseases are nostalgically charged. They tell a story of loss. These diseases, the terms imply, are preventable. Biomedicine solved the problem. There was a golden age when the public listened to doctors, and we thought that we no longer had to worry. That age is gone. Risk is real, again. And, yet, like McCarthy and Carrey's 1989 vaccine schedule, "vaccine preventable" and "historic" are a kind of restorative misnomer. No vaccine is totally effective, and many historic diseases in the United States thrive elsewhere in the world.

In fact, this highlighting of the strength of modern medicine has oddly reinforced anti-vaccination sentiment. Anti-vaccination parents argue that we've defeated these diseases; they're historic and rare; why are we still vaccinating against them? In a *Time* magazine interview, for instance, Jane, a mother whose son spread measles to his school, describes her risk calculation: "We analyze the diseases and we analyze the risk of disease. . . . Looking at the diseases mumps, measles and rubella in a country like the U.S. . . . Children will do fine with these diseases in a developed country that has good nutrition. And because I live in a country where the norm is vaccine, I can delay my vaccines" ("How My"). Thus, we come across our stases: *What is the risk of disease?* And *What is potentially worse, vaccine preventable diseases or harm from the vaccine?*

Such negotiations of risk define participatory medicine because how patients and medical researchers calculate risk is at the heart of informed consent. The Belmont Report requires medical researchers to teach experiment subjects what's at risk in order for participants to make an informed choice. But parents and physicians calculate risk in radically different ways. Offit, for example, statistically weighs the risk of an epidemic over the risk of vaccination. His risk calculation is about protecting the community at large. In contrast, Jane (and Mountain Momma, in the last section) weighs the fear and guilt of causing her child's injury above the risk of a disease happening "naturally." "It felt like they were giving her four shots. It felt like it was too much." Jane describes of vaccinating her four-month old. "The next day she had blood in her stool and it freaked me out." Fear, thus, transforms risk. Science writer Katie Palmer describes, "If someone has a relative who had a bad reaction to a vaccine—or even a great-aunt on Facebook whose friend's daughter became withdrawn after one—the immediacy of that story will carry more cognitive weight than numbers. . . . [M]edical professionals and researchers must figure out how to use information—cold, impersonal facts—in a way that can counteract the power of that primal (and inaccurate) risk calculation" (2). This specific breed of risk felt by anti-vaccination proponents is often called "dread risk," a category of anxiety (fear of flying, for example) in which the alternative is statistically more likely to cause harm than the feared action. You're significantly more likely to get in a car accident than a plane crash, for instance.

And, yet, by refusing private emotions and risk as inaccurate, Palmer and Offit, like Mouffe's neoliberals last chapter, isolate a large population from decision-making. Langdon Winner rejects such cold rhetorics of risk: "It is possible to discuss that harm directly without pretending that you are playing a game of craps. . . . [S]uch terms as 'environmental crisis,' 'dangerous side effects,' 'health hazards,' and the like were gradually redefined as questions 'of risk'" (142). Winner hints at the pain of having one's personal story, one's child in anti-vaccination, calculated as a probability. In this hyper-rational transformation of human to statistic we see why anti-vaccination parents feel ignored, and why sharing personal narratives is so vital to them.

Another of Offit's nostalgic stories relates to the rotavirus vaccine he co-created. Offit reflects fondly upon sculpting the vaccine, the research, and the safeguarding process: "I think what got me interested in this [anti-vaccination] was the fact that I worked with a team of scientists at the Children's Hospital of Philadelphia to develop the rotavirus vaccine. . . . [T]he real education, frankly, came with the 15-plus years it took to do the research of development to make that vaccine." Contrasting this personal nostalgia for fifteen years of vigilant labor is the ease with which the vaccine is dismissed. "When you see what exactly is required to get a vaccine into children it's just daunting," Offit describes, "then when you see it so easily and wrongly dismissed by people who have really little knowledge about what vaccines are or how they work or how they're made. It was hard to watch."

Part of Offit's anger, here, stems from a feeling that he must educate people in order for his vaccines to work. In Goodnight's terms, Offit views his job as science in the technical sphere, but he has to use the rhetoric of the personal and public spheres for his science to function. This never would have happened in the golden age of medicine, he seems to imply. Though in a separate interview ("The Vaccine") Offit says he understands why anti-vax parents fear vaccines, he rejects the possibility that anti-vaccination parental observations are useful for anything. Like a bad user-centered designer, Offit analyzes parents so that he can change their minds and erase their fears. He doesn't listen to, empathize with, or learn from them. In this rejection, Offit performs what Sara Ahmed calls "emotional othering." He ascribes a positive emotion (righteous anger) to himself, whereas he dismisses the fear and anxiety felt by vaccine-hesitant parents as illogical. "Some emotions are 'elevated' as signs of cultivation," Ahmed describes, "whilst others remain 'lower' as signs of weakness" (3).

What's provocative about Offit's emotion, however, is that his anger and many anti-vaccination parents' anger stem from the very same source—being ignored. *Why are we angry?* becomes a stasis. Both parties are nostalgic for a time when they felt in control as medical and parental experts. Such an overlap of emotion welcomes empathic redesign. A modified cultural probe, for example, might be useful. Offit could record something in his day-to-day life (e.g., being ignored by media) that makes him angry and ask anti-vaccination parents to redesign this encounter to highlight listening. Offit might do the same: asking anti-vaccination parents to record a negative encounter with a doctor, which Offit redesigns. In doing so, each party takes the other's perspective—coming to understand one another's expertise. A new community of shared emotion and experience is formed.

## Medical Science's Decision-Making We: "Do Your Homework."

Because of his concurrent rejection and use of emotion, Offit's decision-making we is knotty. One of the first not-we's that Offit identifies is irresponsible media:

> What got me in was an article in the *Philadelphia Inquirer* about the chicken pox vaccine. . . . [H]ere was a vaccine that had the capacity to protect against the 10,000 hospitalizations and roughly 70–100 deaths that occur from chicken pox every year. And there was an article [that said] . . . here are people, researchers, at the CDC that say this about the vaccine (that it's safe and effective), and here's just the local guy who says it's not. . . . I called up the reporter and said . . . "You know, there's not two sides to this story. You know, do your homework." ("Paul Offit")

There are several arguments driving this excerpt on "fake news," from the responsibility of the media to do research before spreading panic to the importance of juxtaposing equally trained sources. But in terms of stasis, Offit's position that "there's not two sides to this story" is notable for its asystasis. Offit's fundamentalist perspective precludes debate. And, yet, refusing to engage opponents that so clearly exist—opponents who have been vocal because they've felt ignored—only makes those opponents louder, angrier, and, psychologically, convinced that they are right (Lerner and Keltner).

Instead, Offit might consider how he can transform his not-we into his we. If Offit is tired of debating uninformed opponents, why not teach the media and vaccine-hesitant parents how to educate themselves? Theoretically, Offit appears on television to do just that. But because he doesn't engage logics beyond medical rationality (because his expertise is restoratively nostalgic), he doesn't allow his opponents expertise. He screams into the wind. Offit might do better by creating agonistic partners through informed dissent, transforming the wind into part of his decision-making we. Teaching an audience how to search WebMD, properly evaluate sources, or even perform citizen science, for example, could be useful. Such training would empower patients and remove the suspicion that medical science is trying to silence parental expertise. But to be truly participatory, beyond teaching parents how to *understand* his point of view, Offit also needs to teach parents how to *disagree with* him in a persuasive fashion. That is, Offit might teach parents how to transform their "chief concern" (patient fears about treatment or illness) into a "chief complaint" (a biomedical description) (Schleifer and Vannatta). What kind of evidence, language, and rhetoric persuades scientists? How can citizens be transformed into active citizen scientists? Offit needs to help parents to be informed and dissent because, from a lack of resources to help parents with autistic children to a lack of equal rights for autistic citizens, there definitely are reasons for parents to feel isolated and ignored and want to dissent.

When asked what advice he has for everyday physicians who work with vaccine-hesitant parents, Offit tells the story of his wife, pediatrician Dr. Bonnie Offit:

> She used to do whatever she could to try to get children vaccinated. She would give parents as much information as she could. . . . "Look, this is why vaccines are good; here's why a choice not to get a vaccine is a risky choice that you shouldn't make for your child." She felt that she probably had about 25% of parents gradually getting the vaccines. . . . [But] she'd had it. She felt like, "I can't send you out into the world where I know that there's an increased risk now of getting these diseases. *Let me love your child.* Don't put me in a position where I have to practice sub-standard care that could result in harm. . . . I can't see you unless you get vaccines. . . ." And she feels now, actually, that she convinces more people because they see just how strongly she feels.

This story further complicates Offit's binary of rationality and emotion. Bonnie Offit begins by doing what her husband advises, giving scientific facts. But because such education earned trivial results, she switches to a more personal and emotional rhetoric: "Let me love your child." In this way, Bonnie Offit and the parents share individual risk. Her identification works. Paul Offit doesn't go so far as to say that one should match emotional discourse with emotional discourse, but the example is clear. Compare his failed refusal of a space in the media for anti-vaccination voices and Bonnie Offit's successful refusal in her office. Yes, these refusals take place in different contexts, public discourse and personal conversation, but what's evident is that Bonnie Offit engages patient techno-logics; her expertise is reflectively nostalgic.

## Aiding Risk Calculation: Creating Opportunities for Informed Dissent and Community

Offit begins his interview by describing what's at risk in vaccine refusals—the return of vaccine-preventable illness. But because he clings to a restorative nostalgia for scientific expertise, part of Offit's failure to see why anti-vaccination thrives is a failure to make risk a stasis question. He doesn't investigate, *What's at risk here?* And *What's the difference in how I perceive risk and how you do?* To answer these questions, we first turn to the "omission bias" (Ritov and Baron; Asch et al.).

Psychologically, when given the choice, people would rather commit a sin of omission (not acting) than take a risky action. In vaccinating, choosing to vaccinate (an action) seems inherently more risky than choosing not to vaccinate (an omission). Several factors encourage this bias. First, not acting seems nostalgically more "natural" than acting. Humans have immune systems for a reason, some parents argue (Poland and Jacobson 859–66), and medical science has eradicated these diseases. Second, in studies of vaccination omission bias, parents said they would feel *more guilty* for a death or illness caused by vaccinating (acting) as opposed to failing to vaccinate, an act of fate/chance (not acting) (Ritov and Baron; Brown et al.). Where a doctor's calculation of risk might be cold, statistical, and communal (there's a higher risk of being harmed by an illness than the vaccine), parental dread risk is a thorny personal algebra. Doctors and parents feel emotion differently and, therefore, calculate risk differently.

Amy Wallace describes that this calculation is compounded by participatory medicine shifting too far towards a patient-is-always-right perspective. If the patient is always right, medical risk becomes a purely personal responsibility: "Improved diagnostic tests, a change in consumer awareness, an aging society determined to stay youthful—all have contributed to the growing perception that risk (of death, illness, accident) is our responsibility to reduce or eliminate. In the old order, risk management was in the hands of your doctor—or God. Under the new dispensation, it's all up to you. What are the odds that your child will be autistic? It's your job to manage them." As described above, by viewing vaccination as a personal health choice, a techno-logic is created in which any health decision (and, therefore, illness) is a personal responsibility. In the correlation between vaccines and autism, as described by Emily Yochim and Vesta Silva, this individualization "suggests that mothers must be hyper-vigilant, fully tuned into their children's minds and bodies, capable of researching medical debates, and in touch with God and their own parenting instincts" (409). Under this moral logic of "healthism" (Crawford), "good mothers," mothers who have a restoratively nostalgic maternal instinct, don't have autistic kids. Physicians need to recognize this personal calculation of risk and the maternal nostalgia it is based in and respond accordingly.

Unfortunately, in a 2012 review, Douglas Opel et al. report that there is no standardized approach to communicating about risk with vaccine-hesitant parents. Though the American Academy of Pediatrics recommends against it, surveys show that almost 30 percent of pediatricians report that, like Bonnie Offit, they would refuse a patient care rather than participating in the health-care of un-vaccinated children (1270). But terminating care only furthers marginalization. The doctors in this study don't seem to distinguish between refusing to engage parents' knowledge of medical science and refusing to engage parents' personal stories. Rather than refusing parental narratives, emotion, and risk, physicians might better understand how their treatments fit into parental logics through empathic co-design.

The field of narrative medicine is one route to such listening. As defined by James Meza and Daniel Passerman, narrative medicine's goal is inviting "the doctor to enter the patient's world and way of knowing an illness narra-tive and inviting the patient to enter the doctor's world and way of knowing scientific evidence. Both the doctor and patient can claim 'knowing' in both these domains, enabling a conversation that results in a co-constructed nar-rative" (xv). Essentially, what narrative medicine programs teach is *reflectively nostalgic expertise*. Where restorative expertise sees only professional epistemic technê as truth, reflectively nostalgic expertise looks back to technical train-ing as but one ideal resource. It seeks to layer other people's training, obser-vations, and pride in their identity as experts into decision-making. In this new participatory model of expertise, informed dissent can play a crucial role.

In 2010, for example, Tom Delbanco, MD, and Jan Walker, RN, started OpenNotes. In their experiment, patients are encouraged to read and respond to the notes their healthcare providers write about them in medical charts. Though these notes have legally been open to patients since 1996, virtually no one asks to see them. Strikingly, Delbanco and Walker found that "80 percent of patients who saw their records reported better understanding of their medical condition and said they were in better control of their health. Two-thirds reported that they were better at sticking with their prescriptions. Ninety-nine percent of the patients wanted OpenNotes to continue" (Winn). Dr. Leana Wen describes engaging in such co-design with a patient: "I sat down next to her and showed her what I was typing. She began pointing out changes. She'd said that her pain had started three weeks ago, not last week. Her chart mentioned alcohol abuse in the past; she admitted that she was under a lot of stress and had returned to heavy drinking a couple of months ago. As we talked, her diagnosis—inflammation of the pancreas from alcohol use—became clear, and I wondered why I'd never shown patients their records before." OpenNotes creates an opportunity for informed dissent: this happened three weeks ago, not last week. In doing so, it layers epistemic technê and mêtis into reflectively nostalgic expertise. Patient and physician expertise both contribute but are not substituted.

But, despite the importance of this type of conversation, doctors do need to walk a careful line and not simply substitute their expertise for a patient's. For years, for instance, anti-vaccination activists argued that thimerosal (a nontoxic Mercury preservative) was the ingredient in vaccines that caused autism. Though this fear was tested and proven false, in 1999 the FDA and CDC attempted to calm worries by simply removing it. But the redesign didn't come to stasis. Questions weren't answered; action was just taken. The removal backfired—becoming a petri dish for conspiracy. Parents felt their distrust of vaccines was validated. Elimination seemingly proved thimerosal caused autism. And because healing and community weren't addressed, anti-vaccination's target soon switched to "immune overload." As seen in the McCarthy and Carrey interview, now, it isn't thimerosal that is the problem, it's that children receive too many vaccines at once. Vaccine anxiety spread because its techno-logic wasn't considered. As the next section illustrates, it's difficult to legislate away fear and anxiety.

## California State Bill 277: A Test Case of Democratic Design

Responding to the Disneyland measles outbreak of 2014 and low vaccination rates across the state, in June 2015 the California legislature passed Senate Bill 277. Authored by Senators Richard Pan and Ben Allen, SB 277 requires children who attend public or private schools and daycares to be vaccinated. Unlike the previous bill (AB 2109), which allowed religious and personal exemptions, SB277 only accepts physician-approved medical excuses. All healthy children must be vaccinated to attend school. As this is one of the few governmental forums in which vaccination has been debated, this final analysis seeks stases in the public hearings leading up to the bill. Before be-

ing signed into law by Governor Jerry Brown, SB 277 received a majority vote
in three committees: health (Does the bill protect public health?), education
(Does the bill promote students' right to education?), and judiciary (Is the bill
lawful?). Though each hearing ostensibly had a distinct concern, when you
watch the debates you see that arguments followed very similar paths. Thus,
I analyze only selections from the final hearing: a heated 3.5-hour senate
judiciary committee presided over by Senator Hannah-Beth Jackson.

All the stases described so far resurface in this debate, but it's pretty
clear that *Who are we?* is the central question. That is, when asked the question, *What are you nostalgic for, why, and to which ends?* each party subtly answers
that they are nostalgic for constitutionally supported deliberative democracy.
But, like Mouffe's democratic and liberal publics last chapter, pro-vaccination
speakers favor protecting communal rights and public health, where anti-vaccination speakers favor individual choice and personal health. Bringing these
two publics together is tricky.

## *"We're very interested in dealing with fact and not fear."*

Senator Jackson begins the committee by defining its stasis: "This bill is now
before the judiciary committee to review the constitutional issues of liberty
rights, parental rights, religious rights, and fundamental interests" ("April").
The hearing is not about vaccine safety. The topic is constitutionality. Beyond
stases, Jackson establishes who her decision-making wes are and what logics
she values: "As a mother and a grandmother of a fabulous 2-year-old, I understand the strong feelings on both sides. . . . [But] *We're very interested in dealing
with fact and not fear . . .* It is very clear in my opinion that there have been
independent studies . . . that do warrant the importance of vaccinations. And,
frankly, I think what we really all want is to find a cure, the cause of autism.
. . . If we could get that we would all be a little more relieved about what the
future holds." Jackson attempts to create community by presenting a personal
parental ethos and separating questions about autism from questions about
vaccines. She admirably reveals her bias and limits the stasis. However, like
Offit, Jackson reductively juxtaposes fact (the domain of science) and emotion
(the domain of mothers and grandmothers) and, thereby, creates an emotional
other of parental narratives that wield fear, which in the case of anti-vaccination, are *all* parental narratives. Certainly, what else *is* anti-vaccination if not
a response to fear?

Like "risk," "fear" is a crucial term for most technological debates. And, in
many ways, it's nostalgia's foil. Where nostalgia is something in the past we
long to recover, fear is something from the past we seek to avoid. Indeed, fear
often spawns nostalgia. The fear of autism and drug safety, for instance, turns

vaccine-hesitant parents back towards old vaccine schedules. "The turning away from the object of fear," Ahmed observes, "also involves *turning towards* the object of love" (68). Senator Jackson, thus, cannot refuse fear any more than she can refuse happiness. Instead, becoming a nostalgic designer, she might ask, *What do we do with fear? What has caused this emotion?* And *How might redesign allay it?*

To engage emotional stasis, however, we also must distinguish "fear" from its murkier cousin "anxiety." Much anti-vaccination anxiety is falsely labeled fear. But where fear has an object that it's attached to, one is afraid of *something*, anxiety is a more nebulous approach to thinking about the world (Ahmed 66). This distinction is seen in shifting anti-vaccination dread from thimerosal, to immune overload, to a loss of parental rights. It's much harder to redesign for such transitory anxiety than it is to redesign a fearsome object. Thus, by asking, *What is each side afraid of?* the nostalgic designer achieves a peculiar, yet productive, conversion of amorphous anxiety into static fear.

## Supporting and Opposing Witnesses: Public Health vs. Self-Governance

To begin the debate proper, Senator Pan (a pediatrician and medical professor), establishes the need for the bill within the stasis of constitutionality. Citing Supreme Court cases (Jacobson v. Massachusetts, 1905) on the legality of mandatory vaccinations and scientific studies showing vaccine safety, Pan describes that "herd immunity" requires a certain number of citizens in a community to be vaccinated to stop a disease. Unfortunately, "recent events, such as the measles outbreak that began in Disneyland last December, has [*sic*] proved that our community immunity is waning to dangerously low levels due to an over three-fold increase use of the personal belief exemption in way too many schools." Thus, though not directly stated, Pan asks the stasis, *What is of higher priority, public health (herd immunity) or individual freedom (personal exemptions)?*

Constitutional law professor Dorit Reiss expands Pan's stasis: *What are the different rights involved in this mediation? How should they be ranked?* "The first is the interest of the parent to make medical decisions for the child," Reiss describes. "The second is the interest of the child to be free of disease and the child's right to health, and the third is the right of the public, which includes citizens, parents, children as well to be free from communicable diseases." Like Pan, Reiss ranks these rights public safety, child's safety, and, only then, parental choice. In doing so, she argues that children have the right to attend school free of disease. This positive right to attend school, according to Reiss, is ranked above anti-vaccination parents' negative right to not vaccinate their

children. This distinction is an implicit critique of the omission bias: choosing
not to act is simultaneously a choice to act upon others by lowering community immunity. The proposing side concludes with a line of public support at
the provided microphones from parents and medical doctors.

In response, Professor Mary Holland, research scholar at NYU's School
of Law, begins the opposing testimony by defining the inherent danger of vaccines as embodied by the U.S. "vaccine court."[10] "[I]n 1986," Holland describes,
"Congress passed the National Vaccine Injury Act, which created a federal
compensation program. And that program has paid out 3 billion dollars and
has compensated over 3,000 victims, including approximately 150 who have
died from vaccines." Indeed, despite extremely low rates of injury, vaccine injury does occur (usually from a rare allergic reaction), which raises the question, *Is it fair to mandate an activity that has any level of risk?* Holland proceeds to her
most persuasive argument. The bill is essentially forced vaccination (students
can't attend school if they aren't vaccinated), which violates informed consent.
"The global standard for ethical modern medicine is prior, free, and informed
consent," Holland states. "Without some measure of realistic choice, and I do
not believe that medical exemptions or homeschooling are a viable option. . . .
This bill will be coercive." Holland argues that unvaccinated students have
both a positive right to attend school and a negative right to do so free from
government intrusion on their bodies. Informed consent is a particularly good
stasis because it is a god memory for practitioners of participatory healthcare.
By referencing it, Holland forms a shared community of nostalgia. She poses:
*How do the right to education and the right to health interact? What role do informed
consent and the PSDA play in this debate?* Finding such god memories and then
framing one's argument in terms of them is a vital (perhaps the key) move of
nostalgic stasis theory and mediation. It builds goodwill through identifying
with an opponent's nostalgic values.

Unfortunately, Holland quickly dashes this rapport: "In employment lack
of consent is forced labor[,] . . . in intimate relations it's called rape, and in
medical treatment it's battery." Senator Jackson interrupts, "Whoa, Whoa,
Whoa, wait a second, rape is a loaded word . . . to analogize this to rape I
think is a little bit off the rails." Where one of the quickest routes to stasis is
phrasing your argument within an opponent's nostalgias, one of the quickest
routes to asystasis is redefining an opponent's techno-logic through negative
extremes and fear. Holland continues, "How will you possibly enforce this
with parents who won't vaccinate and cannot for economic or other reasons
homeschool? Will you be willing to remove the children . . . throw non-
vaccinating parents in prison?" Again, Jackson interrupts: "Where in this
bill does it talk about throwing parents in prison?" And, yet, though anxiety

marks Holland's statements, we shouldn't throw the baby out with the bath water. We actually have an important stasis here: *What will be done with those parents who refuse to vaccinate their children?* And, perhaps more balanced, *How does this bill resolve or inflame the prior causes of anti-vaccination (guilt, fear, curing vs. healing, etc.)? What does this bill concretely solve?* Like the removal of thimerosal, SB 277 seeks a public solution but doesn't resolve the underlying private motivations of anti-vaccination. There's no route to healing provided. Anxiety and fear proliferate.

The opposition concludes with a procession of public support at the microphones that illustrates this anxiety—a line much longer than the supporting faction—primarily consisting of parents and alternative healthcare professionals. Notable among this crowd are parents who say they have vaccine-injured children. This large number is surprising given that only 4,252 people have been accepted as injured by vaccines by the federal vaccine court since 1986 (HRSA). That so many Californian children are vaccine injured seems questionable. It also highlights an ethical question: In welcoming a two-sided debate over the bill, does the hearing inaccurately portray public sentiment? That is, anti-vaccination dread is a tiny *minority* of public opinion—but it appears as a majority in this hearing. Should people be able to, as philosopher Bernard Williams questions, "come in from the outside, speak when they feel like it, make endless irrelevant, or insulting interventions, and so on; they cannot invoke a right to do so, and no-one thinks things would go better in the direction of truth if they did" (217). Still, the mediating nostalgic designer should be hesitant to refuse these testimonies without looking under the hood. Our goal is to ask, *Why are stories being used to construct reality in this way?*

### Q&A: Defining Vaccine Injury, Exemptions, and Acknowledging Fear

To complete the hearing, several senators ask both sides questions. The first query comes from Jackson: "There were a number of people who referenced the fact that their children were vaccine injured. Could you explain what that is?" Definitions of the term "vaccine injured" focus the divide between parental and physician expertise. Pan describes, for example, "It's not a technical term we use in the medical field. . . . [T]here are people who've stated that their children are vaccine injured from conditions that have been disproven to be associated with vaccination." The term also invokes the vaccine court, whose defining power is fraught. To receive compensation from the court, patients sometimes only need a causal claim rather than scientific proof that a child has been injured (see Althen v. SHHS; Werderitsch v. SHHS; Poling v. SHHS). That is, the court values parental stories much more than medical science does. Thus, different branches of the U.S. government (e.g., the CDC and vaccine court) define vaccine injury differently. In terms of mediation, we might ask: *What is the role of the vaccine court in promoting public health? And how might the numerous branches of national health better coordinate?*[11]

The second major question, jointly posed by several senators, might be paraphrased, "How easy or difficult will it be for parents to receive medical exemptions?" Again, responses split along nostalgia and fear. Pan recounts how quickly he has given exemptions in the past. If parents don't receive an exemption from one doctor, he describes, they're free to seek as many second opinions as they wish. But Dr. Tara Zanfleet, an opposing pediatrician, challenges Pan's depiction as a nostalgic fantasy. "Yes, they are free to seek a second opinion," Zanfleet argues. "However, if they are on medicom, and they are assigned a primary physician, they will be paying out of pocket." Pan and Zanfleet exist in a nostalgic contact zone. Pan has a nostalgic vision of granting exemptions. Zanfleet is nostalgically protective of the current laws. Oddly, both sides' restorations invalidate their argument. If medical exemptions will be so easy to get, why write a new bill? If medical exemptions are currently so difficult to get, why defend the current legislation? In this juxtaposition, we, again, find a key failure of many technological deliberative forums. They produce artificially polarized sides that contradict themselves internally because of a refusal to collaborate. Third ways are possible.

## Anxiety, Fear, and Bridging Social Capital

To redesign from this committee, we begin, as Senator Jackson did, with fear. Because anti-vaccination stories are so effective at inspiring anxiety and fear, one logical response from physicians would seem to be countering fearful story with fearful story. Indeed, despite Jackson forbidding fear, one of the supporting witnesses was a woman describing her terrible struggle with polio. And, yet, because anxiety has no object, this tactic backfires. A study by Brendan Nyhan et al. found that the more a pro-vaccination communiqué engages fear of diseases, the *less* likely a hesitant parent was to vaccinate: "[I]mages of sick children increased expressed belief in a vaccine/autism link and a dramatic narrative about an infant in danger [from a vaccine preventable disease] increased self-reported belief in serious vaccine side effects" (835). Creating fear-based narratives without transforming general anxiety to fear of a specific object is perilous. Anxiety sticks to any nearby object.

Anxiety further affects vaccine hesitancy through risk perception. Because vaccines, unlike most other medical treatments, are preventative, given to healthy people rather than those already with a disease to fear, they necessarily create an anxious threat. The closest object for that threat to attach to is not the disease being prevented (which parents either haven't seen or don't view as dangerous) but rather the vaccine itself. As Robert Cialdini puts it, "What's focal is causal. . . . Because we typically allot special attention to the true causes around us, if we see ourselves giving such attention to some factor, we become more likely to think of it as a cause" (51). An intriguing nostalgic complication of such risk assessment is the chicken pox (varicella) vaccine. Because many parents contracted chicken pox when they were young, they see little risk in it and even have a nostalgia for it. Getting chicken pox seems like a natural rite of passage. Yet, as the CDC reports, before the varicella vaccine, 10,500 to 13,000 patients were hospitalized and 100 to 150 died from chicken pox every year (CDC).

Unfortunately, when considering public health, citizens often have a hard time understanding publics outside their own communities of nostalgia. Anti-vaccination sentiment tends to occur in pockets of like-minded individuals and be driven by personal assessments of risk. In California, for instance, private Waldorf schools are at a higher risk of non-vaccination (Osborn). In response, vaccination campaigns must work harder at welcoming anti-vaccination and vaccine-hesitant parents into their decision-making we. In this light, the biggest flaw of the SB 277 hearings is that true public deliberation, collaboration, and engagement is nowhere to be found. Yes, citizens were welcomed to participate (to voice support or rejection), but they were forbidden to tell *personal* stories.[12] Senator Jackson stated, "If people try to go into greater detail, I will cut them off very politely." In this refusal, Jackson essentially refuses parents a place to co-design. She refuses nonscientific social capital, individualizing moral foundations, and, thereby, agonistic community.[13]

In his "Bowling Alone: America's Declining Social Capital," Robert Putnam argues that such rejections are increasingly common. In the past, Americans socialized in groups that seemed to cut across class and political strata, from bowling leagues to Elks lodges.[14] This type of cross-group "bridging" social capital, Putnam observes, is dying. It's increasingly being replaced by "bonding" social capital: associating only with those who think alike and are often of the same class, race, gender, etc. But even bonding social capital is fading, as Putnam and Thomas Sander write: "As of 2004, a quarter of those polled in the United States reported that they lacked a confidant with whom to discuss important personal matters. . . . Since social isolation (that is, the lack of any confidants) strongly predicts premature death, these are sobering statistics" (10). Increasingly, Americans don't have many close friends, particularly close friends with conflicting views. Digitally, this loss is illustrated by Eli Pariser's "filter bubble," an algorithmically determined personalized social sphere in which all the ads, articles, search results, and friends we come across online (think Facebook friends and ads) are tailored to our tastes: "In the filter bubble, there's less room for the chance encounters that bring insight and learning" (15). We need opportunities for *bridging* civic experiences now more than ever. In this light, the problem of anti-vaccination can be solved less by hard persuasion ("Believe in these facts") and more by the indirect soft-persuasion of Burkean identification ("Let's hang out for a while and see what we have in common").

For an example of how bridging deliberative design that reflectively layers multiple expertise might ideally take place, I turn to "Listening to the City," a large-scale public redesign effort that brought together 4,300 New Yorkers in order to brainstorm the design of the Ground Zero memorial: "Relatives of victims, downtown residents, survivors of September 11, emergency workers, business leaders, the unemployed and underemployed . . . sat side-by-side and contributed myriad points of view, debated planners' redevelopment ideas and shared their hopes and concerns about how to reconstruct lives" (Civic). City planning was personalized and bridged across multiple parties. Conflicting nostalgias for a pre-9/11 New York were layered to create a new design. To wrangle these stakeholders, the planners, AmericaSpeaks, split citizens into purposefully diverse tables of ten. Each participant had their own wireless polling keypad, and each table was led by a trained facilitator, who projected the table's findings onto screens across the space. Among large interests represented were the Lower Manhattan Development Corporation, New York Port Authority, small business owners, and big corporations from JP Morgan Chase to Time Warner—conflict mediation was a must.

For instance, architects brought six potential blueprints, but because they innovated while ignoring tradition, these plans were immediately rejected by citizens who felt that they represented an outsider and overly corporate perspective. The rejected plans did, however, serve as agonistic designs to get participants talking about what they wanted: open space for a memorial, a symbolic building that filled the gap in the skyline, housing for all incomes, large and small businesses, and better transportation. The most important part of this type of truly democratic design, I'd argue, is less that everyone gets a say and more that everyone gets a chance to listen to the vox populi. The filter bubble is popped. Ideally such small-scale co-design could take place across the nation. Deliberation duty, a requirement like jury duty, might build the new communities we need.

Nostalgic localization, the use of a community's nostalgia, tradition, and personal memories to make designs fit a preexisting tradition, is another reflectively nostalgic way in which communications designers might co-design with technology-hesitant users. For example, recent research by political economists David Broockman and Joshua Kalla has illustrated that personal and emotional bonding with opposing parties can reduce prejudice. Broockman and Kalla studied how storytelling can sway transphobic voters in a political tactic called "deep canvassing." Rather than spending time citing facts or rationalizing with transphobic voters, a set of door-to-door canvassers shared emotional stories about times they were discriminated against and asked voters to tell similarly emotional memories. Essentially, Broockman and Kalla promote creating communities of shared memory. "A single approximately 10-minute conversation encouraging actively taking the perspective of others," the authors report, "can markedly reduce prejudice for at least 3 months" (220). Unlike current pro-vaccination efforts, canvassers shared and listened to personal memories, which led to identification, bridging social capital, healing, and change. Such success is one of the key takeaways of this chapter: listening to memories (*What are you nostalgic for, why, and to which ends?*) generates empathy and community.

## Conclusions: Redesigning Vaccine Communication and Beyond

This chapter has presented an example of how democratic design works and fails in all its messy specificity—how it blends and bleeds and conflicts across personal, technical, and public spheres. My goal hasn't been to resolve anti-vaccination sentiment or create a perfect vaccine communication design. And despite my attempt at a balanced reporting, my goal hasn't been to claim that anti-vaccination parental mêtis is equivalent to a trained doctor's epistemic technê. I strongly believe, as senator Daniel Patrick Moynihan put it, "Everyone is entitled to his own opinion, but not his own facts" (Weisman). But, I hope that I've illustrated a new lens, nostalgic stasis, by which designers can help mediate technology-hesitant environments through co-design.

The radical speed of technical innovation; a desire for participatory design; a seeming abandonment of old traditions; and feelings of loss, chaos, and uncertainty increasingly generate anxiety over new technologies. *They should.*[15] Humans make technology indeterminate through their diverse responses to change; diverse responses to change are what make technologies human. But the anti-vaccination movement is just one example of what happens when uncertain users craving co-design face designers that aren't prepared to mediate, collaborate, or engage users in personal ways.[16] Increasingly, scientists, doctors, technicians, and designers will need to train in a new public-facing kind of technical communication. We need public intellectuals now more than ever.

One of the key lessons that nostalgic stasis offers these new intellectuals is that successful mediations start from gathering assets—generating hope and community rather than silencing an opponent. The goal of the mediation process, in this light, isn't to argue or persuade but rather to co-create, reincorporating the user audiences that were left out of the original design into a new community of nostalgia. In this way, though the healing/curing distinction discussed earlier in this chapter may seem only relevant to medical design, it applies to all techno-logical conflict. Redesign should be focused on healing, searching out alternative viable pasts and futures, moving forward by addressing underlying problems (anxiety, pain, fear), and double-listening for the hope that is part of all nostalgia.

Ultimately, the best forum for vaccine communication may be one-on-one with a trusted doctor in collaborative programs like Bonnie Offit's emotional conversations, OpenNotes, and deep canvassing. Somewhat paradoxically, to bring users into a nostalgic community, designers have to focus on their deep individual memories and experiences. And, yet, one fact I haven't fully addressed in this chapter is the financial reality of such relationships. Doctors are pressured to treat patients as fast (and with the least discussion) as possible. Today, like so many other formerly human-centered professions, "caring for a patient means walking a tightrope between humanism and consumerism" (Hadler 3). Moreover, there are other stakeholders in design beyond the designer and the user. How, then, do the theoretical redesign suggestions described in this chapter play out in real design situations that must balance a desire for user input, client needs, the designer's training, and the fact that mediation costs money? To answer these questions, we turn to chapter 5.

# Chapter 5

# Nostalgic Negotiations

## Adapting, Adopting, and Refusing Client Expertise

Design expertise cannot be understood by studying actions alone . . . [O]ur research needs to concentrate on perception and recognition . . . [W]e will have to examine conversations and memories as much as drawings.

**Bryan Lawson, "Schemata, Gambits and Precedent"**

I think that a good designer is someone who is humble about what they do and don't know. . . . There are certain things I am an expert in, but it's my job to teach [clients] why I'm the expert in that. And it's also my job to be very honest about the things I'm not an expert in. . . . usually anything related to their business. "So, I need you to teach me all about that so that I can make something that is gonna respond well to that. And I'm gonna teach you all about what I'm gonna do, not so that you can replace me, but so that you understand why you're paying me."

**Grant, graphic designer, *personal interview***

When you say a client doesn't "get it" you might as well be saying, "I couldn't figure out how to get my point across. I am a lazy designer. Please take all my clients."

**Mike Monteiro, *Design Is a Job***

There's a difference between working with users and working with clients. And this difference seems pretty clear: users deploy a design to act in the world; clients fund, facilitate, profit from, and have the final approval of designs.[1] Both of these collaborators make or break democratic design. But though there's been an uptick of training in *user*-centered design over the last three decades, for some reason, explicit training and research in *client*-designer interaction is scarce (Roxburgh; Fleming). Maybe this imbalance springs from designers fashioning themselves as artistic activists (Monteiro). Clients and their money are dirty.[2] Or perhaps the tight spotlight on designer and user in user-centered research led to this neglect of clients, who are left wringing their hands just offstage. The design profession compounds the problem, as architect Dana Cuff critiques: "Comments from the juries for design awards display a lack of concern for clients, the building's functions, or the accommodation of human activity" ("Ethos" 311–12). A focus on art rather than human problems in such awards fosters artists, not designers.

Whatever the cause, in reviewing interviews with auto engineers, graphic artists, architects, and other designers, C. M. Eckert et al. report a sense that design education "does not prepare designers for the practical aspects of running projects or businesses. One of the architects stressed that the difference between a successful project and a failure often lies in the customer/client relationship. . . . [T]hese skills were largely absent from design education" (38). Though it's true that strong studio curricula often incorporate client partners (Lewis and Bonollo; Kalay et al.; Chen et al.), even here, client work is typically mediated by the careful hand of a professor. The struggles of day-to-day client relations (and, thereby, the democratic mediations described in the last two chapters) are masked,[3] yielding greenhorns who easily imagine that design is an ego-driven art (Cuff, "Ethos"). Chasing caricatured heroes like Paul Rand, Dieter Rams, and Steve Jobs,[4] novice designers hope to take client tasks and run, returning in a few weeks with a finished project. In this model, clients pay to benefit from—not fathom, learn about, or contribute to—a designer's expertise (Lawson). As chapter 4 illustrates, this cloister of restorative professional knowledge makes one a bit naive. When students face projects outside of class, there's a culture shock: design (even user-centered design) is client-centered because clients ultimately decide whether designs will be implemented or not. In this light, democratic and inclusive designs rely on client input, and, as this chapter argues, incorporating client input relies on reflectively layering the client's and designer's nostalgic visions of their expertise.

Take the experiences of Lux, a freelance brand designer, fresh out of advertising school. A former boss asked her to redesign the website and identity for his small financial planning firm. But Lux doesn't know much about finance and her client knows even less about branding. From this starting line, Lux describes good design not as an isolated sprint but a relay of co-education: "Financial things, I don't know a whole lot about. . . . So, he was kind of approaching it like *I* was a client . . . A common person who's trying to decipher what this [website] means. . . . You really need to collaborate with your client, and you need to listen to what they want. But, then again, you can't just like totally do anything and everything that they say; you should also add in your input because the collaboration is really what makes a strong [design]." In order for Lux to create the best brand she can, her client teaches his domain of expertise and Lux teaches hers. Each adapts to the other. There are no secluded artists here.

Mason, an early-career ER physician, similarly explains that checking one's expertise at the door and adopting client/patient logics is essential for treatment design. "The hardest part to do for a doctor," Mason describes, "is just to stop and listen": "[A] lot of patients will ask me, 'Oh, do you think I should try [natural therapies]?' . . . I will basically tell the patient, 'As long as we can tell that this is not actively harming you, do whatever you want. Do whatever makes you feel better.' . . . People with really negative attitudes that are getting the standard of care that should treat them, they don't do as well as the people that are super highly positive." Beyond mutual adaptation, then, good client-designer interactions involve adopting client logics, even if one doesn't fully endorse them, layering client and designer traditions into neostalgic innovations.

But though client adaptation and adoption sometimes appear in design literature, a third move, refusing a client's requests, is untouched outside advice that "conflict should be avoided" (Cuff, *Architecture* 182). And, yet, working designers refuse clients all the time. Grant, a university design instructor and graphic designer, describes such an encounter. A client he was creating a logo for brought a bunch of examples from competitors to serve as inspiration. They all looked the same: "And, so, one of the first things I did was I brought them something that looked nothing like the rest. . . . What I was trying to do was talk to them about how, 'Okay, so you brought me these forty logos that look a lot alike. Do you just want to be another one of them? Or is this, you know, an opportunity here to elevate?'" In the end, the client insisted on an uninspired logo. But Grant felt it was his ethical duty to at least attempt to convince the client to reach for something better. Good designer-client contacts often hinge on such tactful refusals.

*Adapt, adopt, refuse*—at first these three moves might seem at odds. *If* client negotiations are taught in design courses, they are usually ranked from good to bad in this order. Yet, all three are essential for professional designers to master. This balance is what democratic expertise and design looks like in practice. Each move breaks with the idyllic designer as solo artist stereotype and replaces it with, as Cuff writes, designer as "the conductor, whose genius unifies the orchestra into great, collective performance" ("Ethos" 306). If design is a nostalgic contact zone and client interaction involves conducting an orchestra of nostalgic ideals, it's crucial to create a sonata of shared expertise in which both clients and designers feel skilled.

In this chapter I, thus, conclude my investigation of nostalgic mediation by exploring how nostalgia assists working designers in escaping the blindfold of restorative professional expertise and reaching towards democratic ideals. To do so, I interview the three early-career professionals introduced above—

Lux, a freelance brand designer working in a large midwestern city; Grant, a graphic designer and university instructor teaching at a major midwestern university; and Mason, a West Coast ER physician. Given that Lux, Mason, and Grant are young, that Mason is a doctor rather than a traditional "designer," that Lux and Grant are sometimes self-employed, and that all client relationships are unique, the descriptions in this chapter aren't meant to be representative of some stereotypical client-designer relationship. Rather, these designers were chosen because there's a gap in research on the client practices of entry-level designers. That is, in this chapter I'm interested in the transition from the epistemic technê of design school training to adaptive client practice. Though each designer told me they lacked formal education in client relations, Lux, Mason, and Grant have all accrued best practices that parallel many of the theoretical ideals discussed in chapter 4. When one listens to their stories, that is, each designer's most successful alliances are based in negotiations of memory, tradition, and expertise—a technique I call *memorial interactivity.*

## Memorial Interactivity: Negotiating Expertise as a Transactive Memory System

*Memorial interactivity* is a method of collaboration in which partners directly reveal, discuss, and negotiate tacit expertise by divulging the episodic nostalgias in which that expertise is based. On an abstract level, Linda Candy and Brigid Costello define *interactivity* as "the behaviour of a system in response to its users over time" (521). Interaction designers forge partial gaps in their creations for users to interrelate, customize, and redesign. The designers of YouTube, for instance, create openings for users to contribute videos, comments, and memories but also restrict users' ability to change features like the logo of the website. Memorial interactivity is a similar set of rhetorical opportunities in which designers open and restrict how clients contribute memories, ideals, and expertise. In memorial interactivity, like all interactivity, designers expose themselves to new knowledge, acquiring contributions they never could have planned alone. They welcome new old ways of viewing the world.

In the prefacing quotes of this chapter, Grant describes, for example, "Things I'm not an expert in are usually anything related to their business. 'So, I need you to teach me all about that so that I can make something that is gonna respond well to that.'" By adapting, adopting, and refusing client memories, client-designer interactions become a careful balance between a designer decentralizing her authority to welcome collaboration and fortifying her authority to interject professional know-how. We called this balance reflectively nostalgic expertise in the last chapter.

In addition to nostalgia, however, careful negotiations of memorial interactivity involve a specific form of communal memory: "transactive memory."
Social psychologist Daniel Wegner explains that transactive memory is the
expertise possessed by each member of an organization and an awareness
of whom to go to for that knowledge (186). Transactive memory is the coor-
dination of individual memories into a collective so that a group has access
to more information than any lone individual. Strong transactive memory
systems (TMS) improve collaborations because cognitive labor is split across
members' domains of expertise (Moreland and Myaskovsky; Lewis; Austin).
And everyone is an expert at something—a peer in a decision-making we,
a member of a community of memory. Within TMS, memorial interactivity aids knowledge sharing by making it overt and destabilized. By sharing
knowledge through nostalgic stories, objects, and texts, memorial interactivity
asks collaborators to not only claim expertise but also to tell stories about the
past experiences, training, and failures decisions stem from. Tacit expertise
becomes an overt reflective negotiation of how past skills fit present scenes. In
this revelation of expertise, designers again ask, *What am I nostalgic for, why, and
to which ends?* In this way, memorial interactivity is how designers welcome,
exclude, assign, explicate, and mystify professional knowledge.

In contrast, historian Jan Goldstein enumerates the traditional features of
a "profession" as an esoteric body of knowledge, exclusive recognition as the
expert in that body, control over that body, and a commitment to service and
the client (175). Often, this final principle conflicts with the others. As we saw
last chapter, it can be difficult for professionals, who define their work upon
a guarded system of restoratively nostalgic training, to accept client memories
or open their expertise to critique (Nathan and Petrosino). That is, professions
definitionally trade in Boym's restorative nostalgia, "reconstructing emblems
and rituals of home [their training] . . . to conquer and specialize time" ("Nostalgia"). Yet, "just when the design profession was coming of age," Cal Swann
writes of the necessity of overcoming such professional bias, "the new design
profession (based, to some extent, on the concept of a mystical gift to provide
creative solutions in a consumer-driven market) also came into question from
a public that was (and still is) increasingly demanding accountability" (49). In
the last chapter we saw this "crisis of confidence in the professional" (Schön)
in the nostalgias of anti-vaccination parents.

Of course, crises of confidence surface in clients as well, manifesting
in clients micro-managing projects, questioning decisions, hiring competing firms, or creating rival designs themselves. When (as I observed in my
research for this chapter), after a designer spends weeks creating a logo, a
client comes to the final meeting with an entirely new concept that they "put

together in PowerPoint," it's difficult to know what to do. This tension is especially true for early-career professionals like Lux, Grant, and Mason, who often work for small clients used to total control over their businesses.[5] Such clients tend to have a nostalgic bootstrapping view of their company's past ("I did it on my own!") that hiring an outside designer threatens. Within such uneasy relationships, it's crucial to grasp how trust, expertise, and memory interact.

In rhetorical theory, the study of *ethos* helps rhetoricians analyze this complex system. Aristotle, for instance, writes that by projecting a strong ethos,[6] "persuasion is achieved by the speaker's personal character when the speech is so spoken as to make us think him credible. We believe good men more fully and more readily than others" (*On Rhetoric* 1.2.4, 1356a). But interactivity complicates ethos, as Kristie Fleckenstein describes: "*[E]thos* depends on an audience's predispositions . . . but those predispositions exist as potential, not as actual systems. The specific predispositions contributing to the evocation of ethos do not exist until that ethos is evoked, harkening back to the constitution of ethos as a living system" (338). That is, ethos and expertise are situational, dialogic, and nostalgic: epideictic meetings of past ideals and present performances. Whom do I trust and distrust? What am I an expert at? What am I nostalgic for? How does this new person fit into my past or alter it? Are they like me? Do they trust me? How clients and designers answer these questions defines their relationship. Depending on nostalgia, expertise is trustworthy to some audiences and not others.

My wife, Krista Kurlinkus, CEO of the technical writing consultancy Write Good, encountered this fact firsthand in her work in the 2014 Elk River chemical spill. During this West Virginia water crisis, a toxic mix of 4-methylcyclohexanemethanol (MCHM) and other coal washing chemicals poured into the Elk River, a major drinking-water supply for the region. When given a government order to flush their water systems, Krista found that some homeowners ignored the advice, listening to the stories of friends and family who said the vapor from flushing made them sick (it did). These residents trusted the words of people they knew over scientific orders from a government that failed them in the past.[7] In contrast, Krista heard from other residents who simply continued to drink the water—trusting that the coal and chemical industries that had supported the region all their lives had their best interests in mind. The designers of the government order failed to consider the nostalgic contact zone in which their message existed. Good client-designer collaborations unearth and respond to such nostalgic borders and bridges—memorial interactivity.

## Adapt: Establishing a Nostalgic Baseline for Collaboration

Because of the sway of user-centered design, the most salient rhetorical move in client-designer interactions is mutual learning; as Wegner describes, "A transactive system begins when individuals learn something about each others' domains of expertise" (191). I call this feat adapting because the designer acclimates to the client's picture of their company whereas the client comes to see the designer's skill at achieving their goals. Adaptation is the mutual portrayal, acceptance, and reflective layering of expertise and the transformation of client and designer that springs from this acceptance. As we've seen, such adaptation is the central move of Aristotelian rhetoric; in Kenneth's Burke words, "You persuade a man only insofar as you can talk his language . . . identifying your ways with his" (*Rhetoric* 55). Unfortunately, as Summer Taylor writes of client-based university courses: "Students frequently fail to understand, accept, or even recognize clients' standards. . . . Clients may not be able to explain their standards effectively with enough detail and direction because they are not accustomed to articulating standards for writing" (113). Starting at the initial meeting, then, Lux, Mason, and Grant all guide co-education. Nostalgic storytelling is a key catalyst they use to galvanize such learning.

### *Client Memories: Who Are You? What Are You Nostalgic For? What's Your Expertise?*

One of the first steps of adaptation, for instance, is the client describing their identity and expertise. That is, as in critical nostos or nostalgic stasis, the designer's first move in memorial interactivity is prompting clients to paint nostalgic stories of themselves, their skills, and their companies. In creating a brand for the financial planner described earlier, for example, Lux began by learning about financial planning: "He knows everything about it, it's his company, and, so, financial things . . . It's kind of like daunting, like a huge thing I don't know. And, so, he was kind of approaching it like *I* was a client, you know. I'm just like, a common person who's trying to decipher what this means." To understand her client, Lux fashions a scenario in which she acts out the role of an ideal customer: "I was a client." In doing so, she not only learns about financial planning but also about her client's model customer relationship. Lux studies how the client views his ideal self—a nostalgic identity—to pinpoint his expertise and objectives. An added benefit of starting her partnership with the client describing his nostalgic ideals is that it makes him feel good about himself, creating a safe space from which to reach to the unknown. We might call this agenda-setting *nostalgic priming*. Lux starts her relationship with the client feeling good, and that good feeling transfers to how the client feels about Lux. If you remember yourself being a happy and good collaborator in the past, you'll be one in the present (Van Tilburg; Cialdini 19–30).

We see nostalgic priming more concretely in Lux's method of inquiry. She asks her client: "How do you want your customers to feel about your brand? How do you want that brand to be positioned in their minds? And what do you want to convey, you know—*how are they going to remember you?*" This last question, particularly, requires the client to consider anticipatory nostalgia. In response, the client depicts his ideal ethos: "He talked about . . . how he wanted people to kind of be able to come to him, and we can help you navigate your finances and find the direction where you want to go." Building from her client's stories, Lux focused on his god memories "navigate" and "direction," proposing a compass-themed website. In putting client memories first, she builds a baseline of trust: the client has confidence in Lux because she respects his experiences (and he trusts his own memories). It's significant, however, that Lux limits her client to reviewing his past. She makes him the expert on his company within the transactive memory system and appoints herself the expert on production. If the client had started by saying, "I think the website should look like X, Y, Z," Lux's expertise as a designer would be more difficult to practice.

Beyond reaching her initial concept, by prompting her client to consider the question "How are they going to remember you?" Lux also asks him to explore the collective memory his company exists within. She builds a nostalgic contact zone: How do you remember your company? How do customers remember it? How do your employees conceive of it? And how do all these memories align or conflict? A strong brand accounts for all these questions, and it's important for the client to learn to adapt his expectations to this larger democratic frame (Newcombe; Green; Luck et al.). Indeed, such a contact zone can help persuade clients to fund user-centered research to discover the answers to these questions. In this way the client, like the designer, is always a collective memory construct. It's impossible to know a client from only one representative, even the CEO (Alvesson et al.). Lux teaches her client to view his company as an entity including, but extending beyond, his personal experiences.

Like Lux, Grant begins by unearthing client values. He often asks clients to imagine their company is writing a personal ad: "Do you see yourselves as a friendly company or you're an efficient company or if you were writing a personal ad for your company, what would that be like, you know? Long walks on the beach or, you know, long hours in the library, what is it?" Essentially, he asks, *What are you nostalgic for and why?* Grant also requests that clients bring in inspirational images, mood boards that spark stories about their traits, ethos, and style. Though one might imagine the best clients bring in precise models to imitate, Grant says that the more abstract the image, the better:[8] "The good ones will bring me inspiration images that have nothing to do with their company. 'And here's a great picture of Mt. Rainier,' you know. It's like, 'What is it that you like about this?'" Grant's clients create what Susan Leigh Star calls "boundary objects," forums of shared communication between client and designer worldviews, expertise, and vocabularies, "a means of representing, learning about, and transforming knowledge to resolve the consequences that exist at a given boundary" (Carlile 442). As seen in OpenNotes in the last chapter, boundary objects are naturally memory objects as well (Orr): souvenirs from which clients and designers tell rich stories. But where a specific example might provide something concrete to act from, an abstract image like Mt. Rainier forces Grant's client to tell detailed stories to explain it.

Again, like Lux, Grant imagines design futures by putting clients' personal ads and mood boards into a nostalgic contact zone. For instance, he sometimes enters abstract words from client stories into a Google Images search to find a bearing: "It's like, 'Well, we're thinking friendly. We're thinking da, da, da.' I'll start, sometimes, if I'm having trouble getting ideas, I'll do Google Image searches for those really abstract words. You know, like, what does 'friendly' *look* like to Google? Okay, well, there's probably a lot of friends and then maybe there's like Friendly's the restaurant, and then there's like, you know, these other things." By using Google Images, Grant crowdsources an image-centric collective memory database, studying what the massive number of Google users associate with the terms, images, and values a company wants to develop. Ultimately, then, Lux and Grant are not inspired by ideas in isolation but by the overt, reflectively nostalgic agonism between their training, the new stories that clients bring, and the larger contexts those stories exist within—memorial interactivity.

### Designer Memories: Who Am I? What Am I Nostalgic For? What's My Expertise?

Though designers might appreciate why it's important to learn who clients are and what they want, reflecting on why designers need to justify their expertise to clients is a bit more tenuous. Didn't the client hire me because I'm an expert? "I think a lot of client negotiation," Grant describes, "is oftentimes me trying to frame what experience I'm bringing. Going like, you know, 'Yes, I know exactly what you're talking about. I've seen it on this site, and this site, and this site.'" Grant uses storytelling to transform his tacit knowledge into explicit experiences and, thereby, build trust. Lux, Mason, and Grant all develop such trust by showing clients who they are and which memories they bring to work.

Mason, for instance, explains that an everyday part of his job is educating patients on medicine, teaching them not only what he is an expert at but also how to adapt their concepts of healthcare to his expertise. He told me the story of two parents coming to the ER with a toddler presenting abdominal pain. Though the pain could be appendicitis, this inflammation (hyper-common in public memory) is relatively rare compared to simple indigestion. Mason doesn't put patients under radiation unless symptoms persist:

> I often wind up having kind of my speech I go through with the parents, basically saying, "So, I don't think this is likely to be appendicitis. Here are the tests that we would usually do. . . . If we CT scan him, it's likely not going to show anything, but he could have appendicitis. . . . If you feel comfortable, we'll basically send you home, these are the things you bring back your kid for. Here are the things you look for. I'm gonna show you on your child the things, you know, where the pain would be. Things he might say; we'll talk about it right now. Do you have any questions?" And let them have their opportunity to ask any questions they might have. I also always give them a handout, basically, with all the same things I just said to them in case that was overwhelming for them or they are, you know, distraught because they're in an ER, where no one really wants to be.

Mason's story epitomizes reflectively nostalgic adaptation: the parents who want an immediate diagnosis must adapt to Mason's expertise, which says to wait. To make this adaptation easier, Mason (contrasting the pro-vaccine doctors last chapter) builds an expert role for the parents by teaching them what to look for. He doesn't simply reject the parents' nostalgia (doctors should diagnose a problem). He explains why they are adapting (avoiding CT radiation) towards a shared goal (health of the child) from explicit expertise (stories of how he has seen appendicitis present itself). In his explanation, the child's body becomes a boundary object of sorts, a shared text over which both Mason and the parents exchange expertise as peers.

Earlier, we saw how Lux and Grant limit the client's initial expertise to self-description. Often, however, clients come in with solutions. Contrasting Grant's expert use of Google, for example, Mason describes:

> It's more the patients where they come in with a preconceived notion in their mind . . . "Hey, I Googled this" or . . . "I have low back pain, and I looked up low back pain on the internet, and it says I need an MRI right now" . . . when the vast majority of low back pains are just sprains. . . . When you Google

something all it ever is going to tell you is that you're about to die or you're dead already. . . . You can look up finger pain, and it will tell you, you have finger cancer. . . . Having more and more medical information and having access to it is definitely a double-edged sword.

In fact, I just did Google "finger pain," and the first website tells me that I could have a broken finger, muscular dystrophy, multiple sclerosis, or tumors. Thus, though Mason says access to internet information is "overall a good thing just because it allows patients to kind of empower themselves and their own medical care," and it gets patients to the ER quicker,[9] he also says it's important to teach patients how to interpret WebMD as a resource of expertise in a larger transactive memory system (see Oermann; Weber et al.; Biermann et al.).[10] Rather than rejecting WebMD as inexpert, Mason instructs his clients on how to reflectively layer their expertise with his. He supports patient expertise but limits it because when patients feel trusted, they trust.

Ultimately, therefore, design isn't arresting magic. Good designers have reasons why they create the way they do and are able to explain them. As Mason's stories illustrate, there are always two parts of presenting a design: the choice and the expertise behind it. Grant describes this two-part exhibition in his work on a photography website:

> We had one point where they were pretty adamant about wanting the navigation to work a certain way. They wanted it to be based all on hovers so that things could just automatically vanish. . . . My point of view on that, knowing that a lot of their clients are probably gonna be looking at this on mobile devices . . . hovers don't work on touch screens very well. So we have to do one of two things. We have to either build it to work for all the devices or build these, like, back-end solutions. . . . And either way we could have done it, but there would have been cost differences.

Like Mason, Grant frames his choice to avoid hover menus in terms of client goals—reaching mobile users and staying within budget. In doing so, he makes the logic and memories behind his expertise discussable and welcomes informed dissent. Grant's clients can more easily deliberate over his *design choice* because it's now a *business choice* (something they are expert in) rather than a mysterious part of Grant's repertoire.

## What Is Adaptation For? Shared Pasts and Shared Goals for the Future

Though adaptive co-education flows throughout the client-designer relationship, it's crucial at the "fuzzy front-end" of design, before a course of action has been selected (Reinertsen). A formal boundary object often associated with this early co-education is the brief, a text co-created by designer and client that describes the problem(s) to be solved, the company as an entity, and basic information about the project (timeline, budget, etc.). Designers Bec Paton and Kees Dorst explain, "The aim of briefing, then, is to reframe both the client's and designer's preliminary appreciation of the situation in order to create an actionable view of the project for both parties. . . . An accepted brief that is understood and agreed upon, should be one in which the designer's and client's frames have come to overlap or align to a certain extent" (575). Though the primary goal of briefing is to define the problem the designer is supposed to address, a shared definition relies on creating a shared transactive memory system and an equitable distribution of expertise to build trust.

Thus, briefing, as a capstone of adaptation, involves each party understanding the other's nostalgic expertise and goals, filtering those logics through their own expertise, and reflecting back that adaptation for discussion. The brief becomes a nostalgic contact zone in which both client and designer understandings of the problem and possible futures change. Management professor Paul Carlile explains that briefs, thereby, serve both practical and political roles: "Practical because it must establish a shared syntax or a shared means for representing and specifying differences and dependencies at the boundary. Political because it must facilitate a process of transforming current knowledge (knowledge that is localized, embedded, and invested in practice) so that new knowledge can be created to resolve the negative consequences identified" (453). To more fully understand how Grant, Mason, and Lux open their expertise to such transformation, we move to our second memorial interactivity move: adoption.

## Adopt: Listening for Expertise and Scaffolding Client Feedback

"Zen philosophy," writes client relations specialist Jeff Gardner, "teaches you to approach every task with a beginner's mind. This is simple when you're trying to teach yourself hyper-astro-meta-particle physics [something new], but not as easy as you think when it comes to something you do all day, every day." In this light, learning clients' points of view, as described in the last section, isn't terribly difficult, but transforming your expertise by seriously adopting those views can be a struggle. Carlile labels the roots of such strife "knowledge boundaries," trappings of professional expertise (lexis, logics, goals) that hamper work with other experts. Mason, for example, describes: "The hardest part to do for a doctor (and they've done studies about how quickly we'll interrupt patients and stuff like that) is just to stop and listen. And that's when you gather the most information. You don't want to bias yourself by kind of saying, 'Oh, it's this,' right away. You want to kind of listen to that full story. . . . 'When did this pain start? What is it like? . . . . What's been going on in your life?.' . . . All that data gathering that you do."

Here, Mason depicts the boundary of "initial concept fixation" (Jansson and Smith; Purcell and Gero; Cheng et al.): designers electing the first solution that comes to mind rather than listening for the full gamut of possibilities available. When designers quickly jump to a conclusion, architects H. T. Haagsma and J. G. Hoendervanger describe, clients also become fixated, limiting the knowledge they can contribute: "The architect, hoping to facilitate the communication, right at the outset of the process comes up with sketch designs. . . . The debate from then on will be centered around the sketch designs, to determine which one is 'prettier.' . . . [I]t should actually be about the more rudimental requirements of the future office building" (4).

Initial concept fixation is a dilemma of restoratively nostalgic expertise. If the designer were open to adopting the knowledge of others, first concepts would rarely become final solutions. To break this fixation, Richard Neustadt and Ernest May suggest the "Goldberg Rule": "Don't ask, 'What's the problem?' Ask, 'What's the story?'" (107). To understand client expertise and critique, designers have to understand the complex stories in which they are moored. In contrast to the Aristotelian logic of adapting, then, adopting is more like the Ratcliffean empathic design of chapter 3. It's more about listening, trusting, and believing and less about teaching and persuading.

## Embracing and Evolving from Client Stories

Mason, for instance, works in a hospital where he frequently treats large Chinese and Russian immigrant populations who use *biopsychosocial* healthcare such as acupuncture and herbalism. A typical *biomedical* response to such therapies, described last chapter, is creating a dichotomy of expert and nonexpert, refusing to address scientifically unproven treatments. In contrast, rather than ignoring alternative therapies, which he doubts because of a lack of double-blind trials, Mason works within his patients' cherished medical traditions. That is, he reflectively adopts client nostalgias in order to create a dialogue of healing rather than a monologue of curing:

> As long as you can identify that the patient isn't actively hurting themselves by their alternative therapy, it's probably ok. . . . So, it's just identifying, you know, what's best for the patient as far as their own mental health, too. So, a lot of patients will ask me, "Oh, do you think I should try acupuncture or reiki?" . . .
> I will basically tell the patient, "As long as we can tell that this is not actively

harming you, do . . . whatever makes you feel better." . . . That even goes along
with kind of the religious aspect of people saying, "Oh, I'm praying about this
stuff." "Absolutely! Pray about it! Whatever makes you feel better is good for
you." I've seen a million times where people with really negative attitudes that
are getting the standard of care that should treat them, they don't do as well
as the people that are super highly positive. Does that mean that these positive
patients don't die? No. But I will say those patients do seem to have a better
quality of life up until the end.

Mason takes the time to understand the narrative of meaning his treatment designs operate within and works with, rather than against, that story
because he understands that there is more to healing than biology. Familial
support, religion, positive mindsets, human touch—these psychological and
social factors transform his work. Mason adopts whatever safely improves
his patients' quality of life because most of the time his treatments and his
patients' therapies don't conflict. Just because Mason isn't an expert at biopsychosocial therapy doesn't mean he excludes the possibility of other experts.
One might call this reception an *empathy for experts*—an ethical responsibility
to recognize and work with expertise one does not understand. Indeed, if
Mason didn't engage patient nostalgias, he might not be getting the entire picture: "I've had patients that will bring in Chinese herbs from back in China
that their grandmother sent them. And they're not getting better; they've just
been sick. So, they kind of finally bring it in, and you'll take this medication
and have it analyzed, and it'll be 80% lead and arsenic. . . . They just light
up under x-ray because they're pretty much lead pills. And, they have chronic
lead poisoning." Had Mason restoratively refused to consider biopsychosocial
therapies, seeing them as an intractable knowledge boundary, he wouldn't
know when those therapies were helping or hindering his treatments. Thus,
Mason shapes a transactive memory system by asking: What traditions are
you engaging? Why are you engaging in them? How does my treatment relate
to your medical nostalgias and the other expertise you trust? *What are you
nostalgic for, why, and to which ends?*

Nostalgia, therefore, helps designers respond to clients within their own
stories—treating them as experts. Mason further adopts patient stories to motivate them: "Whenever I have a patient that's coming in, they have bad
COPD, so, long-term complications of smoking, or something like that. And
you're trying to get them not to smoke, and I'll look and say, 'You know,
you've got grandkids. . . . Do you want to see your grandkids grow up? Or do
you want to be on oxygen not able to do anything?' . . . When it's personal,
you're much more likely to get that message." Here, Mason generates anticipa-

tory nostalgia as a motivating force. By adopting patient nostalgias to unearth what they truly care about and what might be lost if they continue down a course of bad health, Mason finds a shared goal not only in curing the patient but also in helping the patient watch her grandchildren grow up. Layering tradition, community, memory, and medicine (making medicine memorially interactive) helps patients.

Still, it's treacherously easy for designers to restoratively overvalue their training and ignore a client's perspective. It's also easy to persuade a trusting client that the designer is right. But by leaving themselves open to change, designers can discover creative solutions. Lux explains how she provided her financial planner client with numerous logos based on the compass theme she initially proposed. Though she had her favorites, she welcomed informed dissent, and the client ended up convincing her that another option fit his business better: "Something where I would think like, 'Ohhhh, that's going to look really ugly.' . . . But I would still do it because he would want it, and then I would see, ok, if we tweaked it a little bit this way, we could actually make it work, and it's really, you know, a stronger concept. . . . So, his ideas also helped me realize ideas that I thought weren't possible." In listening beyond her expertise, Lux performs what Baruch Hirschberg calls "diplomatic recognition": "When you give other people 'diplomatic recognition' professionally, even as a tactic to soften them up, you end up changing too. Because then you, having recognized them, have to take them more seriously. You can't pretend" (Forester, *Deliberative* 109). By designing a prototype that didn't align with her tastes, Lux discovered a logo that was better than her original. She was open enough to let her client change her mind. Lux didn't abandon her expertise—she just trusted her client had expertise, too.

## Adopting Client Feedback: Structuring Design Critiques

Though adopting client values often happens at the beginning of collaborations, Grant and Lux also described a later stage of adoption: receiving client feedback. Criticism, particularly negative or seemingly bad advice, can be irritating, especially when early-career designers are used to receiving critique solely from professors and colleagues in school. Without structure, design critiques can even feel like the client is challenging the designer's very being. Fortunately, teaching clients to make the logic behind their critiques overt through nostalgic stories—memorial interactivity—makes criticism less painful and more adoptable.

Grant and Lux, for example, both depict their critique processes as highly structured. Neither simply emails a client a sketch and asks, "What do you think?" They recognize that for a boundary object to exist, conversation must happen over it. Stories must be told about it. Thus, Grant and Lux insist on being in the room to frame the different possible solutions they propose in terms of business goals. Deliverables are shored by the expertise that created them. This rule applies to clients as well: "Don't ask, 'What's the problem?' Ask, 'What's the story?'" (Neustadt and May 107). Grant and Lux teach their clients to perform informed dissent by asking that they frame critiques in explicit knowledge of their company, their customers, and the goals of the brief. "I don't like this," isn't a critique; it's a complaint. "I don't like this because I've seen our elderly customers struggling with reading text this small in the past," frames feedback within expert memories. For example, Grant recalls picking a website color:

> The clients who are very connected to their company as a separate entity from them, I think, are the ones that . . . pick, really, the one that is gonna be the best for them. It's the clients that have trouble separating themselves from [their company]. . . . They'll be clients that are like, "Well, I just don't like green. It shouldn't be green, I just don't like green." "You're a recycling company. I mean, you don't *have* to have green, but that might be the one thing that sort of aligns you with your industry."

By reminding clients to give feedback not only from personal opinion but also within the nostalgic contact zone their company exists in, Grant helps his client frame feedback for adoption.

To further encourage adoptable evaluations, Grant prevents initial concept fixation by carefully releasing drafts in stages so that clients comment on one aspect at a time: "Even though they told me they loved bright colors, and it's gotta be electric blue or whatever, I'm gonna show them something that's black, white, navy, gray. Usually just black and white because if I select the wrong blue on one of the columns, that's all they'll see." Grant focuses his clients to help them avoid complaints not pertinent to the task at hand. To explain this process to clients, Grant uses the metaphor of buying a home:

> If it's a website, it's usually starting with a bunch of gray boxes, you know, wire-framing it. Which sometimes catches them off guard. They're like, "Wait, what is all this," you know. And I'm like, "Well, okay, so generally we're gonna have your logo up in this corner. I know your logo is not a gray box, but it's a gray box right now. Right now we're trying to make some really big decisions, you know. We're sort of, like, when you go buy a house, you know? You first make the big decision that you're going to live in Chicago, right? Then you maybe narrow down the big decision of Lincoln Park or Wrigleyville. And then, you narrow down, like, to the school district, right? Like, that's what we're trying to

do here. We're trying to get you in Chicago first. Ok, we're in Chicago and not in Detroit, awesome. What neighborhood do we want to be in?"

Grant's metaphor illustrates that in order to provide adoptable feedback, clients must focus on higher-order concerns first. With his low-fi gray boxes, he is also showing them that, like all his sketches, "The design is not the drawings but is the idea that the drawings (always partially represent)" (Medway 258). In contrast, hi-fi CAD models and full-color prototypes shut down conversations and critique because they seem completed already. But good sketches aren't finished concepts; they are open to challenge, change, and redesign. They are boundary-objects to talk over.

## Why Adopt Client Goals? Summarizing New Perspectives on Your Designs

Pragmatically, perhaps the key rhetorical move of adopting client feedback is the designer rephrasing, summarizing, and presenting feedback to a client through the simple phrase, "Is this what you mean?" As we saw last chapter, finding an audience's god memories and then framing one's argument in terms of them is a vital move of nostalgic mediation. It builds goodwill through identifying with an opponent's nostalgic values. Cuff describes post-meeting memos as one boundary object that structures this act: "Clients receive memos, and if no corrections are made, agreement is presumed. In fact, meeting notes are often far more definite than the meeting itself, so that the memo becomes a tool for expediting progress" (*Architecture* 185). Like the design brief, the meeting memo becomes a nostalgic document, smoothing the potential tension of critiques into an actionable list. In this sense, the responsibility of the designer is almost like that of a ghostwriter, as Deborah Brandt describes: "Whenever possible, ghostwriters expend a great deal of energy trying to capture the 'signature' style of thoughts or values of an author-client. . . . [One ghostwriter explains,] 'I try to make people sound smarter. . . . I try to pull things together structurally where they might have these thoughts but they probably didn't think of them in a cogent way'" (*Rise* 36). One of the ethical commitments of nostalgic summaries, then, is not mischaracterizing client desires. If meeting minutes are well written, clients are flattered to see their expertise come to life; if poorly written, clients lose trust. Philosopher Daniel Dennett gives four rules to avoid such distortion:

1. You should attempt to re-express your target's position so clearly, vividly, and fairly that your target says, "Thanks, I wish I'd thought of putting it that way."

2. You should list any points of agreement (especially if they are not matters of general or widespread agreement).
3. You should mention anything you have learned from your target.
4. Only then are you permitted to say so much as a word of rebuttal or criticism. (34)

Dennett's rules are an avenue for designers to slow their inherent desire to defend initial designs—opening themselves to change through diplomatic recognition. By "re-express[ing] your target's position" through retelling a client's stories, for example, the designer is more likely to empathize with client critiques. Ultimately, then, embedding critique in explicit memory allows one to overcome knowledge boundaries. Of course, though client feedback can be valuable, sometimes it's just plain bad and has to be refused.

## Refuse: Telling a Client When They're Wrong and Its Price

In his *Rhetorical Refusals: Defying Audiences' Expectations*, John Schilb defines "rhetorical refusals" as "an act of writing or speaking in which the rhetor pointedly refuses to do what the audience considers rhetorically normal. By rejecting a procedure that the audience expects, the rhetor seeks the audience's assent to another principle, cast as a higher authority" (3). The opening example of Schilb's book, for instance, is *New Yorker* ballet critic Arlene Croce's review of a performance she refused to see because it featured "victim art," videos of people with terminal illnesses. Though sensationalist, Croce rejects the rhetorically normal (seeing a performance before she reviews it) and supplants it with a higher value (victim art can't be reviewed critically; let's have a conversation about that). Rhetorical refusals differ from standard rejections, then, because they understand a collaborator's logic so well that when they happen, the refused person is instantaneously offered a better solution and usually leaves more satisfied.

In both design and rhetorical education, this ability to tactfully refuse an audience is perhaps the most under-explored move of collaboration. Lux, for instance, remembers, "Well, in advertising they taught us the client is always right, you know; who cares what you think. It's what the client wants." And, yet, as client-relationship specialist Mike Monteiro presents: "Doing good work often requires a few hard conversations. There's a difference between being enjoyable to work with and being 'nice.' Being nice means worrying about keeping up the appearance of harmony at the expense of being straightforward and fully engaged. Sometimes you need to tell a client they're making the wrong call. Part of client services is being able to do that without coming off as a dick. No one is hiring you to be their friend. They're hiring you to

design solutions to problems" (14). Grant follows this logic when he argues
that designers should consider refusals as early as the first client conversation:
"You know, the more designers we have out there who are putting themselves
in those positions to be able to say, like, 'No, I'm not gonna do another
crappy logo.' . . . Who are going to take more ownership and go, 'No let's [do
something else].'" Whenever possible, Grant contends, it's the designer's professional obligation to make sure the project she is undertaking is a good fit
for her skills, will benefit her portfolio, will help her client, and will improve
the world. "In the end," Grant says, "I want them to get what they want. I
want them to get a good solution. And if I'm not the person, you know, if my
aesthetic or my skillset or whatever is just not gonna get them the solution
they're happy with, then I'm not the right designer for the job." Of course,
though learning to refuse is a necessity, being a brute is not. Like good critiques, successful rhetorical refusals are memorially interactive, positioned
within the memories that make their logic explicit.

## Refusing Towards Shared Goals

Above, I described how Lux, Grant, and Mason carefully shepherd adoptable
client feedback. But even the most client-centered designer will admit that
some client feedback is simply wrong. Good designers walk their clients back
from these critiques to the shared business objectives established in the brief.
Grant, for example, describes attempting to free a client's mind from a mundane concept:

> I have a client who I was recently working on her branding, and I was doing
> a logo for them, and they brought me—it was kind of nice, they had done a lot
> of research. They brought me logos from all kinds of their competitors, you
> know, and they all have a very similar feel. They all sort of look a certain way.
> And they're like, "So you know, we're thinking, here's some inspiration," right?
> And, so, one of the first things I did was I brought them something that looked
> nothing like the rest. . . . What I was trying to do was talk to them about how,
> "Okay, so you brought me these forty logos that look a lot alike. Do you just
> want to be another one of them? Or is this, you know, an opportunity here to
> elevate, not just your brand, but elevate the category?" . . . When Apple came out
> with their original iMac, the candy color ones, right? The reason that took off is
> they were like, "Now everyone is gonna know who has a Mac."

Though he might not end up with a logo that is as avant-garde as he'd
like, Grant cunningly provides *provo*types to stretch his clients. His refusal
is *rhetorical* because it substitutes the client's original goal (a logo that fits industry standards) with a higher business goal (a logo that revolutionizes the

industry). Architects Jessica Siva and Kerry London call this style of refusal a "habitus shock": "A state of shock when confronted with the architect who is of a different corresponding habitus and may undergo some form of adjustment similar to individuals experiencing culture shock" (215). Rather than being a negative experience, well-crafted habitus shocks are a resource for client education: "The sojourner develops a new sensitivity and understanding about the host culture and is able to function more competently within the new culture. . . . [Ultimately,] one accepts and enjoys the differences between cultures and is able to function in both the 'old' and 'new' culture" (216).

At Elemental Coffee in Oklahoma City, I watch such rhetorical refusals happen all the time. Customers used to visiting Starbucks ask for chocolate, whipped cream, etc., which this particular cafe, serving only house-roasted pour-over coffee, refuses to provide. The customer and the coffee shop have different nostalgic understandings of what the ideal cup of coffee is. But rather than snobbishly stating, "We don't do that here," the baristas take this refusal as a chance for education. They teach customers how savoring coffee is similar to wine tasting and help customers reach their goal of enjoying the best cup possible. Again, the key marker of a rhetorical refusal is substituting some better standard and explaining the alternative in terms of a co-defined objective. The nostalgic designer finds a collaborator's god memories and poses her argument in terms of that tradition. This is the layering of simultaneously right traditions that defines nostalgic design.

Monteiro describes a similar situation. A potential client asked for concepts from each design firm bidding for a project. Monteiro explained the impossibility of designing anything good, let alone useful, without first doing research on the client and their goals. He refuses the client and interjects his research process as a higher standard: "We told them that if we were just to do some quick sketches without the benefit of discussion and research, the ideas would inevitably be wrong. We'd never be able to guess what was in the clients' heads. And we wouldn't put ourselves in the position where we'd be judged on our mind-reading powers." The client responded, "That all makes a lot of sense. You're hired" (58).

Such rhetorical refusals are vastly different from the standard refusal taught in rhetoric and writing classrooms today: the logical fallacy. Straw man, ad hominem, bandwagon—labeling an opponent's argument a logical (or "rhetorical") fallacy refuses one's opponents by pointing out their flaws in reasoning. What revealing logical fallacies doesn't do is grant the opposing side expertise in a transactive memory system, start a productive collaboration, or, as the last chapter attests, work. This style of refusal is restoratively nostalgic, seeking to replace one ideal with another without reflectively showing how the new ideal speaks to the opponent's goals. Indeed, simply pointing out logical fallacies has been psychologically shown to make opponents grasp to them tighter (see Nyhan and Reifler's "backfire effect"). There's a difference between agonistic and antagonistic refusals.

### Refusals of Voice: Sticking to One's Aesthetic Guns

I began this chapter by criticizing designers who see themselves as isolated artists. But, admittedly, part of what makes great designers great is a cohesive voice, "a designer's distinctive personal and professional way of doing things resulting from a series of decisions made in the process to deliberate the pattern of expression" (Chan 321). Renowned industrial designer Dieter Rams, for example, has influenced generations through a voice in which designs "are neither decorative objects nor works of art. Their design should therefore be both neutral and restrained, to leave room for the user's self-expression." Rams's voice as a designer—minimalist and utilitarian—*refuses* superfluous aesthetics.

To define a cohesive style, *all artistic voice refuses* in this way, defining what it is by way of what it is not. Thus, like expertise, voice is nostalgic—an imagined ideal, pure, authentic self that is lost when one has to adapt to real-world scenarios.[11] Voice seeks to recover this ideal. It's a dialogue of past ideals (who I imagine myself to be as a designer) and present performances (how my imagined identity interacts with client needs). Where adapting and adopting involve designers learning to grant clients expertise, voice is a designer granting herself expertise and the right to artistic pleasure. At its best, voice is reflectively nostalgic—an imagined ur-identity that one reaches towards but can only attain an adaptable version of. At its worst, it's restoratively nostalgic—never budging, never changing, locked in isolated expertise as truth.

Mason, for example, explains that like designers, doctors, too, have unique voices they must balance with patient expectations:

> I've actually worked with doctors that will basically say to a patient, "Yeah, you're feeling short of breath because you are super fat. Lose weight and stop smoking. You're an idiot." And they have a very specific group of patients that they see that LOVE them. They would never have another doctor in a million years. . . . [However,] when one of the other doctors was out of the office, his patients had to go to that doctor that's very the blunt: "This is what you should do; you're dumb; you're ugly," kind of thing. And those patients HATE that, hate it, hate, hate, hate. . . . You know, coming and being like, "Yeah, uh, you need to lose like 40 pounds, what is wrong with you? Stop eating horrible, you fat ass." You know, a certain patient that is not going to go over well, at all. So,

it's actually a lot of the combination between what the patient expects and wants and the doctor's, how they kind of do their clinical practice.

Though Mason's colleague's voice is harsh, it may have rhetorical purpose. It ruptures his patients' nostalgia of what a doctor should say and, in doing so, highlights the importance of his words. It refuses their apathy. It enacts a habitus shock. Sometimes adaptation and adoption are harmful because the designer's perspective is what is needed to see the situation in a new light. It would be unethical to continue to adapt and adopt when a refusal is needed. "When the client's lack of expertise in the field affects the quality of the design," Robert Bowen argues, "we have a responsibility to do everything in our power to convince the client that the design is perfect as it is." Mason's rude colleague might be exactly the kick in the pants some patients need.

For other patients, of course, this refusal is insensitive and deeply *unethical*. Especially, given the unequal power dynamic of doctor and patient, some patients might simply take abuse. One also wonders if Mason's colleague weren't a white male, would he still as effectively wield refusals? Ultimately, Mason describes: "Each doctor has their own style. It's like being an artist. You have your own style of practice. The end result is the same a lot of the times, but the path to get there is a lot different. And he [the blunt doctor] was basically saying that his patients come in one of two categories: either a patient he sees once and never again or a patient he has for twenty years." A strong voice, therefore, may attract a devoted group of clients. But it might also scare them away, like the patients in Mason's story who "hate, hate, hate" his harsh colleague. This pragmatic side of voice—style's relationship to economic risk and reward—isn't often considered in design, rhetoric, or writing classrooms, but it guides Grant, Mason, and Lux through the complexities of client interaction.

Grant describes, for instance, that deciding to enact a refusal of voice is usually related to his financial situation:

> I do tend to work in a particular sort of aesthetic. . . . I like really flat, minimalist [designs]. . . . [T]here have been times where that initial meeting has been, you know, they bring me stuff, and I'm in a position where I'm not like eating dirt, so, I will usually make recommendations if I know someone: "I actually have this friend who does a lot of work that's a lot more like this who would probably be awesome." You know, because that only helps me too. Like, one, it keeps me out of a project that I don't want to do, and, two, I get this reputation.

If Grant isn't in dire economic straits, then, he'll refuse work in order to reaffirm the type of designer he is and develop his ethos as a friend who shares clients. In conjunction with this refusal, however, Grant describes how sometimes he has to deny his voice to make money: "There are times when you'll have certain clients, and those are the not so great clients, that they don't wanna hear how you can elevate their brand. . . . They just want what they want. And at the end of the day it's like, okay, well, I'm going to detach myself emotionally from this work. It's probably not going to stay in my portfolio that long, and I'll buy some mac and cheese. You know, I'll get paid. And, at the end of the day, that's what I gotta do." Again, we find nostalgic loss and pride. The fact that voice is economic—those without power and money frequently cannot afford it—is ignored in much design and writing research. But it anchors all client work. Of course, there are spaces, as seen in chapter 2, for less powerful designers to reshape and refuse the world (knitting while at work) and ethical reasons (e.g., building a home in tech workplaces for other women) to do so. But voice is always grounded in power and, thereby, involves risk. For this reason, Grant's client contracts always have a maintenance of copyright clause that gives him ownership of all the designs that his client didn't choose. Under this clause, all his work, even when he has to bow to client whims, develops his voice as a designer. Later, he revamps these options for other clients or for T-shirts he sells on his website. The refusal of voice, thus, illustrates the intricate balance of art, ethics, and business that is design.

## Why Refuse? Preparing for Enjoying Work and for When Things Go Wrong

The first move described in this chapter is adapting to client expertise, but it would be wrong to ignore the designer's hopes, dreams, and satisfaction. Design's rising audience deference in this era of democratic production doesn't always build a space for the designer's voice. But democratic technologies require it. As explored in chapter 2, designers too often are asked to curb their desire for meaningful work in favor of some larger corporate goal. This has triggered Richard Barbrook and Pit Schultz, for instance, to challenge in their "Digital Artisans Manifesto": "We are the digital artisans. We celebrate the Promethean power of our labour and imagination to shape the virtual world. By hacking, coding, designing and mixing, we build the wired future through our own efforts and inventiveness. . . . Free market policies don't just brutalise our societies and ignore environmental degradation. Above all, they cannot remove alienation within the workplace. Under neo-liberalism, individuals are only allowed to exercise their own autonomy in deal-making rather than through making things. We cannot express ourselves directly by constructing useful and beautiful virtual artifacts." For Barbrook and Schultz, voice is an ethical refusal to sit back and design someone else's bad idea. It's a right to enjoy one's work.

In 1972 the National Council of Teachers of English (NCTE) put out a similar statement on "Students' Right to Their Own Language": "We affirm the students' right to their own patterns and varieties of language—the dialects of their nurture or whatever dialects in which they find their own identity and style. Language scholars long ago denied that the myth of a standard American dialect has any validity. The claim that any one dialect is unacceptable amounts to an attempt of one social group to exert its dominance over another. Such a claim leads to false advice for speakers and writers, and immoral advice for humans." (CCC). Unfortunately, NCTE didn't provide an equivalent pedagogy to teach students how the rhetorical refusal of voice might succeed or fail them in work contexts—the economics of voice.

Pragmatically, readying oneself for the economics of refusals and voice happens up-front, whether that is refusing to design outside of the aesthetic of one's portfolio, refusing to veer from one's preferred design process, or making sure a client knows what happens when a design relationship sours. If adaption is embodied by a co-written brief and adoption is best seen in design meeting memos, the boundary object that best represents the refusal is the contract. For example, lawyer and web developer Jacob Myers places the following cancellation fees and ownership rights clauses in his contracts:

- *Cancellation Fees*: In the event of Cancellation, Designer will be compensated for services performed through the date of cancellation in the amount of a prorated portion of the fees due. Upon cancellation all rights to the website revert to the Designer and all original art must be returned, including sketches, comps, or other preliminary materials
- *Preliminary Works*: Designer retains all rights in and to all Preliminary Designs. Client shall return all Preliminary Designs to Designer within thirty (30) days of completion of the project and all rights in and to any Preliminary Designs shall remain the exclusive property of Designer.

Myers' cancellation or "kill fee" legally protects his right to refuse a client as well as the right of his client to fire him. Similarly, his retention of the copyright of preliminary works and sketches, as with Grant's t-shirts above, allows Myers to reuse the concepts a client rejects. Voice is planned for contractually.

## Conclusions: Aesthetics, Ethics, and Economics

Memorial interactivity builds a forum for democratic design by making the memories behind design expertise explicit and assigning expertise to all collaborators in the transactive memory system. Between creating something the designer is passionate about and getting paid; between understanding one's expertise as a concrete set of guidelines and a skewed nostalgic commitment to professional power; between welcoming clients' knowledge of themselves and refusing clients' sometimes terrible suggestions—client negotiations are a strange jumble of aesthetics, ethics, and economics. Within these tensions, professional expertise is both a boon and a curse, a reflectively nostalgic resource for creativity and a restorative blindfold restricting designers from communing with other experts. Grant, Lux, and Mason each use memorial interactivity to unearth and relieve these tensions.

Though in the past the professions maintained their sense of power through guarding esoteric expertise so that their work appeared by magic, in memorial interactivity professionals reveal the sources of their decisions. In doing so, they rupture their invisible "microphysics of power," as Michel Foucault calls them, but they also gain the faith of an audience who no longer trusts magical expertise. Self-reflective nostalgia reveals, harnesses, questions, and diversifies points of origin. Thus, the three memorially interactive moves that structure Lux, Grant, and Mason's design interactions provide a means to negotiate the push and pull of idealistic and pragmatic needs by creating a clear transactive memory system in which designers and clients recognize and feel comfortable challenging and transforming each other's knowledge. Ultimately, adapting, adopting, and refusing (much like the rhetorical design methods of chapter 3) aren't hyper-distinct rhetorical moves; they're practiced simultaneously. Nostalgia ends up being a strong lens for teaching this balancing, blending, and granting of expertise because it is both very real (memories and lessons learned from design education and past experiences) and self-reflectively unreal (only ever existing in a nostalgic contact zone as read by an audience who often has their own idiosyncratic definition of expertise).

In the larger context of nostalgic design, memorial interactivity aids designers in their ethical responsibility towards inclusivity, welcoming an ever-diverse set of client minds into co-design. But how can designers achieve inclusivity when clients can't pay for user research or participation? You'll notice that in this chapter, for example, I haven't mentioned Lux or Grant performing the rich user-centered and participatory research of chapter 3. That's because they work at small design shops with small clients who can't afford big research budgets. Part of the exigence of the next chapter is to imagine ways that planning for user nostalgia as a form of product personalization can benefit such small design shops with big dreams of inclusivity. Engaging nostalgia, we'll see, can lead to more ethical, interactive, inclusive, and popular designs when deep user research isn't possible.

# III

# Designing for Nostalgia

# Chapter 6

# Nostalgic UX

## Designing for Future Memories

> True, long-lasting emotional feelings take time to develop. . . . What do people love and cherish, despise and detest? Surface appearance and behavioral utility play relatively minor roles. Instead, what matters is the history of interaction, the associations people have with the objects, and the memories they evoke.
>
> **Donald Norman, *Emotional Design***

> When a person buys a *service*, he purchases a set of intangible activities carried out on his behalf. But when he buys an *experience*, he pays to spend time enjoying a series of memorable events that a company stages.
>
> **B. Joseph Pine II and James H. Gilmore, *The Experience Economy***

> It's time for a new generation of products that can age slowly and in a dignified way, become our partners in life, and support our memories.
>
> **Ezio Manzini, *Eternally Yours***

In the epilogue to his *Emotional Design*, Donald Norman asks a question that should haunt designers in our age of fast digital productions: "How can mass-produced objects have personal meaning?" (118). Whether it's college students being driven through enormous lecture courses or the quick death of a cell phone, the speed of mass design often leaves users unfulfilled. In universities (Allenby) this leads to rising dropout rates and falling alumni donations (why be true to your school if you never had a personal conversation with a professor?).[1] In tech, it leads to landfills of toxic junk (why be true to your laptop when the newer, faster, better one is out?). And fighting this drought of long-term attachment is crucial to the democratic technologies this book advocates. Designers can listen for and negotiate with overlooked users and clients, but if design systems don't stick around long enough to gather followers, critics, and collaborators, diversity won't be a platform for revolution. Why invest your time in redesign when your efforts will be obsolete tomorrow? Eric Hsu and Anthony Elliott call this ennui "the detached self": "[P]eople become so resigned to the logics of a high-speed society that. . . .

[They] passively accept that perpetual change is a regular feature of the world in which they live" (402).

Of course, some readers might rightly object to the claim that personal attachment to technology is dwindling. After all, there are millions of special choices that consumers get to make every day: customizable cars, computers, shoes. I make my cell phone personal by putting it in a leather case that no one else has. And Starbucks writes my name on the cup! Yet, despite an explosion of choices, I stand with Norman when he balks, "[M]anufacturers have tried to overcome the sameness of their product offerings by allowing customers to 'customize' them. . . . [Where] the purchaser can choose the color or select from a list of accessories. . . . Are these customizations emotionally compelling? Not really" (*Emotional Design* 118). *Mass customization* (a set of closed decisions wherein users mistake a company's choices for their own) should not be confused for *personalization* (a product's individual and emotional anchoring in our lives). A custom cell phone case is not the same as the vintage guitar entrusted to me by my dad. Mass customization (S. Davis; Pine; Tseng et al.) relies on a logic of speed—individuality through rapid selection; but personalization thrives on slow becoming—an attachment to an artifact's history of interaction. From your grandfather's favorite tattered recliner to a decade old Facebook account, personal designs *record, store,* and *emit* nostalgias of use. Look around. What objects are most meaningful to you?

In their 1981 study *The Meaning of Things*, Mihaly Csikszentmihalyi and Eugene Halton survey this "role of objects in people's definition of who they are, of who they have been, and who they wish to become" (x). To do so, the researchers asked three hundred Chicagoans, "What are the things in your home which are special to you?" (56). Through a rich taxonomy, Csikszentmihalyi and Halton discovered that the most meaningful objects are "contemplative," used for action *and* meditation. And the largest group of these contemplative designs? Tangible mnemonic devices, memory things. Two interviewees describe their favorite possessions, for example: (1) "They are the first two chairs me and my husband ever bought, and we sit in them and I just associate them with my home and having babies and sitting in the chairs with babies"; (2) "It is very old. It was given to me as a present by one of the oldest black families in Evanston. They thought I would take care of it" (60–61). Whereas Csikszentmihalyi and Halton call such possessions "contemplative objects," we might just as easily call them nostalgic designs. And, yet, although the defining objects in our lives so often metamorphose from action to reflection, there's been surprisingly little research on how designers might better plan for memory, increase psychic investment, and aid in this transformation. Which routes lead to memorable designs?

In this concluding chapter I approach this question through a blueprint for personalization I call *nostalgic user experience architecture* (N-UX).[2] If, as Richard Buchanan argues, designers create "a persuasive argument that comes to life whenever a user considers or uses a product," nostalgic UX persuades users to be nostalgic, slow down, and, thereby, awaken to their place in time ("Declaration" 8). To explore N-UX, I catalogue, rhetorically analyze, and derive best practices from designs that afford user memories through three types of interactions:

1. *Narratability:* The appetite to participate in and recount nostalgic stories about designs
2. *Craft:* The positive memories and human connections gained from contributing to the lifecycle of an object
3. *Connoisseurship:* Sharing in communal consumption and a taste for playing with time that require memorable rituals and traditional knowledge as badges of membership

More so than the other methods of this book, nostalgic UX focuses on how nostalgia makes designs profitable because I hope to answer an often-ignored question about democratic design: "Why would those with wealth and power want to support that?" (Westley et al. 121). Personal designs are. popular, and nostalgic designs respond to user desires when the extensive research described in chapters 3 and 4 is not feasible.

At the same time, however, each nostalgic UX interaction also exposes restorative, technocratic, and fundamentalist techno-logics for critical evaluation. Philosopher Hartmut Rosa calls this self-conscious slowing in the wake of fast digital designs *entschleunigung,* deceleration. When a technology runs well we ignore it; "good" tech anaesthetizes users as it speeds on (e.g., Heidegger's "ready-to-hand"; McLuhan's "somnambulism"). I only pay attention to my car, for example, when it interrupts me with noises, lights, or, heaven forbid, smoke. A parallel interruption happens, however, when I make an old family recipe for Sicilian *binulati* from my grandmother's cookbook. I'm more apt to slow down, to think about the processes and people behind my consumption, than I am when I simply buy bread at the store. Nostalgia can be a positive interruption (*efahrung*) of the flow of present experience (*erlebnis*) in the same way my check oil light is a negative one.[3] By promoting such nostalgic calls to attention, the three interactions of this chapter similarly cause user audiences to become aware of how designs exist in time and, thereby, re-embody, re-spatialize, and re-think definitions of technological *eudaimonia*. N-UX wakes us up.

## Nostalgic UX: From Things to Experiences to Memories

With this intention in mind, to explore this rousing force, this chapter steps back from democratic design mediations and ponders how designers (especially at a mass scale) might support memorable experiences with their creations *after* they leave the designer's workbench. In making this turn from process to product, I shift from user-centered, participatory, and rhetorical design to *user experience design* (UX): designs as curations of experience.

Throughout its history, UX has often been a slowing and humanizing force. Yet, its origins can be traced (Buley; Soegaard) to notably dehumanizing Taylorist research on assembly lines, which, within brutalizing speed and division of labor, paid attention to how workers operated in a specific environment over time—worker experience. The slowing, democratic, and humane UX we're interested in, however, arose in response to such speed. In the 1940s Sakichi Toyoda, Kiichiro Toyoda, and Taiichi Ohno visited Ford Motor Company's assembly line. Though they learned critical lessons, they were disappointed by the overwork and waste they saw (Ohno; Womack et al.). Their answer, the Toyota Production System, humanized Fordism by interjecting philosophies such as "respect for people," "work like the tortoise [thoughtfully and consistently] not the hare," and *jidoka* (automation with a human touch). Though Toyota is swift in speed and its celebrated "just-in-time" production, it's slow in its careful ethic. Workers are people. Speed can be humane. This ethic is typified, for instance, in the Andon Cord, an egalitarian device at each Toyota workstation that any employee can pull to halt the assembly line if trouble is spotted.

Shifting from worker to user experiences, throughout the 1960s, '70s, and '80s, proto-UX developed under the many names described in chapter 3 (user-centered design, participatory design, etc.), but it wasn't until the personal computer boom of the 1990s that Donald Norman joined Apple and devised the job title "User Experience Architect" for himself. "I invented the term," Norman recounts, "because I thought human interface and usability were too narrow: I wanted to cover all aspects of the person's experience with a system, including industrial design, graphics, the interface, the physical interaction, and the manual" (Merholz). In Norman's description one sees how UX plans for a fuller range of human interaction than traditional design. UX is the difference, for instance, between a PC and an iMac or an *amusement* park's design of thrilling rides and a *theme* park's curation of rides, restaurants, parking lots, lines, etc.

Over the past twenty years, UX has flourished as marketing (e.g., relationship marketing), business (e.g., Lean), and design (e.g., participatory, empath-

**Figure 6.1.** Thomas Brisebras's "No Coaster Please" table and chairs depict the process of aging. Over time, Brisebras explains, "Each set becomes a unique graphic, reflecting personal and social patterns of use. Like a guest book, No Coaster Please invites guests to inscribe their mark with one of the aluminum pens, contributing to the life story of the furniture." Photo: Thomas Brisebras.

ic, and emotional design) experts shift from working in isolation from one another towards collaboratively designing objects and the contexts they exist within. Ideally, this code submits that products are democratic before their production. But in this chapter, I'm more interested in UX's argument that designs shouldn't be left alone after their release. Future use is planned for: marketing, packaging, ritual, repair, recycling, and resale. Johan Redström famously calls such planning "design-after-design." A computer, for instance, is designed to be reshaped and adapted by its user. UX, therefore, ideally accounts for time and change. It calls forth users' mêtis.

Expanding on this taste for change, *nostalgic UX* invites users to redesign objects by attaching memories to them. That is, it supports commemoration as redesign. Take, for example, designer Thomas Brisebras's "No Coaster Please" table (figure 6.1). The wooden table and chairs are coated with several layers of special colored paint so that as users rest damp cups, spill bowls of soup, or simply rest their hands, the paint gradually wears away, leaving unique histories of interaction. "Each set becomes a unique graphic, reflecting personal and social patterns of use," Brisebras describes. This is what I mean when I say nostalgic UX highlights a design's place in time.

As we've seen, on the consumer's end one of the demands for such lifespan awareness is a sense of isolation from and mistrust of technical experts and a corresponding nostalgic desire for knowledgeable and personal consumption. The consumer-citizens (Featherstone) of the slow food movement, for instance, don't just want a chicken dinner, they want food provenance. They want to know, as one sketch from the TV show *Portlandia* spoofs: "Is that USDA organic, or Oregon organic, or Portland organic? How big is the area where the chickens are able to roam free? . . . A lot of friends? Other chickens as friends?" ("Farm"). Though *Portlandia*'s questions are extreme, given revelations of abysmal animal conditions and the overuse of antibiotics, there's an ethical imperative to know the history, tradition, and collective memory that a chicken (like any technology) exists within. In contrast to the anaesthetizing force of fast food, slow food, as initiated in Folco Portinari's 1989 manifesto, "[P]ropose[s] the vaccine of an adequate portion of sensual gourmandise pleasures, to be taken with slow and prolonged enjoyment. . . . [W]e can begin by cultivating taste[,] . . . by advocating historical food culture and by defending old-fashioned food traditions."

Still, despite a mounting desire for slow experiences, lasting emotions, and object memory, UX is not inevitably time conscious. Very few methods actually measure how a user's experience matures over time (see Vermeeren et al.'s survey). Nostalgia as a topic of UX has been underexplored with the majority of inquiry stemming from marketing. Morris Holbrook and Robert Schindler, for example, describe that "nostalgic bonding," "a consumer's history of personal interaction with a product during a critical period of preference formation that occurs roughly in the vicinity of age twenty (give or take a few years in either direction) can create a lifelong preference for that object" (109). Stephen Brown et al.'s "retro branding" considers the power of this bonding in revived brands—from Star Wars to Throwback Pepsi—to encourage consumers to celebrate an idealized brand past. Similarly, "brand heritage" has consistently been developed as a brand's ability to build customer trust through a symbolic history (Aaker et al.; Urde et al.; Wuestefeld et al.). But though I touch on these concepts, nostalgic UX diverges from *brand-centric* ideals, seeking to understand how products become *meaningful to users*. That is, I follow Pelle Ehn, Elizabet Nilsson, and Richard Topgaard's belief that theories of innovation focus too much on god terms of speed, efficiency, and profit: "Is making it to the market the only thing that really counts?" (2). No. Let's slow down.

## Narratable UX: Scaffolding Wonderful Stories

When asked on the Netflix series *Chef's Table* to describe his most formative food experience, for example, master Italian chef Massimo Bottura is rapt by nostalgia:

> My older brothers . . . were chasing me, and my safety place was in the kitchen, under the table, where my grandmother was rolling pasta. . . . Flour was falling . . . and in that moment I was stealing from under the table the tortellini. So, when they ask me, "What is the plate of your life?" . . . It's the raw tortellino . . . just made one second before, from the hand of my grandmother. That's why food is so important for me because in the many different creations I do you can find that I'm trying to take you in that moment back to when you were a child. (Massimo)

Bottura's meals are clearly nostalgic experiences. They provoke reflection and wonder. And such wonder at the past "is a complex emotion," writes psychiatrist Neel Burton, "involving elements of surprise, curiosity, contemplation, and joy. It is perhaps best defined as a heightened state of consciousness and emotion brought about by something singularly beautiful, rare, or unexpected—that is, by a marvel." We begin our trek into nostalgic UX, then, with wonderful stories because, as seen in Bottura's memory, if there is one feature that marks reflectively nostalgic narratives it's this spark of curiosity that drives us to remember, relive, and recount. Wondrous things cause us to slowly savor the world. In a 2012 survey of such stories, psychologist Elena Stephan et al. corroborate "that nostalgic narratives, compared to ordinary or positive narratives, will be more meaningful (involving abstract construal) and vivid (incorporating concrete elements in the part connecting the event to the present) . . . [and] that nostalgia will engender a sense of authenticity" (8). If a UX feature could be said to be nostalgically wondrous, then, it would call forth vivid personal stories like Bottura's tortellini.

Sam Gosling's "behavioral residue," for instance, is composed of the physical traces an interaction leaves behind that spark others to wonder, What's that? Old movie stubs, an "I Voted" sticker, a marathon T-shirt—behavioral residues are prompts that users tell stories about: "Do you see this scar? I got this skateboarding in 1987." But differing from photographs or purchased memorabilia, behavioral residues happen automatically. They're planned UX features. And meaningful residues are not empty kitsch. "To serve as traces of authentic experience," folklorist Susan Stewart describes, "we do not need or desire souvenirs of events that are repeatable. Rather we need and desire souvenirs of events that are reportable. . . . [T]he souvenir must remain impoverished and partial so that it can be supplemented by a narrative" (135). Thus, the user becomes a narrator. Recovering a memory from a good souvenir requires that you tell a personal story about it. Nostalgia resides in this striving but futile attempt to return to the lost past through wondrous narrative. The gap between the object as symbol (a small bit of sea glass represents my trip to Lake Michigan) and the lived experience (the micro-memories of my trip [a beach picnic, a college road trip, former friends] not overtly seen in the glass) calls for closure—calls for personal story—an invitation I call *narratability*. Narratable UX is a design plan that generates, records, and recalls wonderful stories of use.

## *Rupturing the Present: Generating Surprise, Story, and Nostalgic Wandering*

The archetypical example of such wondrous narratives is an account by French novelist Marcel Proust. One infamous winter day Proust, trapped in a bleak existence, was offered lime blossom tea and madeleine cookies by his mother. "No sooner had the warm liquid, and the crumbs with it, touched my palate," Proust recounts, "a shudder ran through my whole body, and I stopped, intent upon the extraordinary changes that were taking place." The taste of tea and cookie ejects Proust from the present, awakening an involuntary nostalgia and self-reflectiveness. It reminds him of his time in Combray, which he narrates for his reader. Proust is surprised by his own past and urged to tell a story about it. Describing such Proustian wonder, narrative theorists Elinor Ochs and Lisa Capps write, "Although tellers can transform just about anything that happened into a tellable account, events that violate the status quo are prototypically the basis of everyday narration" (253). Remarkable things, that is, are worthy of remark.

Though a designer probably could never plan for the chance nostalgic wonder of Proust's madeleine, one way to compel users to create and share nostalgic stories is through surprise. To reach towards Proustian personalization, however, rather than simple attention-grabbing gimmicks, we need a more subtle type of surprise. *Ruptures of the present*, as we've seen throughout this book, are features like Proust's madeleine, Bottura's tortellini, or Donna's sock-making machine in chapter 2, which throw users out of the smooth flow of the now, causing them to reflect on their identity, a design's construction, and their place in time. Each rupture is a storytelling event.

Under metaphorical design in chapter 3, for example, we saw such a rupture when Oren Teich, COO of the app developer Heroku, required his programmers to make quilts and bind books. Participants were surprised by nostalgia. In Teich's words, the juxtaposition of craft and coding encouraged his team to think in neostalgic ways about the present: "Why do we care about crafts? Because I want you to be thinking not just about 'how do I write the best line of code,' but 'how do I open myself up to world of what's possible'" (Mitroff). This self-reflective opening of one's identity to change is what's particularly useful about ruptures of the present. They transform us. When we experience them, we often reflect on who we are, are not, have been, and wish to become: "[W]e become very aware of our new-ness in this place. . . . We begin to feel and become more aware of ourselves. . . . This is an example of what an *authentic* mode of being might be like" (Coxon, "Fundamental" 19).

The *nostalgic* surprise is especially meaningful because it ruptures the present by way of something that used to be a part of us (the joy of handicraft, a madeleine, a tortellini).[4] It doesn't necessarily seek to create a new memory; instead, it reawakens and links old memories to new experiences. A highly personal neostalgic perspective is stirred whose light transforms the everyday. Teich's programmers encounter nostalgic making, and their daily coding is ruptured. Reliving triggers rethinking. Rhetorician Susan Delagrange calls this effect "critical wonder": "An attitude toward the world . . . that both predisposes us to be amazed and prepares us to desire to learn more about the source of our amazement" (16).

Of course, just because something grabs a user's attention doesn't mean it will continuously promote wonder. Once Teich's employees make their fifth quilt, they probably aren't going to be amazed. You can't have the same surprise twice. One way to encourage enduring rupture, however, is through continual random delivery. Successful long-term service UX, for example, often offers what economist Noriaki Kano calls "delighters" to loyal customers—from a chance hotel upgrade to a free sample included with purchase. Because they are random (as opposed to planned rewards like frequent-flier miles), no one misses delighters if they're not activated, but they make a great difference when present because they feel like gifts, causing people to shout, "Hey, look what I won!" (Heilman et al.). Delighters renovate mundane services, causing users to rethink them, and, thereby, tell stories.

By accounting for time, delighters also create narrative depth—they put users inside product stories. Take a video game that must be played hundreds of times for users to uncover all its "Easter eggs," unexpected secrets containing insider information, cheat codes, and other surprises that improve gameplay (Uribe-Jongbloed et al.). Such a game is enjoyable for first-time users, but it's equally enjoyable on its hundredth play as expert gamers seek to uncover all its content, driven on by the excitement and loss of the original surprise (Moschou and Zaharias). Wondering begets joyful wandering. One finds such Easter eggs in many designs with deep fan bases: vinyl records with secret tracks, Disney parks with hidden references to movies in the landscape, etc. Fertile narratability, thus, involves carefully layered surprises that bloom with time, placing the user in a story where they are an explorer.

To buoy narrative depth, delighters frequently utilize what sixteenth-century rhetorician Baldesar Castiglione calls *sprezzatura*, the art of artlessness. Castiglione wrote his etiquette guide, *The Book of the Courtier*, during the Italian Renaissance, a time when a courtly gentleman's livelihood (from a continued stipend to avoiding conscription) depended on memorable wit in the collective storytelling rituals of the court. A group of courtiers, for instance, might exchange witticisms about "what quality he would most like the person he loves to possess . . . what fault as well" (46). In these games, Castiglione and his ilk had to impress their duke and duchess to survive. But rather than brutishly shouting, "Hey, look at me!" the most exciting surprises, Castiglione instructs, are natural and nonchalant. They engage sprezzatura by making an audience think the speaker is authentic even if he has rehearsed for hours. This story, sprezzatura suggests, is one of a kind, is of the moment, and should be remembered. To develop such ruptures, Castiglione's courtesan slyly proposes a course of conversation (e.g., "If you had to make a fool of yourself, what would you do?" [17]) that leads to a topic in which he can display secretly prepared remarks (36). The courtier doesn't get straight to the point but savors slow storytelling, seemingly wandering nowhere, then falling upon his planned surprise. The courtier, thus, designs a memorable story but also the context it exists within.

Adding sprezzatura to designs generates contexts in which delight thrives. When I lived in Columbus, Ohio, for example, there was a small park that was fairly difficult to find. Only people in the know realized that you had to walk past what seemed like a dead-end street to get to it. Within this park, if you wandered beyond all paved paths, you would reach an underpass. Painted beneath this bridge was a beautiful mural of Ohio's native birds (figure 6.2). When I first fell upon this mural, I was amazed. Delight in exploration. Hidden art. I became a character (a treasure hunter) in the story the park designs. And because of this revelation, I remember, cherish, and talk about it. Surprise generated a nostalgic experience.

Ultimately, what makes ruptures of the present truly valuable for narratability, then, is that people love to share stories about them, playing the role of the trendsetter who has "discovered" a secret. They make us feel special. And people love talking about how they're special. Somewhat paradoxically, surprising, insider, and secret knowledge, like my hidden park, generate more buzz than direct marketing (Ludden et al.; Derbaix and Vanhamme). Playing with this concept, for instance, a set of popular bars (e.g., Please Don't Tell;

**Figure 6.2.** Clint Davidson's mural of Ohio's native birds being examined by explorers Larkyn and Rhys Osborne. Photo: Stacie Osborne.

Bathtub Gin) have modeled themselves after Prohibition-era speakeasies by removing all external signage and hiding mysteriously in the city, a trend called "secret urbanism" (Beekmans). To access San Diego's Nobel Experiment, for example, patrons enter an adjacent restaurant, go to the bathrooms, and push a false beer keg wall. Without prior knowledge of the bar's location, it's completely hidden. In terms of cultural capital, urgency is created by this secret because the patron knows the site won't remain clandestine and, thereby, its pioneer potential ("Look what I discovered") won't remain fresh. Clientele swarm the bar in anticipation of a nostalgic loss when it becomes mainstream. This mourning for the present is Sedikides's "anticipatory nostalgia." When something is rare or fleeting, users know that they will remember it fondly and, thereby, realize that they should take advantage of the opportunity.[5] Narratable UX urges consumers to become story collectors.

## Slow Virality: Recording and Recalling Memorable Digital Stories

But how does a theory of slow rupture apply to digital stories, where speed and obsolescence are the ruling logics? Counterintuitively, one sees narrative deceleration in the success of many viral "slacktivist campaigns,"[6] social media protests critiqued for asking users to quickly click a button rather than rally in the physical world (see Vie; Sortable). Take the Amyotrophic Lateral

Sclerosis (ALS) Association's Ice Bucket Challenge, which swept Facebook in the summer of 2014. To raise funds, in the Ice Bucket Challenge slacktivists poured a bucket of ice water over their heads, recorded a video of it, posted it to Facebook, and challenged their friends to do the same or donate. The dare went viral. About 2.4 million videos were posted by the likes of George W. Bush, Lebron James, and Kermit the Frog. Though only roughly 40 percent of participants donated, the ALS Association raised over $88.5 million in under a month (Stenovec; Goldberg). The challenge caught on for many of the reasons other "slacktivist" campaigns do—it was easy, spoke to people's social currency, and provided a ritualized communal story to enter.

But more than a communal narrative, the Ice Bucket Challenge was easily personalized—ice water was dumped from helicopters; Californians used liquids like milk to speak to the region's drought. Though meme theorists often pose fidelity of replication as the key measure of a meme's success (a good meme keeps the same message over time), this is a designer-centered metric. Rather, the most viral of the viral is virality that personalizes. The nostalgic impossibility of pure replica—the mimetic gap between the original ice bucket video and the copies—makes the meme personal, meaningful, and (ironically) possible. It urges the author to be a character in a collective story while simultaneously moving that story in new directions.

It's this focus on personalization that insulates true digital activism from slacktivist critiques. Ideally, by spending time customizing the meme (like making a sign to wave before a real-world protest), one thinks more about their personal connection to the cause it represents. The aesthetic force of mindful creation (What should I make my ice bucket video about?) battles the anesthetic force of fast replication (simply clicking a button), hence, *slow virality*. Still, social media activists might get so rapt by art and individuality that they lose sight of the collective movement. Whether one sees digital activism as successful, then, depends on what one judges its ends to be: attention gained, money donated, cause won, or lasting concern generated.

Narratability's ideal end is the latter, slow virality that involves revisiting and reflecting into the future. To promote this long-term commitment, such nostalgic UX relies on long-lasting behavioral residue. Canon's "hybrid auto mode" and the iPhone's "live mode" are perfect examples of such mechanisms of memory. Each photographic design automatically takes four-second videos before and after a picture. Photographers, thereby, don't just get a still shot; they also get the voices, playfulness, and posing (a memorable story) that rhetorically position the picture in the context of its production. They digitally capture a snippet of what Walter Benjamin says is impossible, the work of art's aura: "Its presence in time and space, its unique existence at the place where it happens to be" (220). The Ice Bucket Challenge similarly required recording and sharing a video, producing residue in anticipation of nostalgic reflection.

And, yet, I can collect backstories, create memes, and make videos, but if I don't remember them in three months, do they matter? Technologies are increasingly designed to archive stories (Facebook, Instagram, etc.), but a constant collection of memories doesn't make them meaningful. As the millions of unwatched family videos in our combined attics illustrate, we need recall mechanisms to match our glut of records. The best digital archives include recollection mechanisms to bring memories out of the darkness to talk about. Instacube and Pixily, for instance, are picture frames that automatically draw from deep within one's Instagram account for photos—placing them publicly in one's living room as conversation pieces. Features on Facebook like On This Day and Look Back similarly remind users of memories they posted years ago. Still, these Facebook features are easily ignored. What if users didn't get to choose? What if Facebook selected images and posts from years ago and automatically presented them for all to see? Such automation (see Bhömer et al.) might more often rupture the present, forcing users to engage with the past in active, public, and meaningful ways: a parent defending a drunk party photo from ten years ago, for example, or a politician reengaging with a slacktivist video and a formerly activist self.

## Storytelling in Nostalgic Contact Zones

In the larger democratic arena of nostalgic design, such narratability generates personal stories that serve as reservoirs of memory to act in the world: commemoration as redesign. The zenith of nostalgic design is welcoming users to defy dominant techno-logics through such memories. This nostalgic challenge is at the heart of critical nostos, rhetorical design, nostalgic stasis, and memorial interactivity. But narratability isn't inherently democratic or ethical. Just because I create a space for users to post memorable experiences, that doesn't mean I have to redesign from their memories. "There is an immense difference between having permission to speak," Cheryl Glenn writes, "and enjoying the hope that someone might actually listen to you" (84). When designers ignore the nostalgic contact zones they create, however, things get sticky. If a designer scaffolds nostalgic UX, they should be prepared to learn from informed dissent.

In the summer of 2014, for instance, the New York City Police Department started the Twitter hashtag #myNYPD, hoping to garner stories of positive interactions with the city's protectors. Essentially, they created a narratable UX scaffold upon which citizens might record individual stories. Critics pounced. They used an ironic nostalgia to refuse #myNYPD. One user, for example, posted a photo of a woman getting her hair yanked by an officer that reads, "The #NYPD will also help you de-tangle your hair. #myNYPD" (McSwagsalot). Now, the hashtag is solely used for censure. Countering the critique of slacktivism as lazy button clicking, such biting responses highlight the power of digital activism to provide a safer space for the stories of those who are at risk in physical activism. Yarimar Bonilla and Jonathan Rosa write of #Ferguson, for example, "It is surely not coincidental that the groups most likely to experience police brutality, to have their protests disparaged as acts of 'rioting' or 'looting,' and to be misrepresented in the media are precisely those turning to digital activism at the highest rates" (8). All hashtags create such counterpublics and critical stories. They hail mêtis.

Using this mêtis, the NYPD might have embraced agonism and redesigned its UX ethics. Indeed, NYC Police Commissioner William Bratton did respond to the criticism, stating, "I kind of welcome the attention. . . . We really broke the numbers yesterday" (Tracy and McShane). But this was a fast tolerance ("let's move on") rather than a slow wonder ("let's investigate"). Bratton didn't embrace the rupture. His expertise as a police officer wasn't reflectively nostalgic. Instead, like all experts, police forces need to be asking themselves, Who has nostalgic stories of the police, who doesn't, and why has this disparity been created? The activist goal of narratability, then, is creating the platforms for disruptive storytelling and wondering across boundaries upon which democratic redesign relies. Stories spark revolutions. Crafting them changes the world.

## Craft UX: Connection through Participation

And, of course, such crafting can often be fun. In chapter 2, for instance, Donna, Jo, and Kit use of crafting to initiate flow showed us how "there is an inherent pleasure in making," as anthropologist Ellen Dissanayake writes. "We might call this *joie de faire* (like *joie de vivre*) to indicate that there is something important, even urgent, to be said about the sheer enjoyment of making something exist that didn't exist before" (41). In other words, we cherish, take care of, and remember the things we build. In a 2012 study, psychologists Michael Norton, Daniel Mochon, and Dan Ariely researched this emotional fact, calling it "the IKEA effect." In tasks from assembling IKEA furniture to folding origami, subjects esteemed things they constructed, understanding "their amateurish creations as similar in value to experts' creations" (453). When participants priced their designs, they "over-valued" the memorable co-design experience and the competent identity it generated.

As we've seen throughout this book, this desire for co-production is not new; it arises in response to most technological revolutions, and it often represents a second craft drive—a yearning to connect with others across time. In the 1950s, for example, the golden age of the mass consumable, Betty Crocker introduced its instant cake mix. But home bakers immediately rejected it: "The consumer felt no sense of accomplishment, no involvement with the product. It made her feel useless especially if somewhere her aproned mom was still whipping up cakes from scratch" (Goebert and Rosenthal 2). Innovation without tradition had led to alienation. In response, Betty Crocker's UX architects eventually resolved their problem by considering nostalgia, adding a tiny piece of craft labor and, thereby, collective memory, back into the process. Bakers now had to add an egg to the mix, a talismanic act of co-production, connecting them to memories of their mothers.

In chapter 2, I suggested that the current DIY revival arose in part as a resistance to digital technology's intangibility and the bleed of work into home. But craft is also a meaningful story of small-scale production; it's a valuing of skill and people over the work of machines; and it's a deterministic "view that products made using a craft process carry a Benjaminian 'aura' of originality that individuates the consumer, worships tradition through consumption, meshes with local values, and bonds user and producer" (Kurlinkus, "Crafting" 51). Thus, a second way nostalgic designers can support personal connection to designs is through crafty UX, experiences that connect designer, owner, repairer, and inheritor through labor across the lifecycle of a design. In nostalgia, psychologist D. G. Hertz writes, "the mind is peopled" (195).

## Craft as Care: Labor and the Aura of Nostalgic Production

A now classic example of craft that embodies this connection is the mixtape.[7] In *High Fidelity*, novelist and music critic Nick Hornsby depicts the composition of mixtapes as a highly ornate craft. "I spent hours putting that cassette together," Hornby's narrator describes. "Making a tape is like writing a letter—there's a lot of erasing and rethinking and starting again. . . . You've got to kick off with a corker, to hold the attention . . . and then you've got to up it a notch, or cool it. . . . [O]h, there are loads of rules" (88–89). Like Kano's delighter or Castiglione's sprezzatura, in Hornsby's mixtape there's a plan for time and slow delivery—hidden lyrical messages reveal themselves through repeated listening. The technological process of creating the tape parallels the toil of composition. You had to select songs, yes, but you also had to record those songs from one tape or the radio to another cassette—rewinding, fast-forwarding, erasing. For Hornsby what makes the mixtape a craft is not a pure final product but the delicate skill behind it. Craft is care and the creation of a nostalgic image of the composer's effort.

To display this effort, craft is often pocked with "leaked constructedness" (Kurlinkus, "Ethics" 17), sprezzaturic residue of production (from smeared ink on the tape's tracklist to an overly long silence between songs), sometimes purposefully encoded or "leaked," that brings the user's attention to the behind-the-scenes effort of the designer. The Japanese wabi-sabi aesthetic presents a similar story of production by leaving single chips, cracks, and other flaws within pottery. The blemishes of leaked constructedness rupture a pure final product and connect crafter and recipient in what UX researcher Ian Coxon calls "an ecology of care" (TED). They highlight that *I* made this for you, not a machine. Such "honorific marks of hand labor" (Veblen 159) initiate the recipient into the collective memory of the object. This aura is the key difference between a mixtape and a mix playlist, today, and is often mimicked digitally through skeuomorphic mechanisms from digital fonts that appear to be handwritten to Instagram's retro filters (Schrey; Sapio; Bartholeyns). Thus, the craft design differs from the mechanically produced design in that it represents the act of making and, thereby, links the minds and hearts of user and designer. Labor + intricacy + memory = meaning. Or perhaps better put: thoughtful labor = thoughtful UX.

Today, digital UX architects use this formula to evoke affective reactions in their users and, thereby, prevent them from leaving a service through *nostalgic loss aversion*. As mentioned in chapter 1, when a user tries to quit Facebook, for instance, the company deploys N-UX to highlight how "the collection of memories and experiences, in aggregate, becomes more valuable over time" (Eyal 147). When a user deactivates her account, a screen appears with pictures of cherished friends and a message that reads, "Are you sure you want to deactivate your account. . . . Your 1,137 friends will no longer be able to keep in touch with you." Each photograph has a message above it: "Krista will miss you," "NeNe will miss you." Despite the fact that this is a rote customization (an algorithm filled a template), the message still feels personal because it causes users to contemplate the nostalgic "work" invested in their social network. If you quit, you don't care.

Another way nostalgia intertwines itself into the craft equation, therefore, is that so often things that we remember fondly are things we feel we've earned. Every year I see students encountering this fact. In my digital writing course, I teach students two image editing software. One, easel.ly, is a free online infographic program that is simple to use—the other, Photoshop, is more complex and notoriously unintuitive. Students use both programs for roughly the same tasks (data visualization and advertisements). Yet, at the end of the semester the majority of students are fiercely loyal to Photoshop and have often forgotten easel.ly. Why? One reason is that difficult processes initiate students into a community, offer challenge, and, thereby, seem inherently more valuable than simple processes. Loyalty can flow from struggle. Students gaze back nostalgically on challenges.

In a darker light, this nostalgic anaesthetizing of pain, J. J. Skowronski et al.'s "fading affect bias," may also hint at a more dubious loss aversion. Skowronski et al. found that the affects associated with positive memories tend to fade more slowly than those associated with negative memories because positive life stories are more likely to promote social attachments and prepare people to act in the future. People tell positive stories about themselves more than negative ones to make themselves look good to others; as these positive tales are recounted, they reinforce memory (see Kahneman's "focusing illusion"). Remembering is inherently nostalgic. But, in the case of my students, they might also nostalgically transform a negative experience into a positive one so that they feel their time hasn't been wasted. Such strife compounds itself when it snowballs into restorative arguments about rites of passage: "I had to do it; so do you." In 2016, for instance, potential presidential candidate Bernie Sanders argued for offering free college to American youth. A certain group of citizens resisted, contending that because they had to work their way through college or join the military to pay for it, the next generation should as well. For these citizens, their hard work to fund their education was a character-builder, a nostalgic badge of honor that might be invalidated if someone else didn't have to do it. To counter this bias, we journey deeper into the ecology of care and the human connections of slow design.

## Aging Gracefully: Inheritable UX, Design Stewardship, and Repair

Co-founder of the slow design movement Alastair Fuad-Luke explains that slow design "represents a series of diverse opportunities to encourage consumption in which people reflect on what really nourishes them while simultaneously reducing negative environmental, social, and economic impacts" ("Adjusting" 134). Slow design disrupts the throwaway logic of speed by focusing on humans as *homo faber*, who create lasting personal artifices, rather than *animal laborans*, who slave away in an endless, isolated labor of quickly consumed goods. A defining form of slow design that accentuates how things, people, and communities can slowly ripen rather than rot with time is *inheritable UX*, creating products that will last both physically and culturally and, thereby, be passed down generationally. Under this techno-logic, craft is the stewardship of a design that makes consumers aware of its place in time and the other people associated with it. Craft stewardship, that is, promotes mono no aware, an awareness of things brought on by observing their change. If the important objects in our lives are those that collect memories and if collecting memories takes time, the quest for designs that improve with age is imperative.

Revolutionizing aging with grace, for example, Simon Heijdens's *Broken White* is a set of flatware that is pure white when purchased. As it ages, tiny cracks blossom into intricate patterns: "The cracks slowly begin to form a floral decoration that grows like a real flower. . . . [T]he cups or dishes you love most will stand out. . . . [I]t is not a state, but a never-ending process." Where wabi-sabi promotes mono no aware by including purposeful flaws in designs (a chip left in a tea pot), Heijdens's flatware actually depicts the process of *becoming* wabi-sabi. *Broken White* crafts itself. Many products (wine, whisky, blue jeans, beef) get better with age, but it takes shifts in standards of taste (connoisseurship) to actualize this enjoyment of decay. Humans don't naturally enjoy the abrasive taste of wine; appreciation has to be acquired.

Without teaching a taste for such aging, citizens risk the loss of many of the types of meaningful objects Csikszentmihalyi and Halton catalogue in their study. The authors describe, for example, how family bibles create an ecology of care through being crafted across generations (e.g., highlighting favorite passages and adding personal photographs between the pages): "In this respect, the Bible serves as a talisman of continuity. . . . (What would it mean to you not to have this Bible) 'I would feel as though I had lost a friend, because when I open it and read the names of all the children, and they were so young and they all lived to be so old, none of them died at a young age. And when I see their pictures, I see I have good roots.'" (70) But what is the digital family Bible? What do we inherit in an age of speed? What, for instance, might an intergenerational Facebook account—passed down from grandmother to grandson—look like? Currently, there are several "memorialize" and de-activate options for postmortem Facebook accounts, anticipatory design features that encourage users to think about collaborating with their future selves. But I can't read my deceased ancestors' accounts as I do a journal or family bible. What if I could? Such inheritable objects are more than antiques. They are designs that we can use to maintain a sense of self as they age. Wildschut et al. report that "[A]s individuals navigate the many life challenges associated with aging. . . . nostalgia moderated the relationship between age and well-being, such that age was positively associated with indicators of well-being (i.e., positive affect, positive relationships, environmental mastery). . . . [F]requent engagement in nostalgia is a catalyst for successful aging" (815). Indeed, recent research on Alzheimer's by psychologists Sanda Umar, Gary Christopher, and Richard Cheston has suggested that nostalgic storytelling and music leads to patients reporting higher self-esteem, social connectedness, and sense of meaning in their lives.

Products that age with grace (and help their owners do so, as well) are a first step towards inheritable UX, but such designs will inevitably need to be maintained. Another side of craft UX, therefore, is revolution through regeneration. Several manifestos (e.g., "The Maker's Bill of Rights") have been written on the responsibility of designers to create repairable goods: "Meaningful and specific parts lists shall be included. Cases shall be easy to open. Batteries shall be replaceable" (Mr. Jalopy). Other designers offer low-cost repairs themselves. The climbing shoe company Evolv, for example, runs its own cobbler service, YosemiteBum, fixing climbers' favorite shoes while simultaneously creating brand loyalty. A recent shoe repair they did for me cost $45, whereas a new specialized climbing shoe would have been upwards of $200. And new shoes don't have my old memories. Again, there's a certain awakening to a design's place in time as the user becomes aware of how a shoe changes. When someone first buys a shoe, they don't think about its creators. When a shoe is repaired, human connection is promoted.[8]

To make their arguments, repair activists often draw upon a nostalgia for craft production before users were alienated from the creation of their goods. There was a time, for instance, when automobile owners had to repair their own cars. What are the economic, environmental, and cultural benefits of recovering such a period? What if driver's ed courses required students to learn how to change their car's oil? Often, I kick myself for not taking auto-shop in high school—frowned upon as a blue-collar elective for those not college bound. Cultures of maintenance regularly hold this stigma, which is just one of the reasons auto-shop is quickly being replaced by maker labs in contemporary high schools. Consumers think so little about auto repair, in fact, that only since 2012 has the US *Right to Repair Bill* required car manufacturers to give the average citizen access to the same manuals and diagnostics as dealerships. Without such legislation, manufacturers like John Deere can make it impossible (even illegal through copyright law) for consumers to repair designs themselves. Many farmers who "own" John Deere tractors, for example, only own a contract to use the equipment, not the machine itself. This is not inheritability—there's no meaningful passing on of the design here.

In contrast to such compulsory non-ownership, Kyle Wiens, CEO of the repair company iFixit, describes receiving a laptop to resell with a note attached: "Goodbye, iBook. In your death, may you give life to a dozen more computers." This is inheritability, a mode of anticipatory nostalgia that can overcome obsolescence by charging the user with the care of a design so that others can share it in the future. Designing things that last and pass lets users imagine technological inheritors down the line and promotes meaningful afterlives.

Many (if most) countries have stronger repair economies than the United States (Chipchase). When I visited a friend in South Korea, I saw this difference firsthand. Lindsay's laptop keyboard broke. Rather than replacing it (a cost of $50 + shipping), we traveled to Yongsan Electronics Market. Hunting through a group of multistory buildings with hundreds of individual stalls, we sought the area where her brand of keyboard might be found. The search for the craftsman took an hour; the repair took five minutes, cost $10, and didn't result in a keyboard thrown in the trash. Compare this experience to my recent visit to the Apple Store after I slightly cracked my iPhone screen. Apple geniuses told me I would have to replace my $600 phone because the case was dented. They refused to attempt the repair.

Once the realm of a few weekend warriors, as chapter 2 depicts, post millennium there has been a resurgence of DIY and repair culture. Marketing researchers Marco Wolf and Shaun McQuitty report, "The home improvement industry has grown considerably, with U.S.-based sales of $22.5 billion in 1978 (Hornik and Feldman 1982), $38.6 billion in 1987 (Bush, Menon, and Smart 1987), $135 billion in 1996, and $300 billion in 2006 (Tratensek and Jensen 2006)" (195). Again, this drive to repair is often deeply nostalgic. Risto Moisio et al., for example, study the role home repair plays in male identity across white-collar and working-class families. They found that white-collar men often engage in DIY activities in order to identify with the artisan craftsmanship of the past and escape knowledge-based jobs by way of "therapeutic class tourism": "Alex, a university professor by day, explicates this idea of class tourism: '[DIY home improvement is a] chance for me to be something entirely different than a professor for a day or two a week . . . kind of an image of myself as almost being blue-collar for a couple days a week'" (303). But Alex makes a *nostalgic other* out of his working-class counterparts. In fact, blue-collar participants saw DIY not as an escape but a moral duty. Ideally, craft UX directly connects multiple classes of DIYers in spaces from repair classes to open auto-shops. Isolated neoliberal DIY needs to be redesigned as DIT (Do-It-Together). Craft as care means that craft objects call forth owners who care for those who inherit the object, those who repair it, and the larger environment the object lives in—the ecology of care.

## Fetishizing Craft Labor

Thus, there's a difference between making and critical making. This disparity may seem obvious. Not all engineers are philosophers of technology. And, yet, as touched upon in chapter 2, we live in a culture in which craft has become a restorative god memory. Slap the word "craft," "handmade," or "artisan" on a product, and it automatically seems ethical, environmentally friendly, and critically aware. But sweatshops hand make goods, too. For N-UX to be ethical, craft needs to be critically opened as a nostalgic contact zone.

In their book *The Experience Economy*, for example, Joseph Pine and James Gilmore applaud how employees become "actors" in the caring craft labor of UX: workers at Cold Stone Creamery sing every time they receive a tip, and "the grocery clerk should ask himself how he might scan the canned goods with flair, what dramatic voice and entertaining words he might use when asking for a credit card" (158). But, as this quote highlights, the ethics of labor in the experience economy are fraught. Such UX promotes a nostalgic craft connection to artisans without necessarily changing the capitalist system that oppresses them.

Fighting tooth and nail to stay relevant, for example, in 2015 McDonald's began its "pay with lovin'" campaign in which, for a time between the Super Bowl and Valentine's Day, cashiers offered free food if a customer performed a "loving act." Patrons called their mothers and told them they loved them, did a dance for the restaurant, etc. Though this campaign was certainly memorable, it required low-paid foodservice employees to perform a new form of emotional labor. Bryce Covert writes: "They have to come up with cutesy tasks. . . . If someone dances, they have to dance too. . . . [P]oorly paid people [have] to slather a smile onto their face and cover up the real conditions under which they labor. . . . [F]amilies can't survive on the money they make. But the company instead wants its customers to see employees who are genuinely delighted that a mother hugged her son in front of them." This is what happens when craft and care are reduced to features rather than meaningful relationships. A veneer of homo faber masks a core of animal laborans.

Applying a critical eye to craft also illustrates that prestige—even in seemingly democratic maker cultures—gets attached to some forms of making and not others. There's a very gendered and classist reason, for example, why the contemporary "maker movement" has not called itself the "crafter movement" or more deeply linked itself to preexisting high school auto-shop and hot rod customization traditions. In this light, engineer Debbie Chachra warns that maker culture continues a history of cheering on individualist masculine production while forgetting the traditionally feminine modes of teaching, repair, and caregiving that make such production possible. "The cultural primacy of making," Chachra observes, "especially in tech culture—that it is intrinsically superior to not-making, to repair, analysis, and especially caregiving—is informed by the gendered history of who made things. . . . That artifacts are important, and people are not." Again, DIT not DIY.

Ethical craft UX also affords, but doesn't *require*, participation. When the best experiences are only for those who have the time and money to participate, the techno-logical gaps this book opposes expand. Likewise, designers should take seriously Moisio et al.'s distinction between upper- and lower-class repair motivations. John McMurria argues, for instance, that the rise of DIY television from *This Old House* to *Extreme Makeover: Home Edition* promotes a neoliberal agenda in which fixing things becomes an individual moral responsibility and, thereby, living in poverty becomes a moral failure. When a white-collar man redesigns his porch for fun over the weekend, a bootstraps narrative is generated: "Why can't you, lower-class neighbor, fix your house up?"

## Connoisseur UX: A Radical Taste for Time

To promote more thoughtful craft consumption, connoisseurship—apprenticeship in a collective memory of taste—tempers consumption, transforming it into a thoughtful and lasting holy rite. Following on the heels of narratability and craft, connoisseur UX is made of the training that makes slow consumption popular. Savoring finely aged wines, learning to spot a rare antique, carefully training in coffee tasting rituals—connoisseurship is often a taste for slow time. From the Latin *cognoscere* (to get to know) connoisseurs are addicted to learning, reading, and savoring the marks of craftsmanship, repair, Easter eggs, and ecologies of care described earlier. To urge such devotion, a gated tradition is generally posed as threatened or lost in the face of mass culture. Only collective ritual can nostalgically preserve this better past and the values it embodies. Thus, connoisseurship (from seeking out the most authentic taco in town to collecting delicate fly-fishing lures) is always an act of commemoration, a reenactment of a golden age of which all that remains are ritual objects, focused fragments of a lost community we wish to join. Through such reenactment, connoisseurs sharpen their critical skills and reinforce a shared ideology. A community of nostalgia is formed.

The connoisseur's reward for this work is cultural capital (people worship his opinion—which he gleefully shares) and the often-ignored clout to judge and reject the connoisseur object: "Don't drink that sauvignon blanc, it's too metallic." Historically, such capital has been dismissed as elitist (Veblen's "conspicuous consumption"; Bourdieu's "taste"). But in the twenty-first century there's an explosion of pop connoisseur objects (beer, coffee, chocolate) and an increased democratic power to rate goods and services publicly on websites like Amazon and Yelp (Mellet et al.; Vásquez and Chik).

Thus, though taste is often restoratively nostalgic, I'm more interested in it as a reflectively nostalgic process of meaningful savoring. "Whether we can actually tell the difference between cheap and expensive wine may be less important than whether we think that we can," Dan Ariely describes. "We might actually experience more pleasure when drinking an expensive wine, enjoy it more, because we're slowing down, savoring it, paying more attention to its qualities" (Zane). But like the other modes of N-UX, designers employing connoisseurship train consumers in ritual, history, and slow consumption while simultaneously incentivizing the diverse connections of ecologies of care and welcoming resistance. A taste for playing with time can be enlightening.

## Temporal Rituals and Myths

"Break it in half. Unwrap half of the bar and eat it. Then, unwrap the other half and eat it"—in 2013, Kathleen D. Vohs et al. tested how ritual time play affects the consumption of goods from lemonade to carrots (1715). In an experiment where subjects ate chocolate, for instance, some participants were asked to perform the rather empty unwrapping ritual above. Those who did enjoyed the experience more, thought the chocolate tasted better, savored the flavor more, and were willing to pay more for it. Rituals expand the enjoyment of consumption because they make the UX more focused, self-aware, and wondrous. Stop, wait, think—rituals reorganize time.

The history of chocolate connoisseurship, coincidentally, is a perfect example of such temporal reorganization at a massive scale. Anthropologist Susan Terrio describes how in the 1980s, in order to fight off Belgian competitors, French chocolatiers invoked ritual in order to associate themselves in French collective memory with wine and cheese. "Facing the intensified international competition," Terrio writes, "French chocolatiers and cultural taste makers attempted to stimulate new demand for craft commodities by promoting 'genuine,' 'grand cru,' or 'vintage' French chocolate" *that had not existed in the past* (68). In historian Eric Hobsbawm's terms, French chocolatiers "invented tradition" by creating "a set of practices, normally governed by overtly or tacitly accepted rules and of a ritual or symbolic nature, which seek to inculcate certain values and norms of behavior by repetition. . . . [T]hey normally attempt to establish continuity with a suitable historic past" (1).

To reinforce this invented standard, the chocolatiers developed a tasting process based on wine rituals (rub the chocolate, sniff the chocolate, etc.) to teach proper French consumption and gastronomic heritage. Of course, ritual nostalgia also cloaked the fact that France did not have a particularly crafty chocolate history when compared to Belgian rivals. For the previous thirty years, French chocolate had been largely mass-produced. To temporally anchor their ritual, chocolatiers also created a previously nonexistent tasting scale for cocoa beans based on the *terroir* land standards of wine varietals. Thus, there was a specific decision at a specific point to nostalgia-ize chocolate UX. The French make their chocolates meaningful by instructing consumers in an artificial, yet apparently timeless, taste standard that favors French chocolatiers' tastes (bittersweet) over the Belgians' (sweet) (Terrio 70). In this way, chocolate connoisseurship, like all ritual consumption, becomes meaningful by creating a taste for history—connecting people across time in a community of nostalgia.

The creation of quality designs, therefore, does not in itself create a connoisseur following; rather, UX architects plan rituals of consumption (e.g., judging percentages of cacao) that train the connoisseur to distinguish between good and bad designs and, in doing so, teach the apprentice a nostalgic value set. One sees such ritualization in numerous less-cultured products as well: Oreos (twist the cookies, lick the cream, dunk the cookies); Blue Moon beer (add an orange); the shampoo algorithm "lather, rinse, repeat" pushes users to ritualistically wash in a literally endless cycle. Guinness beer goes so far as to provide a fact sheet for an intricate six-step pour, in which bartenders around the world let the drink settle before topping it off. Making consumers wait a little longer for their drink (ideally, 119.5 seconds) builds anticipation that heightens consumption and inducts them into a community of brand memory. Again, we see a play with time.

Differing from overtly marketed connoisseur practices, in media connoisseurship, viewers are usually trained more subtly within designs themselves. For example, cult TV programs written with deep "narrative complexity" (Mittell) such as *Twin Peaks*, *Lost*, and *Breaking Bad* are designed with odd pacing, layered secrets, and a careful use of their serial format to train their fans to revel in and anticipate their mysteries. Critic Jason Mittell calls such connoisseur viewers "forensic fans," those who become addicted to the secrets, internal references, and layers of deep serial plots. A key marker of such programs (and most connoisseur UX) is rewatchability: the capacity to repeatedly watch an episode (or taste a wine) and get new pleasure and information with each viewing.

Of course, though narratively complex programs are sometimes designed to be savored slowly, increasingly, shows are created to be binge watched on services like Netflix with similarly engrossing results. A taste for time doesn't necessarily have to be a taste for the slow. *Breaking Bad*, for example, is a show in which the viewer follows high school chemistry teacher turned meth cook Walter White through fast, gut-wrenching scenes of violence and terror followed by long stretches of boring everyday events. Through repeated cycles, what *Breaking Bad* creator Vince Gilligan calls "hyper-serialization," the show teaches its viewers to look for clues of the upcoming action in the mundane and to revel in the stress such clues foreshadow (Romano). We see an eyeball floating in White's pool in the first episode of season 2 and don't discover to whom it belongs until the last. By watching *Breaking Bad* once a week, viewers appreciate the program's suspense, but by binge watching multiple episodes on Netflix, the viewer more easily sees these connections. Indeed, Gilligan has described designing the show to reward fans who watch it "in a giant inhalation" (Jurgensen). Yes, binge watching is fast, but it is also immersive. It consumes viewers in flow. Intriguingly, such acceleration also often evokes a guilty nostalgic awareness of time, a sense of anticipatory nostalgic loss as you binge a series that you feel you should be savoring. Once you've finished, you can't return.

## A Taste for Activism: Connoisseurship as Civic Action

So far I've presented connoisseurship as a one-way street. Fans learn to become absorbed in the careful craftsmanship of chocolate and television shows. But connoisseurship isn't always so passive. Compare, for instance, the ritualization of chocolate to the activist connoisseurship of coffee. In most modern coffee houses one finds fair trade (beans from growers that pay a picker a living wage) and direct trade (beans in which the coffee house directly knows the grower rather than purchasing through a third party). In both, quality is associated with food provenance: the object memory of, and humans behind, the crop and selecting a bean that connoisseurs can feel good about, a bean with an ethical aura. Coffee connoisseurship (similar to organic farming/ butchering) becomes an activist platform through managing an ecology of care. Though there may be no gustatory difference between ethical and unethical beans, the thoughtful connection involved in this consumption makes the coffee UX more meaningful. In this way, coffee joins other slow foods that make consumers aware of the political, social, and environmental ramifications of consumption.

Italian activist Carlo Petrini, for example, founded the slow food movement in 1986 in response to the "McDonaldization" of Italian cuisine. The appearance of a McDonalds at Rome's historic Piazza di Spagna drew international attention to the movement when Petrini handed out homemade pizzas to counterpoint the restaurant's opening. Over the last three decades, Petrini's crusade has fought for slow issues including local agrobiodiversity, short supply chains (avoiding the pollution involved in shipping foods), organic farming, and farmers markets. Hand-in-hand with slow food's political agenda is its central delivery method—a taste for time. Just as French chocolate tasting favors bittersweet French chocolate, Petrini's slow food values the seasonal, local, and diverse. Olives from one region of Italy taste different than olives from another; slow connoisseurship reveals this difference and the olive's story. This taste is perpetuated by a deeply nostalgic rhetoric of naturalism and folk tradition.

Regrettably, slow food nostalgia is often restorative rather than reflective, failing to embrace those who don't share its ethic. Petrini and Gigi Padovani, for example, depict those who enjoy fast food as ignorant: "[P]eople devoted to fast rhythms and efficiency are mostly stupid and sad" (93). Yet, so few people can afford Petrini's tastes. Organic food and the restaurants that serve it are expensive. Moreover, in its return to a nostalgic peasant culture ideal, slow food, as Kelly Donati interrogates, often fails to engage nostalgic contact zones: "They fail to recognize the conditions of inequity or oppression often inherent within the preservation of tradition—whether they are socio-economic differences limiting access to education and opportunity or a gender tradition in which the labor of women in the kitchen bears the responsibility for maintaining harmony in the family home and preserving the cultural traditions of society" (236). Again, we see the creation of a nostalgic other, fetishizing a lost cultural diversity without welcoming the métis of the citizens who live that tradition. As Krista Ratcliffe's "eavesdropping" taught us in chapter 3, designers cannot use the past without being responsible for it.

Ultimately, although connoisseurs have been depicted as conservative quaffers of wine, whiskey, and cigars (and some are), good nostalgic designers train activist connoisseurs, who recognize their nostalgia as necessarily fictional and open to change and, ideally, use that artificial past to redesign the real future. Andrew Slack's Harry Potter Alliance is a perfect example of such nostalgic resistance. The Harry Potter Alliance organizes fans of J. K. Rowling's Harry Potter series to take part in activism, from transporting medical supplies to Haiti to voting against Maine's anti–marriage equality measure, Proposition 9. What makes the Alliance's fan activism uniquely nostalgic is that it builds from the values of the fictional wizarding world as if it were the lost past of the real world. Slack writes, "Dumbledore advocates for a series of policy reforms . . . that can be applied to our own society. The Ministry's practice of abandoning *habeas corpus* and using 'dementors' (soul-sucking wraiths) to torture and imprison innocent suspects . . . should be replaced by fair trials and humane prisons." Nostalgic designers, thus, make connoisseurship deeper by urging fans to wield tradition.

## Geeking Out: Fan Futures and Connoisseur Contact Zones

The fan devotion and resistance of connoisseurship, however, can be a double-edged sword. Though it's possible for it to lead to inclusivity and the democratization of design, connoisseur culture (especially contemporary "geek" manifestations) is, almost by definition, *combatively* nostalgic. Brand change gets labeled as selling out, and aficionados rue the popularization of their niche.

Star Wars geek-ism is a prime example of such nostalgic resistance. A set of "original" Star Wars fans became so nostalgically bonded to the brand that when it began to transform—particularly with the Jar Jar Binks-laden *The Phantom Menace*—they became brand enemies. Connoisseurship became a platform upon which to resist change and refuse the formerly praised design. In response, the newest wave of Star Wars movies by director J. J. Abrams has self-consciously harnessed nostalgia to welcome back alienated fans through retro branding. Because of its trio of main characters; the recasting of Carrie Fisher, Harrison Ford, and Mark Hamill; and an invocation of plot parallels, 2015's *The Force Awakens* was excitedly hailed as a nostalgic remake of *Episode IV: A New Hope.*

Still, as Paul Nunes and David Light write in *Harvard Business Review*, "It would be one thing if your product's biggest fans loved it unconditionally. But they don't; they expect that love to be rewarded with respect for their preferences." Such resistance riddles the history of mass consumerism from New Coke to Crystal Pepsi. More and more, UX architects recognize this contact zone and, in response, keep the original design in their back pockets to nostalgically recover when it suits them. Disney World, for instance, has recently updated its Tomorrowland theme park, but you can bet they're keeping the classic rides and attractions in storage to nostalgically revive in the future. Indeed, in 1998 Disney World revamped its classic Tiki Room ride by adding newer movie characters to the flock of animatronic birds in the show. This change was universally rejected. Thus, in 2011 the Tiki Room was restored to its former glory from the original audiotapes, once thought to be lost but "rediscovered" after the ride caught fire.

The power claimed by brand connoisseurs is further illustrated in a recent spate of fan-driven revivals (from the show *Futurama* to the soft drink Surge). In 2013, for instance, seven years after its Fox cancellation, the TV show *Arrested Development* was renewed on Netflix. And, yet, like all nostalgics, the show's fans can't return home again. Many were disappointed by the differences they saw in the transition to Netflix. Intriguingly, show creator Mitch Hurwitz states that his goal for the revival was not to please old fans but to create a new audience of connoisseurs: "I don't want to give too much power to any first reaction, either critics' or fans', because I'm hoping it develops an audience over time" (Berkowitz). Hurwitz designs for time. He describes, for example, how changes in the last season of the original series caused similar angry nostalgia: "Every episode of the last season was met with a lot of hostility. People on message boards would say it's not as good as it used

**Figure 6.3.** Raoul Bretzel and Anna Citelli stand next to their *Capsula Mundi*.

to be, or that we ruined it. Now those episodes are embraced by people who don't distinguish between the first 12 and the last nine—they just see it all as *Arrested Development*."

Ultimately, geek fandom might be seen as low-culture connoisseurship. Certainly, despite Petrini and Padovani's objections, fast food and pop culture can be *connaited* as well. Budweiser's 2015 anti-craft beer Super Bowl ad, for instance, pits nostalgia for blue-collar culture against the nostalgia that drives craft beer. The ad's narrator unapologetically states, "Proudly a macro beer. It's not brewed to be fussed over. It's brewed for a crisp, smooth finish. . . . Let them sip their pumpkin peach ale, we'll be brewing us some golden suds." Budweiser promotes a nostalgic anti-taste. That is, it depicts itself as the losing side of a taste war, creating a feeling of personal loss in fans that might be restored through connoisseurship. In doing so, Budweiser generates what Albert Muniz and Thomas O'Guinn call "oppositional brand loyalty" (e.g., Mac vs. PC; Pepsi vs. Coke). It uses taste for another style of beer to promote a war that pits one fandom against another. It relishes the nostalgic contact zone while intensifying loyal consumer identity. Budweiser's UX architects generate a nostalgic protectiveness in fans for the age when Bud was the "King of Beers." If you don't drink Budweiser, the beer your grandfather drank, your memories of your grandfather might disappear as well. If you don't drink, you don't care.

## The End: The Nostalgic Design of Meaningful Deaths

In the end, planning for nostalgic UX leads to lasting product relationships in a digital age where such bonds are increasingly rare. But beyond a taste for time, what ties the three ethics of this chapter together is valuing humanity, whether wondering about the designer behind a well-crafted mixtape, connecting with an auto-mechanic across a car's lifecycle, or communing with a coffee grower through ritual consumption. And although this chapter primarily focuses on the extension of lifecycles and slow consumption, meaningful deaths and endings are equally important to what makes nostalgic UX human. At some point users must admit that all designs (like all people) die. Nostalgic designers plan for natural decay.

Such anticipatory design, for instance, is typified in Anna Citelli and Raoul Bretzel's *Capsula Mundi* (figure 6.3). This *provo*type imagines that when a person dies, she is placed in a large egg-shaped seed capsule. As her body decays it nourishes a tree, pre-chosen by the deceased, planted atop the pod. "The cemetery will be transformed into a place of nature," write Citelli and Bretzel. "One where families can stroll and learn about the natural world, where communities will come together to tend and care for trees. In short, it will become a sacred forest." Death fertilizes life. To an eerier degree, Shiho Fukuhara and Georg Tremmel's *Biopresence* proposes that the deceased's DNA be inserted into an apple tree that will then bear edible fruit as a process of rebirth. Would you eat an apple from your grandmother's tree? Rather than harsh concrete cemeteries that leach formaldehyde and wood varnishes, *Capsula Mundi* and *Biopresence* rupture the present, calling user audiences to pay attention to their place in space and time, promoting gardens of remembrance, connection, meditation, change, and life that echo into the future.

Thus, *Capsula Mundi* and *Biopresence*, like all good nostalgic designs, creatively juxtapose tradition and transcendence, offering designers, clients, and users a chance to rethink the future by rethinking the past. And, in closing, this is what nostalgic design is really all about: the opportunity to escape our current technological timeline by exploring the parallel ideal pasts and futures that surround us every day. To welcome such humanity, the nostalgic designer must seek out nostalgic resistances (critical nostos) and learn to mediate these parallel timelines (nostalgic stasis and memorial interactivity). The results will never be a utopia. But once the nostalgic contact zones between these realities are revealed as provocative resources and the humans who dwell in them are welcomed as co-creators, innovation, inclusivity, and revolution through revolving back is inevitable. We'll more often shape the future by seeking out new old ways of viewing the world. We'll have a chance to think outside of ourselves for lost values, resources, and timelines that might make the future more human.

# Afterword

# From English Major to Designer

In writing this book, I was, admittedly, overwhelmed by the stereotypical authorial phenomenon of seeing everything in the world through my subject. From Donald Trump's push to Make America Great Again to the hand-knitted cat-eared "pussyhats" of those who protested him at the Women's March on Washington, maybe it's just me, but clashing nostalgias are everywhere. This really is the perfect time for designers and rhetoricians to collaborate in learning about, mediating, and layering such traditions. Before we part, then, I want to leave you with some activities that might help instructors and practitioners of design, rhetoric, and writing come together to activate the nostalgic design suggestions made throughout this book. In doing so, I particularly have in mind my own students, English majors in courses like technical communication, digital media composition, and intro to the digital humanities.

Very early on, after reading a proposal for my research, my PhD advisor Cindy Selfe asked a critical question about such students: "How do we prepare young people with the habits of mind and the skills they'll need to debate technological problems productively in a world so addicted to the dominant techno-logics of efficiency and progress, that both designers and users find it difficult to identify positions *outside* these dominant frameworks?" In this afterword, I provide a few concrete answers to this question in hopes that English majors might become designers who use the creativity, empathy, and expertise at engaging fictional worlds developed in other English courses to transform our real one. In a 2016 job ad, the design firm IDEO seeks designers who can do just that: "Human-centered insights and a deep understanding of people and culture are critical to how we do our best work. Design Researchers guide clients and teams through this research to discover, interpret, and communicate insights & opportunities in an inspiring way, while contributing to all phases of the design process. Researchers at IDEO help our teams use design as a way of understanding people and culture while at the same time using what we learn to inspire and inform design." Beyond experience with qualitative research, including interviews, ethnography, and diary studies (and basically everything else described in chapter 3 of this book), IDEO wants someone with:

- The ability to bring your personal interests and passions to the role to provide a unique perspective to research—whether from modern art, trends in architecture, esports, 19th-century history, or whatever gets you going
- Openness to learning from and understanding people who are much different than you and willingness to challenge your own assumptions
- A desire to keeping [*sic*] digging into insights, going beyond the obvious to identify what is truly unique or different about what you're seeing in the world

If these job qualifications don't describe an English major, I don't know of any that would. But scholars, professors, and students of English have to take some initiative to sharpen their literary and rhetorical interests for such design jobs. What follows are a selection of key takeaways and activities based in each chapter of *Nostalgic Design* that might serve as a whetstone to do so.

## Chapter 1. Nostalgic Design: Between Innovation and Tradition

*Nostalgic design* is the rhetorical analysis of, mediation between, and design for multiple user communities with conflicting traditional ideals in order to create more democratic, inclusive, innovative, meaningful, and human designs. Alternative pasts and futures float around us every day—nostalgic design is a set of tools that helps designers access their groundbreaking potential.

### *Key Takeaways of Nostalgic Design*

- Assume citizens are always nostalgic for a reason. Interrogate nostalgia in order to seek out the logical set of values behind the emotion. Ask, *What are* you *nostalgic for, why, and to which ends?*
- *Everyone* is nostalgic for something. Pride, loss, and longing are inescapable, which means that designers need to not only interrogate user nostalgias but also their own traditions, training, and expertise. Ask of yourself, *What am* I *nostalgic for, why, and to which ends?*
- In light of these first two facts, appeals to tradition are not rhetorical fallacies. Teach students to engage and learn from (while not necessarily pandering to) the traditions of the audiences they are creating for rather than simply rejecting or rebutting them.
- Unquestioned traditions often lead to exclusion and alienation, and nos-

talgic ideologies are already and always designed into the technologies that surround us. Awaken users to those arguments; understand how they might subtly exclude users who don't hold them as sacred.

- The layering of numerous traditions leads to revolution. To pragmatically layer traditions, decentralize your own expertise, welcome stakeholders into direct collaboration, and learn to mediate multiple nostalgias and the mêtis therein.

## Nostalgic Pedagogy

1. *Engaging Traditions as Logical*: Many contemporary composition textbooks define appeals to tradition as logical fallacies "in which something is accepted as true or better because it's the 'way it's always been done.' There is no evidence that a specific belief or course of action actually is better. It is just believed to be better because it is the traditional belief or course of action" (SoftSchools). Compare this typical textbook understanding of tradition to the following quote from education theorists Bill Cope and Mary Kalantzis: "Learning is not a matter of 'development in which you leave your old selves behind; leaving behind lifeworlds which would otherwise be framed by education as more or less inadequate to the task of modern life. Rather, learning is a matter of repertoire" (124). What's the difference between how each author understands tradition?

Find three appeals to tradition in contemporary news media (from Twitter to the *New York Times*). Analyze them for the logical moral foundations, god memories, and values they are based in, asking, *What are people nostalgic for, why, and to which ends?* Using Svetlana Boym's restorative and reflective continuum, how would you describe these appeals to tradition? Why? In 2017, for example, Democratic U.S. Senate candidate Doug Jones critiqued his Republican rival Roy Moore for riding a horse and waving a pistol at a campaign event: "I'm a supporter of the Second Amendment. When you see me with a gun, folks, I'll be climbing in and out of a deer stand or a turkey blind, not prancing around on a stage in a cowboy suit" (Samuels). How is nostalgia being used by each candidate to win over conservative Alabama voters? What god memories does the rhetor play to? What community of nostalgia does he seek to join, form, or transform? Who is scapegoated from that community?

*Follow-Up*: "Moral foundations theory," as social psychologist Jonathan Haidt describes it, helps explain how and why morality differs across cultures. Haidt traces five reoccurring foundations that fall in different balances across all societies: care (protecting those we care for), fairness (a desire for an equal application of rules), ingroup loyalty (being loyal to those like us and fighting those against us), authority (respecting tradition and expertise), and purity (virtue through self-control). In one longitudinal study, for example, Haidt found that American liberals and conservatives, unsurprisingly, build their identities upon different foundations (Graham et al.). Where liberals have a two-foundation identity based in fairness and care, conservatives have a balanced five-channel identity. What this means is that many American moral disputes end up being about those three non-overlapping foundations, those conservative "binding foundations" that stress community over the individual: Should we be more loyal to our immediate family and friends? Should we obey authority figures? Should we base our actions on ideas of religious sanctity?

Choose an audience that uses appeals to tradition to reject contemporary science, from global warming to evolution to vaccines. Using Haidt's moral foundations framework, create a one-paragraph text that appeals to this community's traditions while at the same time persuading them that the science is true. For instance, Christopher Wolsko et al. created the following experimental script that successfully persuaded conservatives who didn't believe in global warming: "Show you love your country by joining the fight to protect the purity of America's natural environment. Take pride in the American tradition of performing one's civic duty by taking responsibility for yourself and the land you call home. By taking a tougher stance on protecting the natural environment, you will be honoring all of Creation. Demonstrate your respect by following the examples of your religious and political leaders who defend America's natural environment. SHOW YOUR PATRIOTISM!" (10).

2. *Identifying Nostalgia in Designs:* From Facebook's On This Day to Confederate Civil War memorials to your computer's desktop, many technologies make subtle arguments about how their users should relate to the past. Examine the appeals to tradition made by three technologies that surround you. What argument does each design make about how we should relate to nostalgia, tradition, and memory? Whose nostalgias and memories? How do you know? Would you say these arguments are restorative or reflective appeals? Do they make the user aware of their values or slide by below the radar? Which users are welcomed into this technology's ideal past and which are subtly excluded? How do you know?

*Follow-Up:* Redesign this technology of memory from a different nostalgic point of view, to welcome a different set of users or to encourage reflective rather than restorative nostalgia. What, for instance, might a Confederate memorial that encourages reflective nostalgia look like?

## Chapter 2. Nostalgic Resistances: Remembering as Critical Redesign in Everyday Workplaces

*Critical nostos* is a form of sociological observation by which designers learn from the ways that users resist and redesign technologies by returning home in memory to more comfortable times, actively layering innovation and tradition. This method can be used to identify design inequities, emotional reactions to tech, and the nostalgic repertoires citizens use to innovate in response to uncomfortable designs every day.

### Key Takeaways of Critical Nostos

- Analyze nostalgia to identify gaps in current designs. People are nostalgic when they feel out of place in the present. The nostalgic designer's first goal is to uncover how the current design of things has made some users feel out of place.
- Nostalgia is always a force of redesign. Scout the mêtis and new possible futures nostalgic users are creating in their resistance to things as they currently are. Look for unique innovations, hacks, and redesigns that are occurring in nostalgic contact zones.
- Particularly, search for the nostalgic resistances of those users who are simultaneously technical experts and nostalgics, cutting and trailing-edge users. They are the artists of the nostalgic contact zone, masters of divergent thinking who naturally innovate by layering progress and tradition.
- Read emotions as signs of some grander scheme, as responses to the way the world is designed, rather than simply using them to manipulate user experiences. Nostalgia, like all emotions, acts as a feedback loop (the process of discomfort, loss, and nostalgic response). Ask, Why are you feeling this emotion and to which ends?
- Technology users always exist in multiple communities of nostalgia. Examine temporal anchors (stable points of communal memory users revise their lives upon) for communal values, signs of comfort, and assets/barriers to redesign. Particularly, seek out polysemous identities created at the boundaries of such communities (knitter and mathematician, knitter and computer programmer, woman and craftsman) as revolutionary assets for design.

### Nostalgic Pedagogy

1. *User Innovation Scavenger Hunt*: Designer Tim Brown writes that "Insight . . . does not usually come from reams of quantitative data. . . . A better starting point is to go out into the world and observe the actual experiences of

commuters, skateboarders, and registered nurses as they improvise their way through their daily lives. . . . the shopkeeper who uses a hammer as a doorstop; the office worker who sticks identifying labels onto the jungle of computer cables" (40–41). Find and photograph three ways in which users have hacked their ways around a design problem. Around campus, for instance, we find "desire lines," paths where walkers wear down the grass because sidewalks didn't provide the quickest route to their destination. Similarly, you might notice where users are purposefully breaking the rules. Where do students write messages to one another that they aren't supposed to? Are they writing on bathroom walls and desks? Posting flyers in odd places? Chalking the sidewalks? Why aren't students just using provided bulletin boards? Your goal in this search is to ask, Where and why have citizens innovated, and how can I draw upon this information to improve the world? But here's the twist: one of your three user redesigns must be nostalgic. That is, you must ask, Where is nostalgia being used as a tool for redesign? From your friend who knits in class to a hipster writing on a typewriter at the local coffee shop, how and why do people use nostalgia to reshape their worlds? To help you find such examples, consider the following techno-resistance terms from anthropologist Bryan Pfaffenberger:

- *Countersignification*: Telling new stories and myths about oppressive technologies (e.g., anti-vaccination parents tell personal stories about vaccines harming their children, the appropriation of #myNYPD to critique the police).
- *Counterappropriation*: Gaining access to a technology you are prohibited from using or a technology designed for someone else (e.g., women working in STEM industries or Kit using stories about her dad to write herself into masculine craft traditions).
- *Counterdelegation*: Hacking technologies to subvert their surveillance features (e.g., turning off a fasten seatbelt buzzer in your car).

2. *Expanding Technological Literacy*: Think of a person in your life who you think is truly smart but who you wouldn't consider literate in high-technologies like the internet, web design, etc. (maybe an older relative or friend). Now imagine that you were going to pitch them as the instructor of a multimodal writing or design course. What types of technological and multimodal composing skills beyond the computer might they be able to teach? For example, what might your great aunt's scrapbooking teach the class about visual rhetoric? What might their syllabus and readings look like? Their assignments? Their grading rubric? Remember that the class is multimodal, so assignments and skills will have to go beyond alphabetic text.

3. *Designing Emotions*: The primary way designers relate to emotion is activating positive emotions in users (joy, happiness, excitement) and banishing negative ones (frustration, anxiety, etc.). But emotion is more complex than that. Choose an emotion that is traditionally considered negative (fear, anxiety, sadness) and harness it in a spatial design that affects occupants in an intriguing way. The office building of the software company Procore Technologies, for example, is purposefully designed to be confusing. Most rooms aren't square and the layout is based on a Chinese tangram puzzle in order to create an enriched environment that uses "surprising or changing spatial elements to activate, and thus engage, different parts of the brain and create new neural pathways. When parts of the brain must focus on new stimulus, blood flow increases, as does alertness" (Rhodes). Of course, your design doesn't have to be a positive one. It could be a "dark design" (Dunne and Raby 38). It could, that is, imagine a speculative dystopia that might happen if our society continues down a negative course of action that we are currently following. What if, for instance, a design were created that further encouraged members of opposing political parties to get angrier and angrier at one another?

*Follow-Up*: One place that angry emotional nostalgias appear again and again is in diatribes about "kids these days." Older generations consistently look at younger ones as somehow destroying the world they grew up in. As numerous headlines attest, for example, "Millennials have killed" chain restaurants, big beer companies, napkins, cereal, golf, department stores, etc., etc. Choose a news story that accuses a younger generation of destroying the world. Examine the nostalgic emotions that the article attempts to mobilize. What are they? What are they meant to do? What is the author nostalgic for, why, and to which ends? What missing piece of the world or emotion beyond nostalgic loss does the author's nostalgia highlight?

## Chapter 3. Nostalgic Deliberations: What I Mean When I Say "Democratizing Technology"

*Rhetorical design* is a form of deliberative production that realizes that all design problems are indeterminate, affording many possible solutions. By combining rhetoric and design studies models of democratic deliberation, rhetorical design provokes diverse designers, users, and stakeholders to debate and deliberate over designs before, during, and after their creation. Within such deliberations, rhetorical designers are acutely aware of the ecologies of language, persuasion, and resistance surrounding the production and use of technology and seek to solve problems of power and inequity in order to promote an inclusive mediation process. If deliberative democracy is government by conversation, then rhetorical design is the creation of the productive conversations that lead to inclusive technologies.

## Key Takeaways of Rhetorical Design

- For technology to be democratic, guide stakeholders in debate and deliberation over designs before, during, and after their rollout. It's the rhetorical designer's responsibility to set up forums for and encourage conversations between multiple conflicting viewpoints.
- Within such conversations, attempting to answer the question, *Who are we?* is crucial: What are this new community's values, histories, and collective identities? Who do they believe should be involved in the decision-making collective? And why? To do so, help stakeholders examine their shared and conflicting nostalgias through the analysis of enthymemes, epideictic rhetoric, god memories, and eavesdropping for privilege.
- Guard against passive understandings of users. Deploy the above conversations to explore messy human individuality and offer opportunities to resist the designer through informed dissent. Train and provoke critical user audiences that become agonistic adversaries in deliberation.
- At some point, the conversation has to pause in order for a design to be formed. This means that some user voices will always be left out—pure consensus is impossible and undesirable. But the conversation will always continue even when the designer has left the room. Listen for these excluded citizens. They rarely sit on their hands waiting for their turn. Rather, from knitting at work to generating anti-vaccination stories, omitted users seek their own solutions through unofficial channels. Cyclically redesign from such excluded expertise, again and again.

## Nostalgic Pedagogy

1. *Inviting Collaborative Design (An Instructor Ethic)*: If, as chapter 3 presents, most design in non-student contexts is a deliberative process between clients, users, designers, marketing experts, technology experts, content experts, etc., then university instructors might consider what would happen if students recruited friends and family to take on these other roles in their assignments. In this deliberative design framework, students might choose only one composing position for themselves and learn the key skill of wrangling human composing resources. If a student's roommate were a film production major, for instance, what if the student wrote the script for her video assignment and directed her roommate's production of the video?

2. *User-Centered Redesign*: Compare the user-centered design of the BioLite HomeStove mentioned at the end of chapter 1 to the Bic for Her pens described in chapter 3. What's the difference between how these designs were customized for their users? Now, research a user *un*-friendly design (e.g., a complex DSLR camera with many features or the warning indicator lights on a car's dashboard) and transform it into an easy-to-learn and -use design. Start by researching a specific unskilled user (your ten-year-old sister, for instance), coming to understand her likes and dislikes and knowledge set so that the new design speaks directly to her mêtis. Next, catalogue your user audience's god memories. What are her best technological experiences, and how might this new design incorporate those ideals? Finally, paper prototype your new interface.

*Follow-Up:* Imagine you are a member of the marketing/design team that is attempting to introduce the value of Google Fiber to several untapped communities (see the introductory vignettes of chapter 1). Using the four design types of chapter 3, how would you go about gauging the specific technological values, affordances, and challenges of a specific community? Analyze, for instance, the neighborhood you grew up in. Who would Google need to get on board first? The young, the elderly, schools? Why? Are there some people who might not see the benefit of Google Fiber? Who? Why? How might you create an argument based on their specific needs?

3. *Provotyping*: "It is now easier for us to imagine the end of the world," writes Fredric Jameson, "than to imagine the end of capitalism" ("Future"). In response to this malaise, this book has argued that designers have a responsibility to help their users overcome status quo biases and a simple trust that "experts" will always have their best interests in mind. We called this ethical standard *informed dissent*. Take an everyday experience that is hyper-naturalized (turning on a light bulb, feeding your cat, waking up in the morning to your alarm clock) and transform it into a provotype that makes user audiences question their everyday life.

Designers Daniel Neville-Rehbehn et al., for example, recently asked, "How might we [transform everyday experiences like waiting for the bus in order to] spark more opportunities to learn from different perspectives?" Their response, "Everyday Voting," is a set of installations across a city in which "twice a month, a new question will be posed by the Everyday Voting installations." To vote on the question, "Should Airbnb be allowed to operate in our city?" for instance, citizens just have to participate in everyday actions: walking through a subway turnstile, throwing trash in a public receptacle, or standing on a pad at the local bus stop, each marked, yes, no, or not sure. As the designers write: "Everyday Voting creates the circumstances to turn public spaces into common ground. By getting to know more about each other's point of view we can practice disagreeing instead of dismissing, arguing instead of attacking. We can remind ourselves that not everyone who thinks differently is nuts. . . . Helping people grow more comfortable and confident participating in civic discourse is essential if we want our society to thrive in all its complexity." Start with a utopic *what if* question like Neville-Rehbehn et al.'s and begin creating.

4. *Dismissing Values*: "Nostalgia accounts for the troubling persistence of those dissenting voices—conservatives, agrarians, and traditionalists of various sorts—that oppose the 'progressive' rationalization and mechanization of the means of production," writes Kimberly Smith. "The claim that such opponents are suffering from nostalgia both explains and delegitimates their political stance" (506). Research a recent technological debate (birth control legislation, internet surveillance, net neutrality, military drones). In what ways (and by whom) do some resistant values, morals, ethics, and logics get delegitimized as private, "illogical," or backward while others are freely and publicly discussed? Which values get excluded from deliberations, why, and by whom? Which values (progress and efficiency, for instance) are kept in play? How does this delineation of public ethics and private morality affect the debate?

## Chapter 4. Nostalgic Mediations: Asking the Right Questions in Vaccine Communication

*Nostalgic stasis* is an equitable question asking and storytelling process in which designers draw upon resistant user nostalgias in order to mediate technological debates. Specifically, by jointly asking of users and technical experts, *What are we nostalgic for, why, and to which ends?* nostalgic stasis locates points of hope, healing, and redesign buried in narratives of loss and longing in order to create new loci of community based in shared ideal pasts.

### Steps to Nostalgic Stasis

- Start mediations in stasis, asking questions that all parties can draw from their expertise and personal experiences (whether technical, personal, or public) to answer. Don't dismiss seemingly illogical foundations of knowledge; rather, promote reflectively nostalgic expertise and avoid asystasis by asking, *What are each party's stories and why are they being used to shape the world in this way?* When everyone can contribute to the conversation, a new community is formed.

- To avoid getting mired in conflict, simultaneously ask of each party, *What has been lost?* but also *What do you cherish about the past that can be used to re-design the future?* Nostalgia's twin emotions of loss and pride individualize, contextualize, and humanize technological mediations.
- To ground loss and pride, seek out the technological god memories of each party. What periods of time does each party wish to restore? How ambiguous or specific are those periods? How are they concretely represented? Uncover the values, losses, and hopes that are subsumed beneath these god memories.
- Understand who is included in and excluded from each party's decision-making we and why. Attempt to form a new community of deliberation by having all parties listen to each other's nostalgic stories and the logics therein, breaking expertise dichotomies by welcoming third parties to the table, asking conflicting parties to reframe their arguments through the nostalgias of their opponents, and empathically redesigning from one another's nostalgias. Such new communities seek reflectively nostalgic healing (embracing hope through change) rather than restoratively nostalgic curing (seeking to recover some previously ideal state).
- Avoid dismissing fear, anger, and other negative emotions (creating emotional others). Rather, ask, *Where are these emotions coming from and why?* Validate the human behind these emotions if not the complaint.

## Nostalgic Pedagogy

1. *Nostalgia-typing*: The narrative mediation strategy of "double-listening" (Winslade and Monk) encourages conflict participants to see one another (and themselves) as always existing in multiple life stories (family, occupation, religion, race, generation, hobbies, etc.), listening simultaneously for the problem/conflict story but also for ideal future stories based in other identities, values, and stories of hope outside of that problem. Nostalgia-typing builds upon this approach by asking conflict participants to break out of the conflict narrative by drawing upon ideal times before the problem in order to remember when opponents were collaborators. In this activity, you will choose a technological conflict and:

    i. Catalogue god memories and pre-conflict nostalgias of the two opposing sides.

    ii. Look for overlaps between each party's nostalgic ideals.

    iii. Listen for a third-party's nostalgic ideals to break stale conflict dichotomies.

iv. Finally, propose a nostalgia-type based on these overlapping ideals that pleases all parties.

You could create a nostalgia-type for a political conflict like anti-vaccination, but you also might consider nostalgic conflicts over smaller everyday events like the design of a playground. Recently, for example, there's been an international trend in park design known as "adventure playgrounds" in which parents and designers nostalgic for their own more venturesome childhoods (and disgusted by current safety-obsessed parks) push to make parks exciting again by adding access to hammers, nails, and wood; homemade tree houses; etc. However, through a lens of nostalgic contact zones the nostalgic designer might ask, Who isn't longing for these dangerous parks? Parents with children with disabilities, for example, may be nostalgic for playgrounds but not for the inaccessibility of parks before the Americans with Disabilities Act. Thus, the pure restoration of mid-century playgrounds might be a bad idea, but the nostalgic values of such parks—risk, trial-and-error, free play—might be explored in more accessible nostalgia-types.

2. *Rephrasing Asystatic Questions*: To be in stasis, questions and points of discussion must be answerable through the logics/values of all parties involved. Good conflict mediators are able to transform asystatic questions into static ones in order to keep the flow of conversation running smoothly. Transform the following asystatic questions into equitably static ones that welcome collaboration.

- Why don't you listen to the science on vaccination?
- Why are you forcing my child to take in dangerous toxins through vaccines?
- Why do you want to celebrate slavery through confederate Civil War memorials?
- Why do you want to take away my guns—haven't you heard of the Second Amendment?

Now, research your own technological debate. Find three asystatic questions and equitably rephrase them.

3. *Exploring Expertise and the Decision-Making We*: Choose a design conflict with an argumentative party with whom you *personally* disagree: whether a celebrity, a religious figure, or a scientist. Research why this community believes what it believes by transforming the question, Why do you believe that? into the question, Why do you remember that? Ideally, you would actu-

ally interview a member of this party, but a less direct research investigation might do as well. Your goal is to have this party fill in the phrase: Where I come from, we trust (implicitly have faith in) *fill in the blank* (technology, designers, doctors, police, teachers, priests, et al.) because of these memories, stories, and values: *fill in the blank*. In contrast, we don't trust (implicitly refuse the authority of) *fill in the blank* (children, scientists, poor people, professors, convicts, et al.) because *fill in the blank*. Now, fill in the blanks for your own opinions about the technological conflict. Who do you implicitly trust and distrust? Why?

## Chapter 5. Nostalgic Negotiations: Adapting, Adopting, and Refusing Client Expertise

*Memorial interactivity* is a method of collaboration in which partners directly reveal, discuss, and negotiate their tacit expertise by divulging the episodic nostalgias in which that expertise is based. Such storytelling creates a transactive memory system wherein all stakeholders hold some proficiency so that the group has access to more information than any lone individual. Designers, thereby, expose themselves to new knowledge by asking clients what they are nostalgic for, why, and to which ends and, then, tactfully adapt to, adopt, or refuse those revealed desires.

### Key Takeaways of Memorial Interactivity

- Perform reflectively nostalgic expertise (listening for and incorporating the expertise of others) and ask clients to do the same by welcoming numerous stakeholders into a transactive memory system in which all members demonstrate knowledge through overt memories and stories about what has happened in their pasts.
- Nostalgically prime collaborations by starting with positive client self-descriptions, scenarios, mood boards, and stories of success in order to set an optimistic tone and safe space to reach into new experiences.
- Frame design presentations within the overt memories used to create them. Moreover, position the design in terms of the client's business goals so that clients can critique and comment directly from their expertise. Give clients an expert platform to contribute from.
- When necessary, rhetorically refuse clients by substituting one ideal for a better one. Don't reject a client opinion, critique, or value without substituting and explaining the choice through the client's god memories.
- Consider the ethics and economics of voice, style, and client refusals before you start a new project. Is this client a good fit for you? Do they want an awful design that you aren't willing to create? Or do you need

to adapt to that awfulness to make a living? Make sure these choices are reflected in your contract.

## Nostalgic Pedagogy

*Note*: The best way to get students practicing memorial interactivity is to have them work with actual clients in their writing assignments—creating documents that will be used by people in the future. Because I realize many readers won't have the chance to situate their courses around client work, however, these activities are designed to simulate client interaction.

1. *Nostalgia Mapping*: In this assignment you will redesign the English major to recruit more students. But rather than simply imagining solutions from the depths of your head, you need to learn about what your stakeholders want. To do so, you will begin by mapping out stakeholders' nostalgic visions of the English department. First, go out, find, and interview two unique stakeholders that you don't think your classmates will interview, asking them to tell a nostalgic story about English. Of course, you're going to find conflicting desires. If you asked every professor in the English department what they loved about the major (what are they nostalgic for), for example, each might tell you a different story of what it has meant to them—deep reading of the classics, exposing students to culture, preparing students to be professional writers. But, obviously, professors aren't the only departmental stakeholders. Current and potential students, university administrators, parents, even students in STEM who condemn the major as useless—What are each group's nostalgic ideals? Once we've generated a batch of stories and ideals, as a class we will map a vision for the department into the future by examining the contact zones, conflicts, and convergences we find.

2. *From Peer Review to Charrette (An Instructor Ethic)*: If your writing class-rooms are anything like mine, then peer review typically happens at the end of an assignment. Perhaps a week (or maybe a few days) before the final assignment is due, I ask students to read over one another's drafts in small groups—often using a worksheet I've made to guide them. But typical peer review (Paton; Cahill) leaves out a couple things that chapter 5 promoted. First, sticking peer review at the end of the writing process doesn't get an audience's feedback early enough. And, more importantly, peer review usu-ally doesn't ask: Who are the actual users and clients of this document? Who's going to interact with it? What do they think about its effectiveness? In contrast to the peer review, design classrooms offer the charrette (Per-nice; Eagen et al.), a participatory approach that invites the experts of the

nostalgia map to evaluate the student's design at the proposal, draft, and final stages.

When I require charrettes, for example, I ask each student to invite one expert user affected by their project to their design presentation. But I also ask these invited experts to stick around and reflect on the other student projects as well. That way, we have multiple voices, most of whom the students don't know, contributing to the conversation. These outsiders (like the student designers) are all asked to follow one simple rule—frame their critique in unique expertise, memories, and stories; don't make baseless complaints. One of the big highlights of charrettes is that such outsiders make design review feel real. In response to this outsider advice, charrettes also offer students the chance to mediate and incorporate multiple conflicting client viewpoints into design briefs and memos. That is, beyond simply experiencing conflicting expert advice, I require students to create and submit summative documents of what stakeholders have said.

3. *Situating Rhetorical Refusals*: Imagine you are a doctor whose patient is not following medical advice. For instance, your patient is continuing to smoke despite having chronic emphysema. But this patient is a kind old lady who comes from a medical tradition in which doctors are supposed to be gentle and nice. How do you refuse this woman's health standards and get more aggressive in terms of medical communication? How do you convince her to stop smoking? What rhetorical moves might you make? A habitus shock? Drawing upon what she values (e.g., spending time with her grandchildren)? Something else? What communication factors will you have to take into account?

4. *The Economics of Voice*: If you were a freelance technical writer or designer who had a client who you were not getting along with, what would you do? For instance, what if you had just spent a month on a new ad campaign for a small dog washing business? You had shown your design to numerous colleagues who all love it and are really excited about what you've come up with. Then, your client shoots it down and asks you to design something bland, unoriginal, and not based on user research but rather on an idea their twelve-year-old nephew had. Would you argue for your design? How? Would you go with what the client wants, despite what your expertise tells you? What are the factors you might have to take into consideration before making your choice? Whether you can afford to be fired? How the client might react? What would you include in your designer-client contract in order to protect you and

your work in light of such a situation? Write a letter to your client that takes into account all of these questions.

## Chapter 6. Nostalgic UX: Designing for Future Memories

*Nostalgic user experience architecture* (N-UX) is a set of design features that encourages users to invest memories in designs, thereby making them more meaningful. Such features record, store, and emit nostalgias of use. The three most powerful rhetorical moves of such features are (1) *narratability* (provoking users to record and tell stories about objects), (2) *craft* (urging users to take part in and care about other players in the lifecycle of a product), and (3) *connoisseurship* (training consumers to have a taste for slow, diverse experiences). Ideally, nostalgic UX doesn't just promote consumption but also meaningful reflection on a design's place in time that urges consumers to embrace more responsible (environmentally friendly, repairable, reusable) designs.

### Key Takeaways of Nostalgic UX

- Design for *personalization* (a product's individual and emotional anchoring in users' lives) rather than *customization* (a set of closed decisions wherein users mistake a company's choices for their own).
- Highlight the consumption of time—rupturing the present, purposefully slowing things down, and calling consumers' attentions to the experience as memorable.
- Build room for behavioral residue (physical traces of user interaction to tell stories about). But also build recall mechanisms, spaces for resistant narratives, and ways to pass these stories on to others.
- Connect the people involved in the lifecycle of a product—through leaked constructedness, inheritability, repair, connoisseur education, and meaningful reflection on death. Use nostalgia to "people the mind" (Hertz).

### Nostalgic Pedagogy

1. *Slowing Down User Experiences*: "I'm actually quite a different person, I just never get around to being him," writes Hungarian playwright Ödön von Horváth (Rosa). Email, cell phones, social media, Netflix, one-hour Amazon shipping—so many technologies that surround us are focused on speed. In this assignment, you will take a prototypically fast experience and slow it down, calling users' attentions to the way time flows around them and promoting nostalgic UX values of connection, repair, and environmental care. Take as an example designer Stuart Walker's response to constantly being on call with modern cell phones. His speculative "pouch phone" is a collection of phone parts in a pouch that "allows the product to be incrementally upgraded

as technology advances. . . . In this disassembled state it is not a mobile phone but simply a collection of parts. Thus, it would not interrupt or intrude upon the owner's thoughts or current activities; incoming calls would simply be transferred to a message service" (105). How might you similarly slow a fast, over-connected experience?

2. *Redesign for Aging Gracefully*: Choose a technology that has been purposefully designed to quickly obsolesce or produce a great amount of waste: iPhones, cars, clothing, Keurig coffee. Find a techno-culture that has arisen to resist this obsolescence or a parallel situation (e.g., iFixit, Creative Commons licenses, repair cafes). Building from your research of that culture, redesign the original product to promote inheritability (products that will last long enough to be passed down generationally), graceful aging (products like wine that transform for the better as they age), repair (products that are easily repairable by users or by the company), and fluid deaths (designs that fade elegantly rather than leaving behind toxic corpses when they die).

3. *Encouraging Connoisseur Culture:* Choose a design that has a devoted group of followers or connoisseurs (craft coffee, music, potato chips, etc.). How is this design invested with a memorable aura (marks of craftsmanship, repair, Easter eggs, and ecologies of care) that guides "correct" usage and tastes? How is this aura (and the collective memory structures attached to it) used to generate a community of nostalgic users who invest their time in the design to gain cultural capital? What are the unique steps of ritual consumption that teach the user to enjoy the product? In what ways do such rituals ask their users to rethink the flow of time? Recall, for instance, how "French chocolatiers and cultural taste makers attempted to stimulate new demand for craft commodities by promoting 'genuine,' 'grand cru,' or 'vintage' French chocolate" that had not existed in the past by creating unique tasting rituals and connecting chocolate to French wine (Terrio 68).

Now, choose a product that does not yet have a devoted following and create a strategic plan by which a connoisseur community might be generated. What histories and memories will you attach to the product? How? What rituals and processes do you imagine your connoisseurs doing to mark their membership and expertise?

# Notes

## Why Nostalgia? Why Here? Why Now?

1. Alex Lubben reports in a November 2017 *ViceNews* article, "According to the federal Bureau of Labor Statistics coal, the coal industry has only added about two thousand jobs since Trump took office, up to about fifty-two thousand employed in total, largely due to a brief blip of increased demand for coal from China. (Trump has repeatedly threatened to cut off trade to China if it doesn't cut ties with North Korea)."

## Chapter 1: Nostalgic Design

1. Currently, several Google-sponsored organizations—Connecting for Good, the Kansas City Public Library District, et al.—engage with such local techno-cultures. And several articles, including one written by Aaron Deacon ("Truth"), have recently argued that the digital divide in KC was just an initial gaff. Still, had Google learned from local organizations *before* it marketed its product, its initial failure might have been prevented.

2. See Zeynep Turan's "Material Memories of the Ottoman Empire: Armenain and Greek Objects of Legacy" and the *This American Life* episode "Are We There Yet?"

3. Quite literally, as established in Endel Tulving and Daniel Schacter's work with amnesiacs, the brain cannot envision the future without access to the past.

4. Starting most clearly with Richard Buchannan's "declaration by design" and progressing to Klaus Krippendorff's understanding of design as "making sense (of things)" and to Carl DiSalvo's "adversarial design," the relationship between rhetoric and design has been growing over the last century. Indeed, Buchanan questions specifically "[W]hether design is a modem form of rhetoric—or whether rhetoric is an ancient form of design. . . . In approaching design from a rhetorical perspective, our hypothesis should be that all products—digital and analog, tangible and intangible—are vivid arguments about how we should lead our lives" ("Design" 191, 194). Thus, though parallel conceptions of the politics of technology flow through the social construction of technology, systems theory, and actor-network theory, this book is grounded in the rhetoric of design, which is focused on the ecologies of language,

persuasion, and resistance surrounding the production and use of technology as well as actively solving problems of power and inequity within these systems.

5. For at least a century, the Swiss were thought to be the sole victims of the disease, so much so that physician Johann Scheuchzer theorized that the clanging of cow bells so commonly found in the Alps had affected these soldiers' brains.

6. See Peter Burke's "History as Social Memory" for a foundational juxtaposition of memory and history.

7. And, perhaps because of this charge of reforming history by recovering often *traumatic* diasporic memories (accounts of holocaust survivors, former slaves, and displaced populations at large), the more sanguine mending narratives of nostalgia have been understudied in many fields. In rhetoric and composition, for instance, there are hundreds of analyses of cultural memory and memorials but just eleven articles/chapters on nostalgia and no books.

8. Jameson doesn't hate nostalgia entirely, however, and was one of the first critics to admit its radical potential in his essay "Walter Benjamin, or Nostalgia," writing: "But if nostalgia as a political movement is most frequently associated with fascism, there is no reason why a nostalgia conscious of itself, a lucid and remorseless dissatisfaction with the present on the ground of some remembered plentitude, cannot furnish as adequate a revolutionary stimulus as any other: the example of Benjamin is there to prove it" (68).

9. Rhetorician Kendall Phillips, for instance, traces the nostalgia of liberal filmmaker Michael Moore: "Across his oeuvre, Moore demonstrates a tendency to return to Flint, Michigan, and to reference the idyllic nature of his own childhood era as a counterpoint to the social ills he is investigating" ("I'm" 292).

10. Philosopher of technology Andrew Feenberg calls this "the bias of technology": "Once introduced, technology offers a material validation of the social order to which it has been preformed. . . . [A]pparently neutral, functional rationality is enlisted in support of a hegemony" (*Between* 18). There are always numerous, equally efficient, cost-effective, and innovative designs available. Why we choose one design over the other is a product of power, politics, and culture.

11. In this section I focus on recruiting women to STEM, but most studies on the issue have shown that keeping women in STEM jobs is equally as important. And part of what drives women from STEM has nothing to do with recruiting but rather a culture of sexual harassment, lower pay, and no maternity leave. There are often more insidious forces at play. The dominant techno-logic has to change.

12. Literacy theorist Elspeth Stuckey calls the pain of this dismissal "the violence of literacy": when users become literate in a certain subject they have to conform to the ideologies of its design and, thereby, expel parts of their identities that don't fit with this new system.

13. This discrimination is still seen in the gaming industry. For instance, in 2014's "gamergate" scandal, a prominent female game developer became the victim of sexist

and violent social media attacks after her ex-boyfriend questioned her journalistic ethics online. This attack soon spread to numerous other female game developers.

14. See also the Carnegie Science Center's failed Science with a Sparkle program.

15. For a fuller account of the difference between *episteme* and *techne*, see Richard Parry's "Episteme and Techne" in the *Stanford Encyclopedia of Philosophy*.

16. Conflict is, however, addressed at several points in the handbook. For example, Carl DiSalvo et al.'s chapter briefly mentions "agonism" (200). But mediating arguments is not a mainstay of the book. As described in chapter 3, this lack of debate has begun to be addressed in design theories and methods that deliberately encourage conflict, like DiSalvo's "adversarial designs" and Dunne and Raby's "critical design."

## Chapter 2: Nostalgic Resistances

*Epigraph:* Throughout this book authorial editing of participant quotations will be represented by ellipses except in the case of the removal of empty repetitions and filler terms including "like," "um," etc. For instance, Kit's statement, "I was little and I would help my dad do, like build things because I was always his helper" becomes "I was little and I would help my dad build things because I was always his helper."

1. Donna, Jo, and Kit (pseudonyms) were each selected through chain-referral sampling (Heckathorn). In 2012, each participant was informally observed in her workplace and asked a series of eighteen questions, resulting in, typically, a one- to two-hour interview that produced what Selfe and Hawisher call "technological literacy autobiographies" and what I develop, here, as critical nostos narratives (7). Interviews were, when possible, both audio and video recorded to capture the richness of linguistic markers, physical gestures, and craft processes that went on during these meetings. Despite interviewing one male crafter, I decided to focus this chapter on craft as a feminist art form to highlight critical nostos's power to innovate from excluded voices.

2. At the time of our interview, Donna was playing a knitting game called "AssassiKnit," in which several international knitters, who met online, race to see who can send pieces the fastest back and forth through the mail.

3. See also Kyffin and Gardien's "innovation matrix."

4. A similar reading of emotion can be found in structural appraisal theory, wherein the identification and interpretation of the emotional stimulus is dubbed the primary appraisal and the appraisal of how to respond to that emotion (the nostalgic search of the past in our case) is the secondary appraisal (Demir et al; Lazarus).

5. See Stacey and Tether's work on designing emotion in a cancer care unit.

6. This view of nostalgia departs from Fred Davis's early claims that we cannot be nostalgic for a period we never experienced ourselves (8). Maybe it is true, as Davis argues, that one cannot feel nostalgic for the Revolutionary War, but there is something to be said for an inherited generational nostalgia like stitch 'n bitch.

7. When I did site observations at several indie and alternative craft fairs, I saw this firsthand. Whereas booths run by twenty-something crafters that used cool patterns to create stuffed animals, for example, were swamped with customers, a smattering of booths selling potholders and old-fashioned sweaters run by little old ladies were ignored.

8. Christen points out that the idea of free sharing of memories in the cultural commons also assumes that everyone is starting from equal positions of power: "Should we perpetuate the logic that race, gender, and class aren't part of the digital commons? That somehow technologies and the infrastructures of design—the code—do not work to secure and structure moral and political positions?" (333). Measuring power relations is critical to all contact zones.

## Chapter 3: Nostalgic Deliberations

1. Though the tomato farmers eventually lost the case in a retrial, the UC system responded by founding the Small Farm Center as well as a Fair Political Practices Commission.

2. Buchanan is a student of rhetoricians Richard McKeon and Wayne Booth.

3. This claim is debatable, as many sophists (e.g., Protagoras, Isocrates, Gorgias) and philosophers (e.g., Plato) precede Aristotle.

4. See Porter's *Audience and Rhetoric* vs. Lunsford and Ede's "On Distinctions Between Classical and Modern Rhetoric."

5. Spinuzzi argues that because of the United States' weaker trade unions, as compared to the Scandinavian countries in which participatory design originated, the U.S. has contributed to this weakening of participatory design's emancipatory power for workers ("Lost").

6. Ratcliffe has a beautiful defense against this critique in her book: "Is rhetorical listening, as defined here, too idealistic to have a pragmatic effect? My response is: No, it is not. Dismissing rhetorical listening as too idealistic presumes a focus only on its obvious limitations: That is, rhetorical listening cannot solve all the world's problems, nor can it guarantee perfect communication or even productive communication in all instances. Then again, neither can Aristotle's enthymeme" (26).

7. Ratcliffe reminds readers that rhetorical listening "does not presume a naïve, *relativistic* empathy, such as 'I'm OK, you're OK' but rather an ethical responsibility to argue for what we deem fair and just while questioning that which we deem fair and just" (25).

8. Mouffe considers agonistic democracy decidedly not a form of deliberative democracy. But practically (though it avoids being connected to Habermas and Rawles by rejecting the term) Mouffe's form of democracy involves deliberation. So, I have no hesitation in calling it deliberative.

9. Ratcliffe's work is not neoliberal, and I use empathic design as a juxtaposition to Burke in this section because Ratcliffe's rhetorical listening is much more balanced than the description of liberalism Mouffe lays out.

10. Rhetorician Arabella Lyon persuasively argues that when imagined this large, the decision-making we isn't really about inclusiveness: "The political forces turned loose by human rights talk, even when rights are imagined as universal, are not committed to universalism but rather to competition for dominance by ideologies and cultures made manifest through our globalization" (2). Lyon gives the example of George W. Bush linking abuses of Afghan women's rights to the Taliban as a way to expand U.S. influence in the region (2). The god memory of human rights masks the hegemonies within it.

11. A Mouffian theory of design also seems to square nicely with Erling Björgvins-son, Pelle Ehn, and Per-Anders Hillgren's theory of design "Things": "Originally, 'Things' go back to the governing assemblies in ancient Nordic and Germanic societies. These pre-Christian Things were assemblies, rituals, and places where disputes were resolved and political decisions made. The prerequisite for understanding this journey from things as material object and back to Things as socio-material assemblies is that if we live in total agreement, we do not need to gather to resolve disputes—because none exist. Instead, the need for a common place where conflicts can be negotiated is motivated by a diversity of perspectives, concerns, and interests" (102).

12. So, which is the right solution to the woes of technological democracy? I have no idea. But (imagining I'm in a future workshop) were I to theorize an ideal situation of democratic deliberation based in what we've learned, it would put as many citizens in conversations with professional experts to make real deliberative decisions as possible. That is, it would be a participatory democracy. This utopia might happen through a required duty of citizenship like jury duty. Once a year, citizens would be required to perform a small-scale deliberative duty in which they work with a group of experts and adversaries to write specific bills and laws. This would be an ideal forum for informed dissent, and it would force citizens to leave their filter bubble of like-minded friends and family and experience the vox populi. Though Lippmann might retort that these nonexpert citizens would still likely be manipulated, I think this smaller scale of in-person learning, debate, and voting is less likely to be manipulated by demagogues than large-scale representative voting. It's hard for spin-doctors to spin when citizens can engage them in-person. In this model, governmental decisions would no longer be abstract choices far away from the average voting citizen.

## Chapter 4: Nostalgic Mediation

1. Smallpox scars even mark the mummy of Egyptian pharaoh Ramses V.

2. On a smaller scale, "variolation," inoculating healthy patients directly with

smallpox through injection and/or snorting powdered scabs was practiced for at least two hundred years prior to the smallpox vaccine proper, with somewhat positive results ("Smallpox").

3. Upon investigation it was found Wakefield wrote the article alone. Though Wakefield's continuing arguments are a central catalyst to the anti-vaccination movement, I don't cover his texts here, because I'm more interested in the co-designs of parents and their doctors. For more on Wakefield's rhetoric, see Kolodziejski; Rundblad et al.; and Kirkland.

4. "Anti-vaccination" is a bit of a misnomer, as the movement is a combination of vaccine-hesitant parents and parents who want to choose some vaccines and not others, though the leaders of many vaccine-hesitant organizations are, indeed, completely anti-vaccination.

5. See PJ Smith, SY Chu, and LE Barker's "Children Who Have Received No Vaccines: Who Are They and Where Do They Live?" in *Pediatrics*.

6. Throughout this chapter, stasis questions are italicized whereas non-static questions are not.

7. The McCarthy and Carrey interview is one segment in a larger debate on the program. I choose to highlight only McCarthy and Carrey's contributions, however, because the other nostalgias and techno-logics represented in the debate will be featured elsewhere in this chapter.

8. Participatory medicine is particularly important, here, because when anti-vax parents, who are primarily white, upper-class, and well-educated (Jones et. al), feel a loss of power in their formerly privileged lives, a drive to regain power is created. If deference isn't given to parental experience nor an effort made towards shared decision-making, parents go elsewhere for control.

9. Though I treat Offit without kid gloves here, I do deeply sympathize with him, and something I don't cover are the numerous death threats Offit and other pro-vaccine public figures regularly receive from anti-vaccination parents. Indeed, when I was watching the SB 277 hearings, one of the representatives mentioned that she did not appreciate the threats from anti-vaccination parents.

10. The Office of Special Masters on Vaccine Claims of the United States Court of Federal Claims.

11. Similarly, the CDC website on vaccine risks lists both "rare and real" and "rare and hypothetical" vaccine reactions. The rare and real category describes reactions that have been recorded and proven by science; the rare and hypothetical category describes reactions that have not been recorded or proven through any scientific means. Why include this rare and hypothetical category?

12. Above I mention several anti-vaccination parental stories being recounted at the microphone. Most were cut off by Jackson.

13. Thus, though the bill was successful in that it passed, it was unsuccessful in that it didn't resolve the sources of anti-vaccination and didn't come to stasis. The pres-

ence of several lawsuits and a quick search of #SB277 on twitter shows parental resistance in California is still a very real issue even if vaccination rates of kindergartners went up by 3 percent between the 2015 and 2016 school years (California Department).

14. Putnam's data is full of restorative nostalgia for a time before technology isolated us from bridging social capital. This is one of Everett Ladd's critiques of his work. Ladd compares Putnam's studies to Robert and Helen Lynd's 1920s Middletown studies, which raise the same issue of fading bridging social capital that Putnam does but describe this social change as a response to the new technology of the radio. I don't think this argument against Putnam's work, however, invalidates his useful distinction between bridging and bonding social capital.

15. Admittedly, the majority of this chapter (like its author) tips in favor of medical science rather than anti-vaccination parents. But there are real reasons to be skeptical of technology. In an interview on PBS's *Frontline*, Offit describes the story of John Salamone and his son, David, who received the oral polio vaccine in the 1980s and contracted polio: "[John] looked at countries like in Scandinavian countries, where they never use the oral polio vaccine. . . . and he said: 'Why can't we be one of those countries? Why do I have to give my child a vaccine which can potentially cause polio when there's another vaccine that can be used?' And he then I think, frankly, became the single most important person in moving us from the oral polio vaccine schedule. . . . I think that's an example of consumer activism at its best."

16. Of course, there are important reasons not to collaborate with opponents. I don't mean to suggest, for instance, that extremist groups like Holocaust deniers should be welcomed into redesigning history textbooks. However, when such groups begin to affect the flow of everyday events and/or harm themselves, as in anti-vaccination, redesign is necessary.

## Chapter 5: Nostalgic Negotiations

1. Of course, sometimes (even often) users and clients are one and the same. This is the case in most medical designs, for example.

2. Working in a Department of English, this feeling of the necessary ethical unworldliness of literary criticism similarly leads to students who have skill in research, analysis, empathy, and writing but don't know how to get paid.

3. Even in internships, this direct understanding of client work can be hidden from students; interns (like low-level designers in large firms) rarely work directly with clients.

4. Caricatured because neither Rand, Rams, nor Jobs created in isolation.

5. Indeed, I've specifically chosen Lux, Grant, and Mason because of their small freelance businesses and early-career status. In smaller firms and freelance positions, as reported by Kolleeny and Linn, early-career professionals are much more likely to directly interact with clients than in large companies. And, as Dana Cuff reports in her 1992 book *Architecture: A Story of Practice*: "Most architects do not practice in

corporate-sized organizations: of the 25,000 firms that have one or more employees, half have fewer than five employees; fewer than 10 percent of firms in America have 20 or more employees. Remarkably, there are only 250 firms in the United States with over 50 persons" (155).

6. Aristotle limits ethos to artistic appeals of credibility inside speeches—a speaker's preexisting credibility isn't ethos. I'm more encompassing when I refer to the term, thinking about how trust is created before and after interactions.

7. Including the lax safety checks, under-regulation, and under-preparedness that led to the crisis in the first place.

8. Cheng et al. explain that "designers create more original designs when the presented examples contain more abstract information" (376).

9. Indeed, in 2008 Microsoft published a longitudinal research report on the effect that Googling symptoms has on people's psyche. In doing so, they coined the term "cyberchondria" to describe how, "results show that web search engines have the potential to escalate medical concerns," causing health anxiety that lasts long after the initial search (White and Horvitz). Cyberchondria causes patients to visit their doctor sooner.

10. Bryan Weber et al. report a gap between the huge number of patients that use the internet to look up symptoms and the small number that discuss their findings with a doctor: "Eighty-six percent of adult patients use the Internet for answers to health-related questions (Bylund et al. 2007). However, the percentage of patients who consult with primary health care providers about information from the Internet is estimated at approximately 28%-41%" (1371). This gap suggests that doctors, like Mason, might more often engage the other sources of medical expertise in which patients base their healthcare decisions.

11. There's a deep tradition of researching voice in composition studies that nuance my claims here. The instrumentalist view of voice (from Cicero to Strunk and White) argues that style is decoration to a preexisting thought: "Ideas exist wordlessly and can be dressed in a variety of outfits, depending on the need for the occasion," but those outfits do not fundamentally change the composer's idea (Milic 141). In contrast, the deterministic view (from Quintilian to Hugh Blair to Robert Kaplan) correlates style directly with ideology. As LuMing Mao argues, "Alternative discourses . . . are less acceptable or less valued not because their discursive tendencies are deficient, but because the ideologies they are grounded in challenge the dominate ideology" (115). Finally, social constructivist theories of style see voice as performative. Such a claim for performativity is forcefully seen when Jacqueline Jones Royster's colleague applauds, "How wonderful it was that you were willing to share with us your 'authentic voice,'" to which Royster longs to respond, "All my voices are authentic" ("When the First" 1123, 1124).

## Chapter 6: Nostalgic UX

1. Though the amount of money universities receive from donors and alumni keeps increasing, the number of alumni donating decreases. From 1990 to 2013, for instance, the percentage of graduates who donated to their universities was halved, from 18 to 9 percent (Allenby 26).

2. An earlier version of this chapter appeared as "Memorial Interactivity: Scaffolding Nostalgic User Experiences" in Liza Potts and Michael Salvo's edited collection *Rhetoric and Information Architecture*. In that chapter, I call this concept "memorial interactivity," but, as you saw in the last chapter, I've shuffled these terms a bit.

3. Emily Keightley and Michael Pickering explain this difference: "Erlebnis and Efahrung, where the former refers to immediate experience in the moment it is lived, and the latter to the point where experience is evaluated and the process through which we learn from accumulated experience in our biographical journey. The contrast is between a moment in time and movement across time, with the movement involving the cumulative quality of crystallised knowledge" (26–27).

4. This feeling of authenticity, which involves some discomfort, is related to philosopher Jane Bennett's "enchantment": "Surprise itself includes both a pleasant, charming feeling and a slightly off-putting sense of having been disrupted. . . . In enchantment, these two are present in just the right measures so as to combine, fortuitously, in a way that engenders an energizing feeling of fullness and plentitude. . . . Enchantment begins with the step-back immobilization of surprise but ends with a mobilizing rush" (104).

5. This method of word of mouth is not perfect. Sarit Moldovan et al. describe that in order to protect the uniqueness of their brand, early adopters of products sometimes deploy a "share and scare" tactic—telling others about the delight of the product while simultaneously scaring them away from trying it by mentioning negative features like high price, danger, etc.

6. The statistics on slacktivism tell a much different story than the term implies: slacktivists are two times more likely to volunteer, two times more likely to ask for donations, and "four times more likely to encourage others to sign a petition" (Sortable). See also Stephanie Vie's "In Defense of 'Slacktivism': The Human Rights Campaign Facebook Logo as Digital Activism."

7. Interestingly, nostalgia for analog music began almost immediately after the CD was introduced into popular culture; see David Lander's 1983 *Rolling Stone* lament "Digital Discontent."

8. In 2017 Sweden sought to boost such repair and care economies. Swedish repair services for products from bikes to shoes are now taxed at a lower rate. Individuals even receive income tax breaks when they repair broken items themselves.

# References

Aaker, J., et al. "If Money Doesn't Make You Happier, Consider Time." *Journal of Consumer Psychology*, vol. 21, no. 2, 2011, pp. 126–30.

AAUW Educational Foundation Commission on Technology, Gender, and Teacher Education. *Tech-Savvy: Educating Girls in the Computer Age.* American Association of University Women Educational Foundation, 2000.

Adamson, Glenn. *Thinking Through Craft.* Bloomsbury Academic, 2007.

Ahmed, Sara. *The Cultural Politics of Emotion.* Routledge, 2004.

Allenby, Dan. "Class Exodus." *AlumniParticipation*, 2014, pp. 26–30. annualgiving.com/wp-content/uploads/2014/11/Class-Exodus_Currents_October-2014.pdf.

Akhtar, Salman. "The Immigrant, the Exile, and the Experience of Nostalgia." *Journal of Applied Psychoanalytic Studies*, vol. 1, no. 2, 1999, pp. 123–30.

Alexander, Jonathan, and Julia R. Lupton. "Letter from the Editor." *Computers and Composition*, vol. 33, 2014, pp. v–xv.

Almquist, Julka, and Julia Lupton. "Affording Meaning: Design-Oriented Research from the Humanities and Social Sciences." *Design Issues*, vol. 26, no. 1, 2010, pp. 3–14.

Alvesson, Mats. "Unpacking the Client(s): Constructions, Positions and Client–Consultant Dynamics." *Scandinavian Journal of Management*, 2009, vol. 25, no. 3, pp. 253–63.

Andersen, Kurt. *Fantasyland: How America Went Haywire: A 500-Year History.* Random House, 2017.

Anderson, David E. "British Peace Women: 'We're Just Ordinary Mums.'" United Press International, 1 Mar. 1983, www.upi.com/Archives/1983/03/01/British-peace-women-Were-just-ordinary-mums/9606415342800/.

Anders, George. *You Can Do Anything: The Surprising Power of a "Useless" Liberal Arts Education.* Little, Brown and Company, 2017.

Apel, Heino. "The Future Workshop." 2004, www.die-bonn.de/publikationen/online-texte/index.asp.

"April 28 2015 California Senate Judiciary Hearing SB277." *YouTube*, uploaded by Kara Rhodes Kitano, 28 Apr. 2015, www.youtube.com/watch?v=oKvlYrT7gec.

"Are We There Yet?" *This American Life,* narrated by Ira Glass, National Public Radio, 29 July 2016.

Aristotle. *On Rhetoric: A Theory of Civic Discourse.* Translated by George A. Kennedy, 2nd ed., Oxford UP, 2007.

Aristotle. *Politics.* Translated by Ernest Baker, Oxford UP, 1995.

Asch, David A., et al. "Omission Bias and Pertussis Vaccination." *Medical Decision Making,* vol. 14, no. 2, 1994, pp. 118-23.

Assmann, Jan, and Aleida Assmann. *Schrift und Gedächtnis: Beiträge zur Archäologie der literarischen Kommunikation.* Fink, 1987.

Austin, John R. "Transactive Memory in Organizational Groups: The Effects of Content, Consensus, Specialization, and Accuracy on Group Performance." *Journal of Applied Psychology,* vol. 88, no. 5, 2003, pp. 866-78.

Autistic Self Advocacy Network. "Position Statements." autisticadvocacy.org/home/about-asan/position-statements/.

Ball, Linden, et al. "Cognitive Processes in Engineering Design: A Longitudinal Study." *Ergonomics,* vol. 37, 1994, pp. 1753-86.

Banks, Adam. *Digital Griots: African American Rhetoric in a Multimodal Age.* SIU P, 2011.

Barbrook, Richard, and Pit Schultz. "'Digital Artisans Manifesto,' European Digital Artisans Network." *The Craft Reader,* edited by Glenn Adamson, Berg Publishers, 2010, pp. 317-20.

Barron, Brigid. "Learning Ecologies for Technological Fluency: Gender and Experience Differences." *Journal of Educational Computing Research,* vol. 31, no. 1, 2004, pp. 1-36.

Bartholeyns, Gil. "The Instant Past: Nostalgia and Digital Retro Photography." *Media and Nostalgia: Yearning for the Past, Present and Future,* edited by Katharina Niemeyer, Springer, 2014, pp. 51-69.

Barton, David. *Literacy: An Introduction to the Ecology of Written Language.* 2nd ed., Blackwell Publishing, 2007.

Bateson, Gregory. *Steps to an Ecology of the Mind.* U of Chicago P, 1972.

Beekmans, Jeroen. "Trend 2: Secret Urbanism And New Exclusivity." *Pop Up City,* 25 Jan. 2015, popupcity.net/trend-2-secret-urbanism-and-new-exclusivity.

Benjamin, Walter. "The Work of Art in the Age of Mechanical Reproduction." *Illuminations: Essays and Reflections,* Schocken, 1969.

Bennett, Jane. *The Enchantment of Modern Life: Attachments, Crossings, and Ethics.* Princeton UP, 2001.

Berkowitz, Joe. "How Mitch Hurwitz Revived 'Arrested Development' on Netflix, and Why the Show Belongs There." *Fast Company,* 23 May 2015.

Björgvinsson, Erling, et al. "Agonistic Participatory Design: Working with Marginalised Social Movements." *CoDesign: International Journal of CoCreation in Design and the Arts,* vol. 8, no. 2-3, 2012, pp. 127-44.

Black, Anthea, and Nicole Burisch. "Craft Hard Die Free: Radical Curatorial Strategies for Craftivism." *Extra/Ordinary: Craft and Contemporary Art,* edited by Maria Elena Buszek, Duke UP, 2011, pp. 204–21.

Blackwell, Alan. "The Reification of Metaphor as a Design Tool." *ACM Transactions on Computer-Human Interaction,* vol. 13, no. 4, 2006, pp. 490–530.

Blomquist, Åsa, and Mattias Arvola. "Personas in Action: Ethnography in an Interaction Design Team." *Conference: Proceedings of the Second Nordic Conference on Human-Computer Interaction,* 2002, pp. 197–200.

Bødker, Susanne, et al. "A Utopian Experience: On Design of Powerful Computer-Based Tools for Skilled Graphical Workers." *Computers and Democracy—A Scandinavian Challenge,* edited by G. Bjerknes, P. Ehn, and M. Kyng, Gower, 1987, pp. 251–78.

Boehner, Kirsten, et al. "How HCI Interprets the Probes." *Proceedings of the SIGCHI Conference on Human Factors in Computing Systems,* 2007, pp. 1077–86.

Bonilla, Yarimar, and Jonathan Rosa. "#Ferguson: Digital Protest, Hashtag Ethnography, and the Racial Politics of Social Media in the United States." *American Ethnologist,* vol. 00, no. 0, 2015, pp. 4–16.

Bonnett, Alastair. *Left in the Past: Radicalism and the Politics of Nostalgia.* Continuum, 2010.

Bonsiepe, Gui. "Persuasive Communication: Towards a Visual Rhetoric." *Uppercase 5,* edited by Theo Crosby, Whitefriars Press, 1963, pp. 19–34.

Bowen, Robert. "How to Convince the Client That Your Design Is Perfect." *Smashing Magazine,* 6 Oct. 2010, www.smashingmagazine.com/2010/10/how-to-convince -the-client-that-your-design-is-perfect/.

Boym, Svetlana. *The Future of Nostalgia.* Basic Books, 2001.

Boym, Svetlana. "Nostalgia and Its Discontents." *The Collective Memory Reader,* edited by Jeffrey Olick, et al., Oxford UP, 2011, pp. 452–57.

Brandt, Deborah. *The Rise of Writing: Redefining Mass Literacy.* Cambridge UP, 2014.

Brandt, Deborah. "Sponsors of Literacy." *College Composition and Communication,* vol. 49, no. 2, 1998, pp. 165–85.

Bratich, Jack Z., and Heidi M. Brush. "Fabricating Activism: Craft-Work, Popular Culture, Gender." *Utopian Studies,* vol. 2, no. 2, 2011, pp. 233–60.

"Breaking Down Ideological Battle Lines." *RadioTimes,* hosted by Marty Moss-Coane, 23 May 2017.

Brisebras, Thomas. "No Coaster Please." *DesignsOn,* IDEO, www.designs-on.com/ time/no-coaster-please/.

Brizee, H. Allen. "Stasis Theory as a Strategy for Workplace Teaming and Decision Making." *Journal of Technical Writing and Communication,* vol. 38, no. 4, 2008, pp. 363–85.

Broockman, David, and Joshua Kalla. "Durably Reducing Transphobia: A Field Experiment on Door-to-Door Canvassing." *Science,* vol. 352, no. 6282, 2016, pp. 220–24.

Brooke, Robert. "Underlife and Writing Instruction." *College Composition and Communication*, vol. 38, no. 2, 1987, pp. 141–53.

Brown, Katrina, et al. "Omission Bias and Vaccine Rejection by Parents of Healthy Children: Implications for the Influenza A/H1N1 Vaccination Programme." *Vaccine*, vol. 28, no. 25, 2010, pp. 4181–85.

Brown, Stephen, et al. "Sell Me the Old, Old Story: Retromarketing Management and the Art of Brand Revival." *Journal of Customer Behavior*, vol. 2, 2003, pp. 85–98.

Brown, Tim. *Change by Design*. Harper Collins, 2009.

Bryson, Krista. *The Rhetorics of Advocacy in Appalachia*. Dissertation, The Ohio State University, 2015.

Buchanan, Richard. "Declaration by Design: Rhetoric, Argument, and Demonstration in Design Practice." *Design Issues*, vol. 2, no. 1, 1985, pp. 4–22.

Buchanan, Richard. "Design and the New Rhetoric: Productive Arts in the Philosophy of Culture." *Philosophy and Rhetoric*, vol. 34, no. 3, 2001, pp. 183–206.

Buchanan, Richard. "Human Dignity and Human Rights: Thoughts on the Principles of Human-Centered Design." *Design Issues*, vol. 17, no. 3, Summer 2001, pp. 35–39.

Buchanan, Richard. "Rhetoric, Humanism, and Design." *Discovering Design: Explorations in Design Studies*, edited by Richard Buchanan and Victor Margolin, U of Chicago P, 1995, pp. 23–68.

Budweiser. "Brewed the Hard Way" commercial. *YouTube*, uploaded by Six Fifty ml, 3 Feb. 2015, https://www.youtube.com/watch?v=2uJKhkwTG64.

Buley, Leah. *The User Experience Team of One: A Research and Design Survival Guide*. Rosenfeld, 2013.

Burke, Kenneth. *Attitudes toward History*. U of California P, 1937.

Burke, Kenneth. *A Grammar of Motives*. U of California P, 1945.

Burke, Kenneth. *Language as Symbolic Action*. U of California P, 1966.

Burke, Kenneth. *The Philosophy of Literary Form*. U of California P, 1973.

Burke, Kenneth. *A Rhetoric of Motives*. U of California P, 1950.

Burke, Peter. "History as Social Memory." *Memory, History, Culture and the Mind*, edited by Thomas E. Butler, Blackwell, 1989, pp. 97–113.

Burton, Neel. "A Study of Wonder." *Psychology Today*, 2 Dec. 2014, www.psychologytoday.com/blog/hide-and-seek/201412/study-wonder.

Bush, Robert A., and Joseph P. Folger. *The Promise of Mediation: The Transformative Approach to Conflict*. 2nd ed., Wiley, 2004.

Buszek, Maria Elena, editor. *Extra/Ordinary: Craft and Contemporary Art*. Duke UP, 2011.

Butler, Peggy O. (@iPeggy). "Yikes! I'm a girl & actually know OS Assembler language & have 'hacked' your MVS operating systems. Try again please!" *Twitter*, 7 Dec. 2015, 9:19 a.m., twitter.com/iPeggy/status/673884574921936896.

Cabannes, Yves. "From Community Development and *Mutirao* to Housing Finance and *Casa Melhor* in Fortaleza, Brazil." *Environment and Urbanization*, vol. 9, no. 1, 1997, pp. 31–58.

Cahill, Lisa. "Reflection on Peer-Review Practices." *Strategies for Teaching First-Year Composition*, edited by Duane Roen et al., NCTE, 2002, pp. 301–06.

California Department of Public Health. "California's Kindergarten Vaccination Rates Hits New High." 4 Apr. 2017, www.cdph.ca.gov/Programs/OPA/Pages/NR17-032.aspx.

Candy, Linda, and Brigid Costello. "Interaction Design and Creative Practice." *Design Studies*, vol. 29, no. 6, 2008, pp. 521–24.

Carlile, Paul R. "A Pragmatic View of Knowledge and Boundaries: Boundary Objects in New Product Development." *Organization Science*, vol. 13, no. 4, 2002, pp. 442–55.

Casakin, Hernan Pablo. "Metaphors in Design Problem Solving: Implications for Creativity." *International Journal of Design*, vol. 1, no. 2, 2007, pp. 21–33.

Casey, Edward. "Public Memory in Place and Time." *Framing Public Memory*, edited by Kendall Phillips, U of Alabama P, 2004, pp. 17–45.

Castiglione, Baldesar. *The Book of the Courtier*. Penguin Books, 1967.

CCC. "Students' Right to Their Own Language." *College Composition and Communication*, vol. 25, no. 3, 1974, updated 2003, www.ncte.org/cccc/resources/positions/srtolsummary.

CDC. "Monitoring the Impact of Varicella Vaccination." *Centers for Disease Control*, 1 July 2016, www.cdc.gov/chickenpox/surveillance/monitoring-varicella.html.

Ceccarelli, Leah. "Manufactured Scientific Controversy: Science, Rhetoric, and Public Debate." *Rhetoric and Public Affairs*, vol. 14, no. 2, 2011, pp. 195–228.

Chachra, Debbie. "Why I Am Not a Maker: When Tech Culture Only Celebrates Creation, It Risks Ignoring Those Who Teach, Criticize, and Take Care of Others." *The Atlantic*, 23 Jan. 2015.

Chan, Chiu-Shui. "An Examination of The Forces that Generate a Style." *Design Studies*, vol. 22, no. 4, 2001, pp. 319–46.

Charon, Rita. *Narrative Medicine: Honoring the Stories of Illness*. Oxford UP, 2006.

Chen, N., et al. "Place, Time and The Virtual Design Studio." *ACADIA '94*, 1994, pp. 115–32.

Cheng, Peiyao, et al. "A New Strategy to Reduce Design Fixation: Presenting Partial Photographs to Designers." *Design Studies*, vol. 35, no. 4, 2014, pp. 374–91.

Chicago, Judy. *Through the Flower: My Struggle as a Woman Artist*. Author's Choice Press, 2006.

Children's Medical Center. "Vaccinations." 2017, cmcpediatrics.com/programs/vaccination/.

Chipchase, Jan. "The Anthropology of Mobile Phones." *TED*, Mar. 2007, www.ted.com/talks/jan_chipchase_on_our_mobile_phones.

Cho, Erin, and Youn-Kyung Kim. "The Effects of Website Designs, Self-Congruity, and Flow on Behavioral Intention." *International Journal of Design*, vol. 6, no. 2, 2012, pp. 31–39.

Christen, Kimberly. "Gone Digital: Aboriginal Remix and the Cultural Commons." *International Journal of Cultural Property*, no. 12, 2005, pp. 315–45.

Church, Scott H. "Digital Gravescapes: Digital Memorializing on Facebook." *The Information Society*, vol. 29, 2013, pp. 184–89.

Cialdini, Robert. *Pre-Suasion: A Revolutionary Way to Influence and Persuade.* Simon and Schuster, 2016.

Citelli, Anna, and Raoul Bretzel. *Capsula Mundi.* www.capsulamundi.it/en/.

Civic Alliance. *Listening to the City: Report of Proceedings.* 2002, www.icisnyu.org/admin/files/ListeningtoCity.pdf.

"Clear RX Medication System." *Adler Design.* www.adlerdesign.com/project/clear-rx-medication-system/.

Clemmensen, T. "Four Approaches to User Modelling—A Qualitative Research Interview Study of HCI Professionals' Practice." *Human Computer Interaction in Latin America*, vol. 16, no. 4, 2004, 799–829.

Clinton, Hillary (@hillaryclinton). "The science is clear: The earth is round, the sky is blue, and #vaccineswork. Let's protect all our kids. #GrandmothersKnowBest." *Twitter*, 2 Feb. 2015, 7:45 p.m., twitter.com/HillaryClinton/status/562456798020386816.

Clynes, Manfred. *Sentics: The Touch of the Emotions.* Anchor Press, 1978.

Collins, Harry. *Are We All Scientific Experts Now?* New Human Frontiers, 2014.

Condit, Celeste Michelle. "The Rhetorical Construction of Public Morality." *Quarterly Journal of Speech*, vol. 73, no. 1, 1987, pp. 79–97.

Coombes, Rebecca. "Vaccine Disputes." *British Medical Journal*, vol. 338, 2009, pp. 1528–31.

Coontz, Stephanie. *The Way We Never Were: American Families and the Nostalgia Trap.* Basic Books, 2016.

Cope, Bill, and Mary Kalantzis, editors. *Multiliteracies: Literacy Learning and the Design of Social Futures.* Routledge, 2000.

Covert, Bryce. "A Job at McDonald's Now Includes Singing and Dancing on Demand." *The Nation*, 2 Feb. 2015, www.thenation.com/article/job-mcdonalds-now-includes-singing-and-dancing-demand/.

Covino, William A. *Magic, Rhetoric, and Literacy: An Eccentric History of the Composing Imagination.* SUNY P, 1995.

Coxon, Ian. "An Ecology of Care." *YouTube*, uploaded by tedxtalks, 1 Apr. 2016, www.youtube.com/watch?v=A_TlURzWzrs.

Coxon, Ian. "Fundamental Aspects of Human Experience: A Phenomo(logical) Explanation." *Experience Design: Concepts and Case Studies*, edited by Peter Benz, Bloomsbury, 2015, pp. 11–22.

Crawford, Matthew. *Shop Class as Soulcraft: An Inquiry into the Value of Work.* Penguin, 2010.

Crawford, Robert. "Healthism and the Medicalization of Everyday Life." *International Journal of Health Services*, vol. 10, no. 3, 1980, pp. 365–88.

Cree. "Cree Led Light Bulbs 1879 USA" commercial. *YouTube,* uploaded by PERPER-IDIS SPYRIDONAS, 30 June 2013, www.youtube.com/watch?v=LPn8EodTjQA.

Crowley, Sharon. *Toward a Civil Discourse: Rhetoric and Fundamentalism.* U of Pittsburgh P, 2006.

Csikszentmihalyi, Mihaly. *Flow: The Psychology of Optimal Experience.* Harper and Row, 1990.

Csikszentmihalyi, Mihaly and Eugene Halton. *The Meaning of Things: Domestic Symbols and the Self.* Cambridge UP, 1981.

Cuff, Dana. *Architecture: The Story of Practice.* MIT P, 1991.

Cuff, Dana. "The Ethos and Circumstance of Design." *Journal of Architectural and Planning Research,* vol. 6, no. 4, 1989, pp. 305–20.

Curtis, Diane. "Suit Challenges 'Progress at Any Cost.'" *The Argus-Press,* 26 Mar. 1984, news.google.com/newspapers?nid=1988&dat=19840326&id=UEIiAAAAIBAJ &sjid=UK0FAAAAIBAJ&pg=1184,2106995.

Cytowic, Richard, and David Eagleman. *Wednesday is Indigo Blue: Discovering the Brain of Synesthesia.* MIT P, 2011.

Damasio, Antonio. *Descartes' Error: Emotion, Reason, and the Human Brain.* Penguin Books, 2005.

Dant, Tim. *Materiality and Society.* Open UP, 2005.

Dator, Jim. "From Future Workshops to Envisioning Alternative Futures." *Futures Research Quarterly,* vol. 9, no. 3, 1993, pp. 108–12.

Davis, Fred. *Yearning for Yesterday: A Sociology of Nostalgia.* Free Press, 1979.

Davis, Stanley M. *Future Perfect.* Addison-Wesley, 1987.

Deacon, Aaron. "The Truth About Google Fiber and the Digital Divide in Kansas City." KC Digital Drive, 3 Apr. 2015.

De Certeau, Michel. *The Practice of Everyday Life.* U of California P, 1984.

Delagrange, Susan H. *Technologies of Wonder: Rhetorical Practice in a Digital World.* Computers and Composition Digital Press, 2011.

Delbanco, Tom, et al. "Open Notes: Doctors and Patients Signing On." *Annals of Internal Medicine,* vol. 153, no. 2, 2010, pp. 121–26.

Demir, Erdem, et al. "Appraisal Patterns of Emotions in Human-Product Interaction." *International Journal of Design,* vol. 3, no. 2, 2009, pp. 41–51.

Dennett, Daniel. *Intuition Pumps and Other Tools for Thinking.* Norton, 2013.

Derbaix, Christian, and Joëlle Vanhamme. "Inducing Word-of-Mouth by Eliciting Surprise? A Pilot Investigation." *IAG–LSM Working Papers,* 2001, pp. 1–36.

Derkatch, Colleen. "Does Biomedicine Control for Rhetoric? Configuring Practitioner-Patient Interaction." *Rhetorical Questions of Health and Medicine,* edited by J. Leach and D. Dysart-Gale, Lexington Books, 2011, pp. 129–53.

Derrida, Jacques. *Archive Fever: A Freudian Impression.* U of Chicago P, 1998.

Desmet, Pieter, and Paul Hekkert. "Special Issue Editorial: Design and Emotion." *International Journal of Design,* vol. 3, no. 2, 2009, pp. 1–6.

Detienne, Marcel, and Jean-Pierre Vernant. *Cunning Intelligence in Greek Culture and Society.* Translated by Janet Lloyd, Humanities Press, 1978.

Dindler, C., et al. "Mission from Mars." *Proceedings of the 2005 Conference on Interaction Design and Children,* 2005, pp. 40–47.

DiSalvo, Carl. *Adversarial Design.* MIT P, 2015.

DiSalvo, Carl. "Design, Democracy and Agonistic Pluralism." *Design and Complexity: Proceedings of the Design Research Society Conference,* edited by D. Durling, 2010, Université de Montréal.

DiSalvo, Carl, et al. "Toward a Public Rhetoric through Participatory Design: Critical Engagements and Creative Expression in the Neighborhood Networks Project." *Design Issues,* vol. 28, no. 3, 2012, pp. 48–61.

Dissanayake, Ellen. "The Pleasure and Meaning of Making." *American Craft,* vol. 55, no. 2, 1995, pp. 40–45.

Dolmage, Jay. "Metis, Mêtis, Mestiza, Medusa: Rhetorical Bodies across Rhetorical Traditions." *Rhetoric Review,* vol. 28, no. 1, 2009, pp. 1–28.

"Donald Trump Rally in Charleston, West Virginia." *YouTube,* posted by West Virginia Public Broadcasting, 6 May 2016, www.youtube.com/watch?v=1xtynB-kb24.

Donati, Kelly. "The Pleasure of Diversity in Slow Food's Ethics of Taste." *Food Culture and Society an International Journal of Multidisciplinary Research,* 2005, pp. 227–42.

Dunne, Anthony, and Fiona Raby. *Speculative Everything: Design, Fiction, and Social Dreaming.* MIT P, 2013.

Eagen, Ward M., et al. "The Design Charrette in the Classroom as a Method for Outcomes-Based Action Learning in IS Design." *Information Systems Education Journal,* vol. 6, no. 19, 2008.

Eckert, C. M., et al. "Shared Conversations Across Design." *Design Issues,* vol. 26, no. 3, 2010, pp. 27–39.

Ehn, Pelle. *Work-Oriented Design of Computer Artifacts.* Lawrence Erlbaum Associates, 1989.

Ehn, Pelle, et al. *Making Futures: Marginal Notes on Innovation, Design, and Democracy.* MIT P, 2014.

Ehn, Pelle, and Morten Kyng. "The Collective Resource Approach to Systems Design." *Computers and Democracy: A Scandinavian Challenge,* edited by G. Bjerknes, P. Ehn, and M. Kyng, Gower, 1987, pp. 17–58.

Ehrenreich, Barbara, and Deirdre English. *Witches, Midwives & Nurses: A History of Women Healers.* The Feminist Press, 1973.

Emilson, Anders, and Per-Anders Hillgren. "Connecting with the Powerful Strangers: From Governance to Agonistic Design Things." *Making Futures: Marginal Notes on Innovation, Design, and Democracy,* edited by Pelle Ehn, et al., MIT P, 2014, pp. 63–84.

Emilson, Anders, et al. "Designing in the Neighborhood: Beyond (and in the Shadow of) Creative Communities." *Making Futures: Marginal Notes on Innovation, Design, and Democracy*, edited by Pelle Ehn, et al., MIT P, 2014, pp. 35–61.

Engel, George. "The Need for a New Medical Model: A Challenge for Biomedicine." *Science*, vol. 196, no. 4286, 1977, pp.129–36.

Erll, Astrid. *Memory in Culture*. Palgrave Macmillan, 2011.

European Commission. "Factsheet on the 'Right to be Forgotten' Ruling." ec.europa .eu/justice/data-protection/files/factsheets/factsheet_data_protection_en.pdf.

Eyal, Nir. *Hooked: How to Build Habit-Forming Products*. Penguin, 2014.

Faga, Barbara. *Designing Public Consensus: The Civic Theater of Community Participation for Architects, Landscape Architects, Planners, and Urban Designers*. Wiley, 2006.

"Farm." *Portlandia*, season 1, episode 1, IFC, 21 Jan. 2011.

Farrell, Thomas B. "The Tradition of Rhetoric and the Philosophy of Communications." *Communication*, vol. 7, 1983, pp. 151–80.

Featherstone, M. *Consumer Culture and Postmodernism*. Sage, 1991.

Federici, Silvia. *Caliban and the Witch*. Autonomedia, 2004.

Feenberg, Andrew. *Between Reason and Experience: Essays on Technology and Modernity*. MIT P, 2010.

Feenberg, Andrew. "Democratic Rationalization: Technology, Power and Freedom." *Dogma*, www.dogma.lu/txt/AF_democratic-rationalization.html.

Feinberg, Matthew, and Robb Willer. "The Moral Roots of Environmental Attitudes." *Psychological Science*, vol. 24, no.1, 2013, pp. 56–62.

Feygina, I., et al. "System Justification, the Denial of Global Warming, and the Possibility of 'System-Sanctioned Change.'" *Personality and Social Psychology Bulletin*, vol. 36, no. 3, 2010, pp. 326–38.

Fields, Corey D. "Not Your Grandma's Knitting: The Role of Identity Processes in the Transformation of Cultural Practices." *Social Psychology Quarterly*, vol. 77, no. 2, 2014, pp. 150–65.

Fleckenstein, Kristie. "Cybernetics, *Ethos*, and Ethics: The Plight of the Bread-and -Butter-Fly." *Journal of Advanced Composition*, vol. 25, no. 2, 2005, pp. 323–46.

Fleming, David. "Design Talk: Constructing the Object in Studio Conversations." *Design Issues*, vol. 14, no. 2, 1998, pp. 41–62.

Forester, John. "Beyond Dialogue to Transformative Learning: How Deliberative Rituals Encourage Political Judgment in Community Planning Processes." *Political Dialogue: Theories and Practices*, edited by Stephen Esquith, Rodpoi, 1996, pp. 295–334.

Forester, John. *The Deliberative Practitioner: Encouraging Participatory Planning Processes*. MIT P, 1999.

Foucault, Michel. *Discipline and Punish: The Birth of the Prison*. Pantheon, 1977.

Franch, Sage (@TheTrendyTechie). "How to make progress in equality: start treating women like modern human beings instead of the 1950s housewife trope.

#HackAHairDryer." *Twitter,* 7 Dec. 2015, 9:19 a.m., twitter.com/theTrendyTechie/status/673884583314657280.

Friedland, William H., and Amy Barton. "The Harvesting Machine Saved Tomatoes for California." *Society,* 1976, pp. 35–43.

Friess, Erin. "Personas as Rhetorically Rich and Complex Mechanism for Design." *Rhetoric and Experience Architecture,* edited by Liza Potts and Michael J. Salvo, Parlor Press, 2017, pp. 111–21.

Friess, Erin. "The Sword of Data: Does Human-Centered Design Fulfill Its Rhetorical Responsibility?" *Design Studies,* vol. 26, no. 3, 2010, pp. 40–50.

Fuad-Luke, Alastair. "Adjusting Our Metabolism: Slowness and Nourishing Rituals of Delay in Anticipation of a Post-Consumer Age." *Longer Lasting Products: Alternatives to the Throwaway Culture,* Routledge, 2010, pp. 133–55.

Fuad-Luke, Alastair. *Design Activism: Beautiful Strangeness for a Sustainable World.* Routledge, 2009.

Fukuhara, Shiho, and Georg Tremmel. *Biopresence: Human DNA Trees as Living Memorials.* www.biopresence.com/index.html.

Fuss, Diana. *Essentially Speaking: Feminism, Nature and Difference.* Routledge, 1989.

Gagnon, Caroline, and Valérie Côté. "Learning From Others: A Five-Year Experience on Teaching Empathic Design." *DRS 2014: Design's Big Debates.* Design Research Society Biennial International Conference, edited by Y-K Lim et al., Umeå Institute of Design, 2014.

Gardner, Jeff. "8 Strategies for Successful Relations with Clients." *Smashing Magazine,* 9 Oct. 2008, www.smashingmagazine.com/2008/10/strategies-for-successful-client-relations/.

Gauntlett, David. *Making Is Connecting: The Social Meaning of Creativity, from DIY and Knitting to YouTube and Web 2.0.* Polity, 2011.

Gaver, Bill, et al. "Design: Cultural Probes." *Interactions,* vol. 6, no. 1, 1999, pp. 21–29.

Gee, James, et al. *The New Work Order: Behind the Language of New Capitalism.* Westview Press, 1996.

Glenn, Cheryl. *Unspoken: A Rhetoric of Silence.* SIU P, 2004.

Goebert, Bonnie, and Herma Rosenthal. *Beyond Listening: Learning the Secret Language of Focus Groups.* Wiley, 2002.

Goffman, Erving. *Stigma: Notes on the Management of Spoiled Identity.* Simon and Schuster, 1986.

Goldstein, Jan. "Foucault among the Sociologists: The 'Disciplines' and the History of the Professions." *History and Theory,* vol. 23, no. 2, 1984, pp. 170–92.

Goldberg, Eleanor. "'Ice Bucket Challenge' Breaks $50 Million in ALS Donations (and Raises over $10 Million in 1 Day)." *Huffington Post,* 22 Aug. 2014.

Goodnight, Thomas G. "The Personal, Technical, and Public Spheres of Argument: A Speculive Inquiry into the Art of Public Deliberation." *Argumentation and Advocacy,* vol. 48, 2012, pp. 198–210.

Gosling, Samuel, et al. "A Room with a Cue: Personality Judgments Based on Offices and Bedrooms." *Journal of Personality and Social Psychology*, vol. 82, no. 3, 2002, pp. 379–98.

Graham, J., et al. "Liberals and Conservatives Rely on Different Sets of Moral Foundations." *Journal of Personality and Social Psychology*, vol. 96 no. 5, 2009, pp. 1029–46.

Grainge, Paul. *Monochrome Memories: Nostalgia and Style in Retro America*. Praeger Publishers, 2002.

Green, S. "A Metaphorical Analysis of Client Organisations and the Briefing Process." *Construction Management and Economics*, vol. 14, no. 2, 1996, pp. 155–64.

Greer, Betsy. "Craftivism." *Encyclopedia of Activism and Social Justice*, edited by Gary L. Anderson and Kathryn G. Herr, SAGE Publications, 2007.

Gross, A. G. "Why Hermagoras Still Matters: The Fourth Stasis and Interdisciplinarity." *Rhetoric Review*, vol. 23, no. 2, 2004, pp. 141–55.

Grosse-Hering, Barbara, et al. "Slow Design for Meaningful Interactions." *CHI '13 Proceedings of the SIGCHI Conference on Human Factors in Computing Systems*, 2013, pp. 3431–40.

Guaman Poma de Ayala, Felipe. *The First New Chronicle and Good Government*. Translated by Roland Hamilton, U of Texas P, 2009.

Haagsma, H. T., and J. G. Hoendervanger. "The Language of the Client versus the Language of the Architect in Workspace Design." Groningen, 2012.

Hackney, Fiona. "Quiet Activism and the New Amateur: The Power of Home and Hobby Crafts." *Design and Culture*, vol. 5, no. 2, 2013, pp. 169–93.

Hadler, Nortin. *By the Bedside of the Patient: Lessons for the Twenty-First-Century Physician*. U of North Carolina P, 2016.

Haidt, Jonathan. *The Righteous Mind: Why Good People Are Divided by Politics and Religion*. Vintage, 2013.Halbwachs, Maurice. *On Collective Memory*. U of Chicago P, 1992.

Hallnäs, Lars, and Johan Redström. "Slow Technology—Designing for Reflection." *Personal and Ubiquitous Computing*, vol. 5, 2001, pp. 201–12.

Halstead, Sarah. "Toward Community Innovation, Resilience and Sustainability." Create West Virginia, 28 Jun 2016, www.createwv.org/single-post/2016/06/28/Toward-Community-Innovation-Resilience-and-Sustainability.

Halstead, Sarah. "Wanted: Digital & Social Media Volunteers to Help Preserve Family History, Oral Histories, & Connect." Create West Virginia, 17 July 2016, www.createwv.org/single-post/2016/07/17/WANTED-DIGITAL-SOCIAL-Media-Volunteers-to-Help-Preserve-Family-History-Oral-Histories-Connect.

Hartelius, E. Johanna. *The Rhetoric of Expertise*. Lexington Books, 2010.

Hauser, Gerard. *Vernacular Voices: The Rhetoric of Publics and Public Spheres*. U of South Carolina P, 2008.

Hauser, Gerard, and Chantal Benoit-Barne. "Reflections on Rhetoric, Deliberative Democracy, Civil Society, and Trust." *Rhetoric & Public Affairs*, vol. 5, no. 2, 2002, pp. 261–75.

Heckathorn, Douglas. "Respondent-Driven Sampling and Deriving Valid Population Estimates from Chain Referral Samples of Hidden Populations." *Social Problems*, vol. 49, no. 1, 2002, pp. 11–34.

Heijdens, Simon. *Broken White / Blanc Cassée*. 2004.

Heilker, Paul. "Autism, Rhetoric, and Whiteness." *Disability Studies Quarterly*, vol. 32, no. 4, 2012.

Heilker, Paul, and Melanie Yergeau. "Autism and Rhetoric." *College English*, vol. 73, no. 5, 2011, pp. 485–97.

Heilman, C. M., et al. "Pleasant Surprises: Consumer Response to Unexpected In-Store Coupons." *Journal of Marketing Research*, vol. 39, no. 2, 2002, pp. 242–52.

Hepper, Erica, et al. "Pancultural Nostalgia: Prototypical Conceptions across Cultures." *Emotion*, vol. 14, no. 4, 2014, pp. 733–47.

Hertz, D. G. "Trauma and Nostalgia: New Aspects of the Coping of Aging Holocaust Survivors." *Israeli Journal of Psychiatry and Related Sciences*, vol. 27, 1990, 189–98.

Hobsbawm, Eric. *The Invention of Tradition*. Cambridge UP, 2012.

Hoey, Brian. "Capitalizing on Distinctiveness: Creating WV for a New Economy." *Journal of Appalachian Studies*, vol. 21, no. 1, 2015, pp. 64–85.

Hofer, Johannes. "Medical Dissertation on Nostalgia." First published 1688. Translated by Carolyn K. Anspach, *Bulletin of the History of Medicine*, vol. 2, 1934, pp. 376–91.

Holbrook, Morris, and Robert Schindler. "Nostalgic Bonding: Exploring the Role of Nostalgia in the Consumption Experience." *Journal of Consumer Behaviour*, vol. 3, no. 2, pp. 107–27.

Hollwich, Matthias. "Can Architecture Help the Elderly Age Gracefully?" Interview by Jenara Nerenberg. *CO.Design*, www.fastcodesign.com/1662258/can-architecture-help-the-elderly-age-gracefully.

Hornby, Nick. *High Fidelity*. New York: Riverhead Books, 1996.

"How My Son Spread the Measles." *Time*, 25 May 2008, content.time.com/time/health/article/0,8599,1809403,00.html.

HRSA. "Data and Statistics." U.S. Department Health and Human Services, 1 Sep. 2015, www.hrsa.gov/vaccinecompensation/data/.

Hsu, Eric L., and Anthony Elliott. "Social Acceleration Theory and the Self." *Journal for the Theory of Social Behavior*, vol. 45, no. 4, 2014, pp. 397–418.

Hui, Mary. "After Protests, Princeton Debates Woodrow Wilson's Legacy." *The Washington Post*, 21 Nov. 2015, www.washingtonpost.com/news/grade-point/wp/2015/11/23/after-protests-princeton-debates-woodrow-wilsons-legacy/.

Hulkko, S., et al. "Mobile Probes." *Proceedings of the Third Nordic Conference on Human-Computer Interaction*, ACM Press, 2004, pp. 43–51.

Huppatz, D. J. "Designer Nostalgia in Hong Kong." *Design Issues*, vol. 25, no. 2, 2009, pp. 14–28.

Hutcheon, Linda. "Irony, Nostalgia, and the Postmodern." *University of Toronto English Library*, 19 Jan. 1998.

Hutcheon, Linda, and Mario J. Valdés. "Irony, Nostalgia, and the Postmodern: A Dialogue." *Poligrafías 3 (1998-2000)*, pp. 18-41.

Hutchinson, Thomas, editor. *Whole Person Care. A New Paradigm for the 21st Century.* Springer, 2011.

Hutchinson, Tom, and James Brawer. "The Challenge of Medical Dichotomies and the Congruent Physician-Patient Relationship in Medicine." *Whole Person Care: A New Paradigm for the 21st Century*, edited by Tom Hutchinson, Springer, 2011, pp. 31-44.

Huyssen, Andreas. *Twilight Memories: Marking Time in a Culture of Amnesia.* Routledge, 1995.

IDEO. "Design Researcher (IDEO New York)." www.ideo.com/jobs.

Irvine, Judith, and Susan Gal. "Language Ideology and Linguistic Differentiation." *Regimes of Language: Ideologies, Polities, and Identities*, edited by Paul Kroskrity, School of American Research P, 2000, pp. 35-83.

Jameson, Fredric. "Future City." *New Left Review*, vol. 21, 2003.

Jameson, Fredric. *Postmodernism or, The Cultural Logic of Late Capitalism.* Duke UP, 1991.

Jameson, Fredric. "Walter Benjamin, or Nostalgia." *Salmagundi*, vol. 10/11, Fall 1969-Winter 1970, pp. 52-68.

Jansson, D., and Smith, S. "Design Fixation." *Design Studies*, vol. 12, no. 1, 1991, pp. 3-11.

"Jenny McCarthy and Holly Robinson Peete Fight to Save Their Autistic Sons." *The Oprah Winfrey Show*, Chicago, 18 Sep. 2007.

"Jenny McCarthy's Autism Fight." *Larry King Live*, CNN, 2 Apr. 2008.

Jenss, Heike. *Fashioning Memory: Vintage Style and Youth Culture.* Bloomsbury Academic, 2017.

Jjo54321. "If only. . . ." *Amazon.* 28 Aug. 2012.

Johnson, Robert R. *User-Centered Technology: A Rhetorical Theory for Computers and Other Mundane Artifacts.* State University of New York P, 2008.

Jones, Abbey, et al. "Parents' Source of Vaccine Information and Impact on Vaccine Attitudes, Beliefs, and Nonmedical Exemptions." *Advances in Preventative Medicine*, vol. 2012, pp. 1-8.

Jones, Joshua A. "From Nostalgia to Post-Traumatic Stress Disorder: A Mass Society Theory of Psychological Reactions to Combat." *Inquiries*, vol. 5, no. 2, 2013, pp. 1-31.

Jørgensen, Marianne. "Pink M.24 Chaffee: A Tank Wrapped in Pink." *Pink M.24 Chaffee*, marianneart.dk/.

Jungk, Robert, and Müllert, Norbert. *Future Workshops: How to Create Desirable Futures.* Institute for Social Inventions, 1987.

Jurgensen, John. "Binge Viewing: TV's Lost Weekends." *The Wall Street Journal*, 13 July 2012, www.wsj.com/articles/SB10001424052702303740704577521300806686174.

Kahneman, Daniel. *Thinking, Fast and Slow*. Farrar, Straus, and Giroux, 2011.

Kalan, Molly. "Expressions of Grief on Facebook: The Complicated Nature of Online Memorialization for the Bereaved." *Interface*, vol. 1, no. 1, 2015, pp. 1-15.

Kalay, Yehuda, et al. "Designer-Client Relationships in Architectural and Software Design." *Computing in Design—Enabling, Capturing and Sharing Ideas: ACADIA Conference Proceedings*, U of Washington P, 1995, pp. 383-403.

Kantor, Jodi, and David Streitfeld. "Inside Amazon: Wrestling Big Ideas in a Bruising Workplace." *New York Times*, 15 Aug. 2015.

Kaphar, Titus. "Can Art Amend History?" *TED2017*, Apr. 2017.

Kaptchuck, T. J., and D. M. Eisenberg. "The Persuasive Appeal of Alternative Medicine." *Annals of Internal Medicine*, vol. 129, no. 12, 1998, pp. 1061-65.

Keightley, Emily, and Michael Pickering. *The Mnemonic Imagination: Remembering as Creative Practice*. Palgrave Macmillan, 2012.

"Kid Politics." *This American Life*, narrated by Ira Glass, National Public Radio, 14 Jan. 2011.

Kirkland, Anna. "Credibility Battles in the Autism Litigation." *Social Studies of Science*, vol. 42, no. 2, 2012, pp. 237-61.

Kolleeny, Jane. F, and Charles Linn. "Lessons from the Best-Managed Firms: Small, Medium, and Large: Size Affects Firm Culture." *Architectural Record*, vol. 190, no. 6, 2002, pp. 1-6.

Kolodziejski, Lauren R. "Harms of Hedging in Scientific Discourse: Andrew Wakefield and the Origins of the Autism Vaccine Controversy." *Technical Communication Quarterly*, vol. 23, no. 3, 2013, pp. 165-83.

Kolstad, Charles D. "What Is Killing the Coal Industry?" *Stanford Institute for Economic Policy Research*, Mar. 2017, siepr.stanford.edu/research/publications/what-killing-us-coal-industry.

Koskinen, Ilpo, et al., editors. *Empathic Design: User Experience in Product Design*. IT Press, 2003.

Kraft, Jessica Carew. "Who Is a Maker?" *Bright*, 5 Oct. 2015, medium.com/bright/who-is-a-maker-603aca72118f#.r03anqe1b.

Krippendorff, Klaus. "On the Essential Contexts of Artifacts or on the Proposition That 'Design Is Making Sense (Of Things).'" *Design Issues*, vol. 5, no. 2, 1989, pp. 9-39.

Krippendorf, Klaus, and Reinhart Butter. "Product Semantics: Explaining the Symbolic Qualities of Form" *Innovation*, vol. 3, no. 2, 1984, pp. 4-9, repository.upenn.edu/asc_papers/40.

Kristensson, P., et al. "Harnessing the Creative Potential among Users." *Journal of Product Innovation Management*, vol. 21, no. 1, 2004, pp. 4-14.

Kurlinkus, William. "Crafting Designs: An Archaeology of 'Craft' as God Term." *Computers and Composition*, vol. 33, 2014, pp. 50-67.

Kurlinkus, William. "An Ethics of Attentions: Three Continuums of Classical and Contemporary Stylistic Manipulation for the 21st Century Composition Classroom." *The Centrality of Style*, edited by Michael Duncan and Star Medzerian, Parlor Press and WAC Clearinghouse, 2013, pp. 9–36.

Kyffin, Steven, and Paul Gardien. "Navigating the Innovation Matrix: An Approach to Design-led Innovation." *International Journal of Design*, vol. 3, no. 1, 2009, pp. 57–69.

Ladd, Everett Carll. *The Ladd Report*. Free Press, 1999.

Ladino, Jennifer. "Longing for Wonderland: Nostalgia for Nature in Post-Frontier America." *Iowa Journal of Cultural Studies*, no. 5, 2004, pp. 89–109.

Ladino, Jennifer. *Reclaiming Nostalgia: Longing for Nature in American Literature*. U of Virginia P, 2012.

Lakoff, George, and Mark Johnson. *Metaphors We Live By*. U of Chicago P, 1980.

Lander, David. "Digital Discontent." *Rolling Stone Magazine*, 1983.

Lauttamäki, Ville. *Practical Guide for Facilitating a Futures Workshop*. Finland Futures Research Centre, 2014, www.utu.fi/fi/yksikot/ffrc/kehittamispalvelut/futuresfocus/Documents/futures-workshops.pdf.

Lawson, Bryan. "Schemata, Gambits and Precedent: Some Factors in Design Expertise." *Design Studies*, vol. 25, no. 5, 2004, pp. 443–57.

Lazarus, R. S. *Emotion and Adaptation*. Oxford UP, 1991.

Lerner, Jennifer S., and Dacher Keltner. "Fear Anger and Risk." *Journal of Personality and Social Psychology*, vol. 81, no. 1, 2001, pp. 146–59.

Lewis, K. "Knowledge and Performance in Knowledge-Worker Teams: A Longitudinal Study of Transactive Memory Systems." *Management Science*, vol. 50, no. 11, 2004, pp. 1519–33.

Lewis, W. P., and E. Bonollo. "An Analysis of Professional Skills in Design: Implications for Education and Research." *Design Studies*, vol. 23, no. 4, 2002, pp. 385–406.

Lindner, Matt. "Block. Mute. Unfriend. Tensions Rise on Facebook after Election Results." *Chicago Tribune*, 9 Nov. 2016.

Lippmann, Walter. *Public Opinion*. Free Press, 1922.

Lord, M. G. "ART VIEW; Women's Work Is (Sometimes) Done." *New York Times*, 19 Feb. 1995, www.nytimes.com/1995/02/19/arts/art-view-women-s-work-is-some-times-done.html.

Lothian, Sayraphim. "Craft Activism—the Greenham Common Women's Peace Camp." *Craftivism*, 22 Feb. 2014, craftivism.com/blog/week-3-of-48-weeks-of-historical-craftivism-greenham-common-womens-peace-camp/.

Lowenthal, David. "Nostalgia Tells It Like It Wasn't." *The Imagined Past: History and Nostalgia*, edited by Christopher Shaw and Malcolm Chase, Manchester UP, 1989, pp. 18–32.

Lübbe, Herman. "Der Fortschritt und das Museum." *Bewahren und Ausstellen, Die Forderung des Kulturellen Erbes in Museen*, edited by A. Hermann and K. G. Saur, 2004, pp. 231-53.

Lubben, Alex. "A Coal Industry Executive Thinks God Intervened to Elect Trump." *ViceNews*, 28 Nov. 2017.

Luck, R., et al. "Project Briefing for Accessible Design." *Design Studies*, vol. 22, no. 3, 2001, pp. 297-315.

Ludden, Geke. "Surprise as a Design Strategy." *Design Issues*, vol. 24, no. 2, 2008, pp. 28-38.

Lunsford, Andrea, and Lisa Ede. "On Distinctions between Classical and Modern Rhetoric." Educational Resources Information Center, 1982, pp. 1-29.

Lyon, Arabella. *Deliberative Acts: Democracy, Rhetoric, and Rights*. Penn State UP, 2013.

MacIntyre, Alasdair. *After Virtue*. U of Notre Dame P, 1981.

Madsen, Kim. "A Guide to Metaphorical Design." *Communications of the ACM*, vol. 3, no. 12, 1994, pp. 57-62.

Manzini, Ezio. "Design Culture and Dialogic Design." *Design Issues*, vol. 32, no. 1, 2016, pp. 52-59.

Manzini, Ezio. *Design when Everybody Designs: An Introduction to Design for Social Innovation*. MIT P. 2015.

Manzini, Ezio. *Eternally Yours: Visions on Product Design*. 010 Uitgeverij, 1997.

Mao, LuMing. "Re-Clustering Traditional Academic Discourse: Alternating with Confucian Discourse." *Alt Dis: Alternative Discourses and the Academy*, edited by Christopher Schroeder, Helen Fox, and Patricia Bizzell, Boynton/Cook Publishers, Inc., 2002, pp. 112-25.

Margolis, Jane, and Allan Fisher. *Unlocking the Clubhouse: Women in Computing*. MIT P, 2003.

Marinker, Marshall. *From Compliance to Concordance: Achieving Shared Goals in Medicine Taking*. Royal Pharmaceutical Society, 1997.

Martinez, Jack. "Princeton Protesters Demand Removal of Woodrow Wilson's Name." *Newsweek*, 20 Nov. 2015, www.newsweek.com/princeton-woodrow-wilson -protest-black-students-396717.

Marx, Karl. "Montesquieu LVI." Translated by The Marx-Engels Institute, *Neue Rheinische Zeitung*, no. 202, 1849.

Mascaro, Lisa. "In Alabama, The Heart of Trump Country, Many Think He's Backing the Wrong Candidate in Senate Race." *Los Angeles Times*, 21 Sep. 2017.

"Massimo Bottura." *Chef's Table*, season 1, episode 1, Netflix.

Massumi, Brian. "Notes on the Translation and Acknowledgments." *A Thousand Plateaus: Capitalism and Schizophrenia*, by Gilles Delueze and Felix Guattari. U of Minnesota P, 1987.

Mattelmäki, T., and K. Battarbee. "Empathy Probes." *Proceedings of the 3rd Conference on Participatory Design*, 2001, pp. 266-71.

McKenzie, John M. "Reading Resistance to Kenneth Burke: 'Burke the Usurper' and Other Themes." *K.B. Journal*, vol. 7, no. 1, 2010, www.kbjournal.org/mckenzie.

McKeon, Richard. "The Uses of Rhetoric in a Technological Age: Architectonic Productive Arts." *The Prospects of Rhetoric*, edited by Lloyd Bitzer and Edwin Black, Prentice-Hall, 1971, pp. 44–63.

McMurria, John. "Desperate Citizens and Good Samaritans: Neoliberalism and Makeover Reality TV." *Television and New Media*, vol. 9, no. 4, 2008, pp. 305–32.

McSwagsalot, Cocky (MoreAndAgain). "The #NYPDwill also help you de-tangle your hair. #myNYPD." *Twitter*, 23 Apr. 2014, 2:40 p.m.

Medway, Patricia. "Imagining the Building: Architectural Design as Semiotic Construction." *Design Studies*, vol. 24, no. 3, 2003, pp. 255–73.

Mellet, Kevin, et al. "A 'Democratization' of Markets? Online Consumer Reviews in the Restaurant Industry." *Valuation Studies*, vol. 2, no. 1, 2014, pp. 5–41.

Merholz, Peter. "Peter in Conversation with Don Norman about UX & Innovation." *Adaptive Path*, 13 Dec. 2007, adaptivepath.org/ideas/e000862/.

Meza, James P., and Daniel S. Passerman. *Integrating Narrative Medicine and Evidence-Based Medicine: The Everyday Social Practice of Healing.* Radcliffe Publishing, 2011.

Middleton, David, and Derek Edwards. "Introduction." *Collective Remembering*, edited by David Middleton and Derek Edwards, Sage Publications, 1990, pp. 1–22.

Middleton, David, and Derek Edwards. "Conversational Remembering: A Social Psychological Approach." *Collective Remembering*, edited by David Middleton and Derek Edwards, Sage Publications, 1990, pp. 23–45.

Milic, Louis T. "Theories of Style and Their Implications for the Teaching of Composition." *College Composition and Communication*, vol. 16, 1965, pp. 66–69.

Miller, Carolyn. "Foreword." *Rhetorics and Technologies*, edited by Stuart Selber, U of South Carolina P, 2010, pp. ix–xii.

Mitroff, Sarah. "Getting Crafty: Why Coders Should Try Quilting and Origami." *Wired*, 2013, www.wired.com/business/2013/03/heroku-waza/.

Mittell, Jason. "Forensic Fandom and the Drillable Text." *Spreadable Media*. 2013.

Mnookin, Seth. *The Panic Virus: A True Story of Science, Medicine, and Fear.* Simon and Schuster, 2011.

Mogensen, Preben. "Towards a Provotyping Approach in Systems Development." *Scandinavian Journal of Information Systems*, vol. 4, 1992, pp. 31–53.

Moisio, Risto, et al. "Productive Consumption in the Class-Mediated Construction of Domestic Masculinity: Do-It-Yourself (DIY) Home Improvement in Men's Identity Work." *Journal Of Consumer Research*, vol. 40, 2013.

Moldovan, Sarit, et al. "'Share and Scare': Solving the Communication Dilemma of Early Adopters with a High Need for Uniqueness." *Journal of Consumer Psychology*, vol. 25, no. 1, 2015, pp. 1–14.

Monteiro, Mike. *Design Is a Job.* A Book Apart, 2012.

Moreland, R. L., and L. Myaskovsky. "Exploring the Performance Benefits of Groups Training: Transactive Memory or Improved Communication?" *Organizational Behavior and Human Decision Processes*, vol. 82, no. 1, 2000, pp. 117–33.

Moreman, Christopher M., and A. David Lewis, editors. *Mortality and Beyond in the Online Age*. Praeger, 2014.

Moschou, Eirini, and Panagiotis Zaharias. "UX-Curve Revisited: Assessing Long-Term User Experience of MMOGs." *CHI 2013*, 2013, pp. 298–316.

Mouffe, Chantal. *The Democratic Paradox*. Verso, 2000.

Mountain Mama. "How I Gave My Son Autism." *The Thinking Mom's Revolution*, 29 Aug. 2014, thinkingmomsrevolution.com/how-i-gave-my-son-autism/.

Mr. Jalopy. "The Maker's Bill of Rights." *Make*. 1 Dec. 2006.

Mulgan, Geoff. "Design in Public and Social Innovation: What Works and What Could Work Better." *Nesta*, Jan. 2014, pp. 1–7.

Muniz, Albert M. Jr., and Thomas C. O'Guinn. "Brand Community." *Journal of Consumer Research*, vol. 27, no. 4, 2001, pp. 412–32. JSTOR, www.jstor.org/stable/10.1086/319618.

Myers, Jacob. "Short Form Design Contract." *Docracy*, www.docracy.com/5152/short-form-design-contract.

"Natasha Jen: Design Thinking Is Bullshit." *Vimeo*, uploaded by 99U, 2 Aug. 2017, vimeo.com/228126880.

Nathan, Mitchell, and Anthony Petrosino. "Expert Blind Spot among Pre-Service Mathematics and Science Teachers." *American Educational Research Journal*, vol. 40, no. 4, 2003, pp. 905–28.

National Science Foundation. "Women, Minorities, and Persons with Disabilities in Science and Engineering: 2013." 2013, www.nsf.gov/statistics/wmpd/.

Neustadt, Richard, and Ernest May. *Thinking in Time: The Uses of History for Decision-Makers*. Free Press, 1988.

Neville-Rehbehn, Danielle, et al. "Everyday Voting." *DesignsOn*, IDEO, designson.ideo.com/citizenship/?work=24-everyday_voting.

Newcombe, R. "From Client to Project Stakeholders: A Stakeholder Mapping Approach." *Construction Management and Economics*, vol. 21, no. 8, 2003, pp. 841–48.

Nichols, Tom. *The Death of Expertise: The Campaign Against Established Knowledge and Why It Matters*. Oxford UP, 2017.

Nielsen, Janni, et al. "Embedding Complementarity in HCI Methods and Techniques—Designing for the 'Cultural Other.'" *Human Work Interaction Design: Designing for Human Work*, vol. 221, 2006, pp. 93–102.

Niesche, Richard, and Malcolm Haase. "Emotions and Ethics: A Foucauldian Framework for Becoming an Ethical Educator." *Educational Philosophy and Theory*, 2010, 1–13.

Nora, Pierre. "Between Memory and History: Les Lieux de Memoire." *Representation*, vol. 26, 1989, pp. 7–24.

Norman, Donald. *The Design of Everyday Things.* Basic Books, 1988.

Norman, Donald. *Emotional Design: Why We Love (or Hate) Everyday Things.* Basic Books, 2005.

Norman, Donald. "Human-Centered Design Considered Harmful." *Interactions,* vol. 12, no. 4, 2005, pp. 14–19.

Norman, Donald A., and Stephen W. Draper, editors. *User Centered System Design: New Perspectives on Human-Computer Interaction.* Lawrence Erlbaum Associates, Inc., 1986.

Norton, Michael, et al. "The IKEA Effect: When Labor Leads to Love." *Journal of Consumer Psychology,* vol. 22, 2012, pp. 453–60.

Nuland, Sherwin. *How We Die: Reflections of Life's Final Chapter.* Vintage, 1995.

Nunes, Paul, and David Light. "Star Wars, Disney, and the Fandom Menace." *Harvard Business Review,* 28 Jan. 2013.

Nyhan, Brendan, et al. "Effective Messages in Vaccine Promotion: A Randomized Trial." *Pediatrics,* vol. 133, no. 4, 2014, pp. 835–42.

Ochs, Elinor, and Lisa Capps. *Living Narrative: Creating Lives in Everyday Storytelling.* Harvard UP, 2002.

Oermann, M. H. "Using Health Web Sites for Patient Education." *Journal of Wound, Ostomy and Continence Nursing,* vol. 30, no. 4, 2003, pp. 217–23.

Ohno, Taiichi. *Toyota Production System: Beyond Large Scale Production.* Productivity Press, 1988.

Opel, Douglas, et al. "Characterizing Providers' Immunization Communication Practices during Health Supervision Visits with Vaccine-Hesitant Parents: A Pilot Study." *Vaccine,* vol. 30, no. 7, 2012, pp. 1269–75.

Orr, J. *Talking about Machines: An Ethnography of a Modern Job.* Cornell UP, 1996.

Osborn, John C. "How Many Kindergarteners Opted Out of Vaccines at Your School?" *EdSource: Highlighting Strategies for Student Success,* 10 Feb. 2015., edsource. org/kindergarten-vaccine-database/.

Palmer, Katie. "How to Get Silicon Valley's Anti-Vaxxers to Change Their Minds." *Wired,* 2 Dec. 2015, www.wired.com/2015/02/get-silicon-valleys-unvaccinated -change-minds/.

Papanek, Victor, and James Hennessey. *How Things Don't Work.* Pantheon Books, 1977.

Pariser, Eli. *The Filter Bubble: What the Internet Is Hiding from You.* Penguin, 2011.

Parry, Richard. "Episteme and Techne." *Stanford Encyclopedia of Philosophy,* 11 Apr. 2013, plato.stanford.edu/entries/episteme-techne/.

Paton, Bec, and Kees Dorst. "Briefing and Reframing: A Situated Practice." *Design Studies,* vol. 32, no. 6, 2011, pp. 573–87.

Paton, Fiona. "Approaches to Productive Peer Review." *Strategies for Teaching First-Year Composition,* edited by Duane Roen et al., NCTE, 2002, pp. 290–300.

"Paul Offit on the Dangers of the Anti-Vaccine Movement." *Medscape,* 27 Apr. 2011, www.medscape.com/viewarticle/741343.

Paulos, Eric, and Tom Jenkins. "Urban Probes." *Proceedings of the SIGCHI Conference on Human Factors in Computing Systems*, ACM Press, 2005, pp. 341–50.

Perelman, Chaim, and Lucie Olbrechts-Tyteca. *The New Rhetoric: A Treatise on Argumentation*. U of Notre Dame P, 1969.

Pernice, Kara. "Charrettes (Design Sketching): ½ Inspiration, ½ Buy-In." Nielsen Norman Group, 2013.

Petrini, Carlo, and Gigi Padovani. *SlowFood Revolution*. Rizzoli, 2005.

Pfaffenberger, Bryan. "Technological Dramas." *Science, Technology, and Human Values*, vol. 17, no. 3, pp. 282–312.

Phillips, Kendall, editor. *Framing Public Memory*. U of Alabama P, 2004.

Phillips, Kendall. "'I'm Sorry to See It Go': Nostalgic Rhetoric in Michael Moore's *Capitalism: A Love Story*." *Michael Moore and the Rhetoric of Documentary*, edited by Thomas Benson et al., SIUP, 2013, pp. 290–323.

Picard, Rosalind. *Affective Computing*. MIT P, 2000.

Pine, Joseph B. II. *Mass Customization*. Harvard Business School P, 1993.

Pine, Joseph B. II, and James H. Gilmore. *The Experience Economy*. Harvard Business Review P, 2011.

Poland, Gregory, and Robert Jacobson. "The Clinician's Guide to the Anti-Vaccinationists' Galaxy." *Human Immunology*, vol. 73, no. 8, 2012, pp. 859–66.

Porter, James E. *Audience and Rhetoric: An Archeological Composition of the Discourse Community*. Prentice-Hall, 1992.

Portinari, Folco. "Slow Food Manifesto." 1986.

Postma, Carolien E., et al. "Challenges of Doing Empathic Design: Experiences from Industry." *International Journal of Design*, vol. 6, no. 1, 2012, pp. 59–70.

Prabhu, Girish. "Global Innovative Design for Social Change: Girish Prabhu's Statement." The 12th International Conference on Human-Computer Interaction, 2007, Beijing.

Pratt, Andy, and Jason Nunes. *Interactive Design: An Introduction to the Theory and Application of User-Centered Design*. Rockport Publishers, 2012.

Pratt, Mary Louise. "Arts of the Contact Zone." *Profession*, vol. 91, pp. 33–40.

Prelli, Lawrence, editor. *Rhetorics of Display*. U of South Carolina P, 2006.

Proust, Marcel. *Swann's Way: In Search of Lost Time, Vol. 1*. Penguin, 2004.

Pullman, George. "Deliberative Rhetoric and Forensic Stasis: Reconsidering the Scope and Function of an Ancient Rhetorical Heuristic in the Aftermath of the Thomas/Hill Controversy." *Rhetoric Society Quarterly*, vol. 25, 1995, pp. 223–30.

Purcell, A. T., and J. S. Gero. "Design and Other Types of Fixation." *Design Studies*, vol. 17, no. 4, 1996, pp. 363–83.

Putnam, Robert. "Bowling Alone: America's Declining Social Capital." *Journal of Democracy*, vol. 7, no. 1, 1995, pp. 65–78.

Putnam, Robert, and Thomas Sander. "Still Bowling Alone? The Post-9/11 Split." *Journal of Democracy*, vol. 21, no. 1, 2010, pp. 9–16.

Raby, Fiona. "Evidence Dolls." *Design Interactions at the RCA*, design-interactions 2007–2014.rca.ac.uk/fiona-raby/evidence-dolls.

Rams, Dieter. "Dieter Rams: Ten Principles for Good Design." *Vitsoe*, www.vitsoe.com/ us/about/good-design.

Rasmussen, Wayne D. "Advances in American Agriculture: The Mechanical Tomato Harvester as a Case Study." *Technology and Culture*, vol. 9, no. 4, 1968, pp. 531–43.

Ratcliffe, Krista. *Rhetorical Listening: Identification, Gender, and Whiteness.* SIU P, 2005.

Redström, Johan. "Re-definitions of Use." *Design Studies*, vol. 29 no. 4, 2008, pp. 410–23.

Reynolds, Simon. *Retromania: Pop Culture's Addiction to Its Own Past.* Faber and Faber, 2011.

Reynolds, Simon. "Total Recall: Why Retromania Is All the Rage." *The Guardian.* 2 June 2011, www.theguardian.com/music/2011/jun/02/total-recall-retromania-all -rage.

Rhodes, Margaret. "The Startup That Designed Its Office to Confuse Workers." *Wired*, 30 June 2015.

Riechers, Angela. "Evoking Memories: Communicating via Memory in Design." *Print*, 10 July 2015, www.printmag.com/in-print/evoking-memories-communicating-via -memory-in-design/.

Ritivoi, Andreea Deciu. *Yesterday's Self: Nostalgia and the Immigrant Identity.* Rowman and Littlefield Publishers, 2002.

Ritov, Ilana, and Jonathan Baron. "Reluctance to Vaccinate: Omission Bias and Ambiguity." *Journal of Behavioral Decision Making*, vol. 3, no. 4, 1990, pp. 263–77.

Rittel, Horst W. J., and Melvin M. Webber. "Dilemmas in a General Theory of Planning." *Policy Sciences*, vol. 4, 1973, pp. 155–69.

Rogers, Everett. *Diffusion of Innovations.* Free Press, 1995.

Romano, Andrew. "Why You're Addicted to TV." *Newsweek*, 15 May 2013.

Rosa, Hartmut. *Social Acceleration: A New Theory of Modernity.* Columbia UP, 2015.

Rosen, Jeffrey. "Response: The Right to Be Forgotten." *Stanford Law Review*, Feb. 2012.

Rosenfield, Lawrence W. "The Practical Celebration of Epideictic." *Rhetoric in Transition: Studies in the Nature and Uses of Rhetoric*, edited by Eugene E. White, U of California P, 1989, pp. 131–53.

Routledge, Clay, et al. "Nostalgia as a Resource for Psychological Health and Well-Being." *Social and Personality Psychology Compass*, vol. 7, no. 11, 2013, pp. 808–18.

Roxburgh, Mark. "Negotiating Design: Conversational Strategies between Clients and Designers." *Form/Work*, vol. 6, 2003, pp. 65–80.

Royster, Jacqueline Jones. "Academic Discourses or Small Boats on a Big Sea." *Alt Dis: Alternative Discourses and the Academy*, edited by Christopher Schroeder, Helen Fox, and Patricia Bizzell, Boynton/Cook Publishers, Inc., 2002, pp. 23–30.

Royster, Jacqueline Jones. "When the First Voice You Hear Is Not Your Own." *College Composition and Communication*, vol. 47, no. 1, 1996, pp. 29–40. JSTOR, www.jstor .org/stable/358272.

Rundblad, Gabriella, et al. "An Enquiry into Scientific and Media Discourse in the MMR Controversy: Authority and Factuality." *Communication and Medicine*, vol. 3, no. 1, 2011, pp. 69–80.

Ruskin, John. "The Nature of Gothic." *The Stones of Venice Vol. II*. Villanova University, 1853, www47.homepage.villanova.edu/seth.koven/gothic.html.

Saffer, Dan. *The Role of Metaphor in Interaction Design*. MA Thesis, Carnegie Mellon University, 2005.

Samuels, Brett. "Jones Mocks Moore for 'Prancing around on a Stage in a Cowboy Suit.'" *The Hill*, 12 Dec. 2017.

Sanders, Elizabeth. "From User-Centered to Participatory Design Approaches." *Design and the Social Sciences*, edited by J. Frascara, Taylor and Francis Books Limited, 2002, pp. 1–8.

Sapio, Giuseppina. "Homesick for Aged Home Movies: Why Do We Shoot Contemporary Family Videos in an Old-Fashioned Way?" *Media and Nostalgia: Yearning for the Past, Present and Future*, edited by Katharina Niemeyer, Springer, 2014, pp. 39–50.

Sartwell, Crispin. *Political Aesthetics*. Cornell UP, 2010.

Satchell, Christine and Dourish, Paul. "Beyond the User: Use and Non-Use in HCI." *OZCHI 2009: Design: Open 24/7: 21st Annual Conference of the Australian Computer-Human Interaction Special Interest Group (CHISIG) of the Human Factors and Ergonomics Society of Australia (HFESA)*, University of Melbourne, 2009.

Schilb, John. *Rhetorical Refusals: Defying Audience's Expectations*. SIU P, 2007.

Schleifer, Ronald, and Jerry Vannatta. *The Chief Concern of Medicine: The Integration of the Medical Humanities and Narrative Knowledge into Medical Practices*. U of Michigan P, 2013.

Schmitz, Thomas A. "Plausibility in the Greek Orators." *The American Journal of Philology*, vol. 121, no. 1, 2000, pp. 47–77.

Schön, Donald. "The Crisis of Professional Knowledge and the Pursuit of an Epistemology of Practice." *Competence in the Learning Society*, edited by John Raven and John Stephenson, Peter Lang, 2001, pp. 185–207.

Schön, Donald. *The Reflective Practitioner: How Professionals Think in Action*. Temple Smith, 1983.

Schrey, Dominik. "Analogue Nostalgia and the Aesthetics of Digital Remediation." *Media and Nostalgia: Yearning for the Past, Present and Future*, edited by Katharina Niemeyer, Springer, 2014, pp. 27–38.

Sedikides, Constantine, et al. "Nostalgia Counteracts Self-Discontinuity and Restores Self-Continuity." *European Journal of Social Psychology*, vol. 45, 2015, pp. 52–61.

Sedikides, Constantine, et al. "Nostalgia: Conceptual Issues and Existential Functions." *Handbook of Experimental Existential Psychology*, edited by J. Greenberg, S. Koole, and T. Pyszczynski, Guilford Press, 2004, pp. 200–14.

Sedikides, Constantine, et al. "To Nostalgize: Mixing Memory with Affect and Desire." *Advances in Experimental Psychology*, vol. 51, 2015, pp. 189–273.

Selfe, Cynthia L. "Students Who Teach Us." *Writing New Media: Theory and Applications for Expanding the Teaching of Composition*, edited by Anne Frances Wysocki et al., Utah State UP, 2004, pp. 43–66.

Selfe, Cynthia L. *Technology and Literacy in the Twenty-First Century: The Importance of Paying Attention*. SIU P, 1999.

Selfe, Cynthia L., and Gail E. Hawisher. *Literate Lives in the Information Age: Narratives of Literacy from the United States*. Lawrence Erlbaum Associates Publishers, 2004.

Selfe, Cynthia L., and Richard J. Selfe Jr. "The Politics of the Interface: Power and Its Exercise in Electronic Contact Zones." *College Composition and Communication*, vol. 45, no. 4, 1994, pp. 480–504.

Selwyn, N. "Apart from Technology: Understanding People's Non-Use of Information and Communication Technologies in Everyday Life." *Technology in Society*, vol. 25, 2003, pp. 99–116.

Sennett, Richard. *The Culture of the New Capitalism*. Yale UP, 2007.

Sharrock, W. W., and R. J. Anderson. "The User as a Scenic Feature of the Design Space." *Design Studies*, vol. 15, no.1, 1994, pp. 5–18.

Shaver, Katherine. "Female Dummy Makes Her Mark on Male-Dominated Crash Tests." *The Washington Post*, 25 Mar. 2012, www.washingtonpost.com/local/traf ficandcommuting/female-dummy-makes-her-mark-on-male-dominated-crash -tests/2012/03/07/gIQANBLjaS_story.html.

Shea, Marybeth, and Cameron Mozafari. "Communicating Complexity in Transdisciplinary Science Teams for Policy: Applied Stasis Theory for Organizing and Assembling Collaboration." *Communication Design Quarterly Review*, vol. 2, no. 3, 2014, pp. 20–24.

Shipka, Jody. *Towards a Composition Made Whole*. U of Pittsburgh P, 2011.

Siva, Jessica, and Kerry London. "Habitus Shock: A Model for Architect-Client Relationships on House Projects Based on Sociological and Psychological Perspectives." *Proceedings of the CIB W096 Architectural Management*, pp. 209–20.

Skowronski, John J., et al. "The Fading Affect Bias: Its History, Its Implications, and Its Future." *Advances in Experimental Social Psychology*, vol. 49, 2014, pp. 163–218.

Slack, Andrew. "Harry Potter and the Muggle Activists." *In These Times*, 26 Oct. 2007, inthesetimes.com/article/3365/harry_potter_and_the_muggle_activists.

"Smallpox: A Great and Terrible Scourge." *NIH: U.S. National Library of Medicine*, www .nlm.nih.gov/exhibition/smallpox/sp_variolation.html.

Smith, Kimberly. "Mere Nostalgia: Notes on a Progressive Paratheory." *Rhetoric and Public Affairs*, vol. 3, no. 4, 2000, pp. 505–27.

Smith, Philip, et al. "Children Who Have Received No Vaccines: Who Are They and Where Do They Live?" *Pediatrics*, vol. 114, no. 1, 2004.

Soegaard, Mads. "The History of Usability: From Simplicity to Complexity." *Smashing Magazine*, 23 May 2012, www.smashingmagazine.com/2012/05/the-history-of-us ability-from-simplicity-to-complexity/.

SoftSchools. "Appeal to Tradition Examples." www.softschools.com/examples/falla cies/appeal_to_tradition_examples/487/.

Sortable. "The Rise of Slacktivism." Infographic.

Spinuzzi, Clay. "Lost in the Translation: Shifting Claims in the Migration of a Research Technique." *Technical Communication Quarterly*, vol. 14, no. 4, 2005, pp. 411–46.

Spinuzzi, Clay. "The Methodology of Participatory Design." *Technical Communication*, vol. 52, no. 2, 2005, pp. 163–74.

Steers, Mai-Ly, et al. "Seeing Everyone Else's Highlight Reels: How Facebook Usage Is Linked to Depressive Symptoms." *Journal of Social and Clinical Psychology*, vol. 33, no. 8, 2014, pp. 701–31.

Stenovec, Timothy. "The Reasons the Ice Bucket Challenge Went Viral." *Huffington Post*, 19 Aug. 2014.

Stephan, Elena, et al. "Mental Travel into the Past: Differentiating Recollections of Nostalgic, Ordinary, and Positive Events." *European Journal of Social Psychology*, 42, 2002, pp. 290–98.

Stewart, Susan. *On Longing: Narratives of the Miniature, the Gigantic, the Souvenir, the Collection*. Duke UP, 1993.

Stoller, Debbie. *Stitch 'n Bitch: The Knitter's Handbook*. Workman Publishing Company, 2003.

Strauss, Carolyn F., and Alastair Fuad-Luke. "The Slow Design Principles: A New Interrogative and Reflexive Tool for Design Research and Practice." *Changing the Change: Design Visions, Proposals, and Tools*, edited by Carla Cipolla and Pier Paolo Peruccio, 2008, pp. 1–14.

Stuckey, Elspeth. *The Violence of Literacy*. Boyton/Cook Publishers, 1991.

Sturken, Marita. "Memory, Consumerism and Media: Reflections on the Emergence of the Field." *Memory Studies*, vol. 1, no. 1, 2008, pp. 73–78.

Sun, Huatong. *Cross-Cultural Technology Design: Creating Culture-Sensitive Technology for Local Users*. Oxford UP, 2012.

Swann, Cal. "Action Research and the Practice of Design." *Design Issues*, vol. 18, no. 1, 2002, pp. 49–61.

Takeuchi, Hirotaka, et al. "The Contradictions That Drive Toyota's Success." *The Harvard Business Review*, June 2008.

Tandoc, Edson, et al. "Facebook Use, Envy, and Depression among College Students: Is Facebooking Depressing?" *Computers in Human Behavior*, vol. 43, 2015, pp. 139–46.

Taylor, Summer Smith. "Assessment in Client-Based Technical Writing Classes: Evolution of Teacher and Client Standards." *Technical Communication Quarterly*, vol. 15, no. 2, 2009, pp. 111–39.

Ten Bhömer, Martijn, et al. "4Photos: A Collaborative Photo Sharing Experience." *Proceedings: NordiCHI 2010*, 2010, pp. 52–61.

Terdiman, Richard. *Present Past: Modernity and the Memory Crisis.* Cornell UP, 1993.

Terrio, Susan J. "Crafting Grand Cru Chocolates in Contemporary France." *American Anthropologist*, vol. 98, no. 1, 1996, pp. 67–79.

Thompson, Craig, and Zeynep Arsel. "The Starbucks Brandscape and Consumers' (Anticorporate) Experiences of Glocalization." *Journal of Consumer Research*, vol. 31, 2004, pp. 631–42.

Toobin, Jeffrey. "The Solace of Oblivion: In Europe, the Right to Be Forgotten Trumps the Internet." *The New Yorker*, 29 Sep. 2014, www.newyorker.com/maga zine/2014/09/29/solace-oblivion.

Tracy, Thomas, and Larry McShane. "Commissioner Bill Bratton on #myNYPD Disaster: 'I Kind of Welcome the Attention.'" *New York Daily News*, 23 Apr. 2014, www.nydailynews.com/new-york/nyc-crime/no-blamed-mynypd-debacle-sources -article-1.1766121.

Tseng, M. M., et al. "Design for Mass Personalization." *Manufacturing Technology*, vol. 59, 2010, pp. 175–78.

Tulving, Endel. "Memory and Consciousness." *Canadian Psychology*, vol. 26, 1985, pp. 1–12.

Tuomi, Ilkka. "Data Is More Than Knowledge: Implications of the Reversed Knowledge Hierarchy for Knowledge Management and Organizational Memory." *Journal of Management Information Systems*, vol. 16, no. 3, 2000, pp. 107–21.

Turan, Zeynep. "Material Memories of the Ottoman Empire: Armenian and Greek Objects of Legacy." *Global Memoryscapes: Contesting Remembrance in a Transnational Age*, edited by Kendall Phillips and G. Mitchell Reyes, U of Alabama P, 2011, pp. 173–94.

Umar, Sanda, et al. "The Psychological Impacts of Nostalgia for People with Dementia: Study Protocol." Research protocol 26/03/15, version 1.4.

Urde, Mats, et al. "Corporate Brands with a Heritage." *Journal of Brand Management*, vol. 15, 2007, pp. 4–19.

Uribe-Jongbloed, Enrique, et al. "The Joy of the Easter Egg and the Pain of Numb Hands: The Augmentation and Limitation of Reality through Video Games." *Palabra Clave*, vol. 18, no. 4, 2015.

"Vaccine War, The." *Frontline*, PBS, 27 Apr. 2010, www.pbs.org/wgbh/frontline/film/ vaccines/.

Van Dijck, José. *Mediated Memories in the Digital Age.* Stanford UP, 2007.

Van Hinte, E. *Eternally Yours: Time in Design.* 010 Publishers, 2004.

Van House, Nancy, and Elizabeth F. Churchill. "Technologies of Memory: Key Issues and Critical Perspectives." *Memory Studies*, vol. 1, no. 3, 2008, pp. 295–310.

Van Mensvoort, Koert. "Innovative Nostalgia." *Next Nature Network*, 1 Jan. 2014, www.nextnature.net/2014/01/innovative-nostalgia-design-the-future-by-refer ring-to-the-past/.

Van Tilburg, Wijnand, et al. "The Mnemonic Muse: Nostalgia Fosters Creativity through Openness to Experience." *Journal of Experimental Social Psychology*, vol. 59, 2015, pp. 1–7.

Vásquez, Camilla, and Alice Chik. "'I Am Not a Foodie . . . ': Culinary Capital in Online Reviews of Michelin Restaurants." *Food and Foodways*, vol. 23, no. 4, 2015, pp. 231–50.

Vealey, K. "Making Dead Bodies Legible: Facebook's Ghosts, Public Bodies and Networked Grief." *Gnovis*, vol. 11, no. 2, 2011.

Veblen, Thorstein. *Theory of the Leisure Class*. 1899. Penguin, 1979.

Velázquez, Daniela. "Lessons from Google's First Rollout of Google Fiber." *Fast Company*, 6 Feb. 2015, www.fastcompany.com/3036659/elasticity/lessons-from-googles -first-rollout-of-google-fiber.

Vermeeren, Arnold, et al. "User Experience Evaluation Methods: Current State and Development Needs." *Proceedings of the NordiCHI Conference*, 2010, pp. 521–30.

Vidal, René Victor Valqui. *The Future Workshop: Democratic Problem Solving*. Informatics and Mathematical Modelling, 2005, pp. 1–21.

Vie, Stephanie. "In Defense of 'Slacktivism': The Human Rights Campaign Facebook Logo as Digital Activism." *First Monday*, vol. 19, no. 4, 2014.

Vinsel, Lee. "Why Carmakers Always Insisted on Male Crash-Test Dummies." *Bloomberg*, 22 Aug. 2012, www.bloomberg.com/view/articles/2012-08-22/why-car makers-always-insisted-on-male-crash-test-dummies.

Vohs, Kathleen, et al. "Rituals Enhance Consumption." *Psychological Science*, vol. 24, no. 9, 2013, pp. 1714–21.

Volcovici, Valerie. "Awaiting Trump's Coal Comeback, Miners Reject Retraining." *Reuters*, 2 Nov. 2017.

Von Hippel, Eric. *Democratizing Innovation*. MIT P, 2005.

Walker, Stuart. "Wrapped Attention: Designing Products for Evolving Permanence and Enduring Meaning." *Design Issues*, vol. 26, no. 4, 2010.

Wallace, Amy. "How Panicked Parents Skipping Shots Endanger Us All." *Wired*, 19 Oct. 2009, www.wired.com/2009/10/ff_waronscience/.

Weber, Bryan A., et al. "Educating Patients to Evaluate Web-Based Healthcare Information: The GATOR Approach to Healthy Surfing." *Journal of Clinical Nursing*, vol. 19, no. 9–10, 2010, pp. 1371–77.

Wegner Daniel. "Transactive Memory: A Contemporary Analysis of the Group Mind." *Theories of Group Behavior*, edited by Mullen B, Goethals GR Springer-Verlag, Springer, 1986, pp. 185–208.

Weisman, Steven. "An American Original." *Vanity Fair*, n.d., www.vanityfair.com/ news/2010/11/moynihan-letters-201011.

Wen, Leana. "When Patients Read What Their Doctors Write." *NPR*, 17 Aug. 2014, www.npr.org/sections/health-shots/2014/08/14/340351393/when-patients-read -what-their-doctors-write.

Westley, Frances et al. *Getting to Maybe: How the World Is Changed*. Vintage Canada, 2007.

White, Ryen W., and Eric Horvitz. "Cyberchondria: Studies of the Escalation of Medical Concerns in Web Search." *Microsoft Research*, 2008, www.microsoft.com/en-us/research/publication/cyberchondria-studies-of-the-escalation-of-medical-concerns-in-web-search/.

Whittemore, Stewart. *Rhetorical Memory: A Study of Technical Communication and Information Management*. U of Chicago P, 2015.

Wiens, Kyle. "Unfixable Computers Are Leading Humanity down a Perilous Path." *Wired*, June 2012, www.wired.com/2012/06/apples-unfixable-devices/.

Wildschut, Tim, et al. "Nostalgia: Content, Triggers, Functions." *Journal of Personality and Social Psychology*, vol. 91, no. 5, 2006, pp. 975–93.

Williams, Bernard. *Truth and Truthfulness: An Essay in Genealogy*. Princeton UP, 2002.

Wilson, Louise. "Cyberwar, God, and Television: An Interview with Paul Virilio." *Digital Delirium*, edited by Arthur and Marilouise Kroker, St. Martin's Press, 1997, pp. 41–48.

Winner, Langdon. *The Whale and the Reactor: A Search for Limits in an Age of High Technology*. U of Chicago P, 1986.

Winslade, John and Gerald Monk. *Narrative Mediation: A New Approach to Conflict Resolution*. Jossey-Bass, 2000.

Wolf, Marco, and Shaun McQuitty. "Circumventing Traditional Markets: An Empirical Study of the Marketplace Motivations and Outcomes of Consumers' Do-It-Yourself Behaviors." *Journal of Marketing Theory and Practice*, vol. 21, no. 2, 2013, pp. 195–209.

Wolsko, Christopher, et al. "Red, White, and Blue Enough to Be Green: Effects of Moral Framing on Climate Change Attitudes and Conservation Behaviors." *Journal of Experimental Social Psychology*, vol. 65, 2016, pp. 7–19.

Womack, James P. et al. *The Machine That Changed the World: The Story of Lean Production—Toyota's Secret Weapon in the Global Car Wars That Is Now Revolutionizing World Industry*. Free Press, 2007.

World Design Organization. "BioLite Homestove." http://wdo.org/site-project/biolite-homestove/.

Wuestefeld, Thomas, et al. "The Impact of Brand Heritage on Customer Perceived Value." *der markt: International Journal of Marketing*, vol. 51, no. 2, 2012, pp. 51–61.

Yochim, Emily, and Jessica Silva. "Everyday Expertise, Autism, and 'Good' Mothering in the Media Discourse of Jenny McCarthy." *Communication and Critical/Cultural Studies*, vol. 10, no. 4, 2013, pp. 406–26.

Zane, J. Peder. "In Pursuit of Taste, en Masse." *New York Times*, 11 Feb. 2013, www.nytimes.com/2013/02/12/business/connoisseurship-expands-beyond-high-art-and-classical-music.html.

Zhou, Xinyue, et al. "Nostalgia: The Gift That Keeps on Giving." *Journal of Consumer Research*, vol. 39, no. 1, 2012, pp. 39–50.

Zielinski, Siegfried. *Deep Time of the Media: Toward an Archaeology of Hearing and Seeing by Technical Means*. MIT P, 2008.

Zipprich, Jennifer, et al. "Measles Outbreak—California, December 2014–February 2015." *CDC*, vol. 64, no. 6, 2015, pp. 153–54.

Zuckerberg, Mark, and Priscilla Chan. "A Letter to Our Daughter." *Facebook*, 1 Dec. 2015, www.facebook.com/notes/mark-zuckerberg/a-letter-to-our-daughter/101533 75081581634/.

# Index

A/B testing, 89
acceleration, 6, 26, 166–67, 189, 210.
    *See also* speed
access, 31–34, 69–72
accountability, 92–93, 142. *See also*
    rhetorical listening
acting together, 87–88
Adamson, Glenn, 44, 48
adapt, 144–49
adaptability, new capitalist, 54–55,
    61, 64
Adler, Deborah, 94
adopt, 149–55
adversarial design, 22–23, 97–102. *See
    also* agonistic design; informed
    dissent; Mouffe, Chantal
affect, 59–60. *See also* emotion; feed-
    back loop
aging, 181; with grace 169–70, 181–82,
    211; new, 42, 95–96; in place,
    42–43
agonism, 22–23, 38, 98–101, 104, 158.
    *See also* informed dissent; provoke
agonistic design, 23, 99–102, 135. *See
    also* informed dissent
Ahmed, Sara, 124, 130
Allen, Ben, 128
Almquist, Julka, 85–86
alternative medicine. *See* biopsycho-
    social healthcare
Alzheimers, 182–83
Amazon, 54–55, 86, 101–2, 186
AmericaSpeaks, 135

Andersen, Kurt, 28
Andon Cord, 168
anger, 121, 123–24
anticipatory design, 43, 182, 193
anticipatory nostalgia, 42, 116, 145,
    151, 189; designs that encourage,
    17, 40, 175, 183, 193
anti-taste, 193
anti-vaccination, 106–37, 218n4; sto-
    ries, 113–17
anxiety, 107, 128, 130, 132, 133–34,
    220n9
Appalachia, 8–9, 10–11, 66, 143, 213n1
appeal to tradition, 10–11, 196, 198. *See
    also* rhetorical fallacy
Apple, 168, 184
appropriation, 44, 52, 72–73, 200
*argumentum ad antiquitatem*, 10
Ariely, Daniel, 178, 187
Aristotle, 37–38, 83–86, 88, 103, 143,
    220n6
*Arrested Development*, 191–93
arresting magic, 109–10, 148, 162. *See
    also* fundamentalism; restorative
    nostalgia
asystatic freeze, 112, 118, 124, 131,
    206
audience analysis, 35–40, 83–89, 143,
    205–7
aura, 42, 176, 179, 180, 189, 211. *See
    also* leaked constructedness
authenticity, 17–18, 26, 57, 66, 171, 173,
    220n11

autistic, 114–21; citizens, 120; identity, 120–21; rhetoric, 121; rights, 116; Self Advocacy Network, 120; shiny, 120–21
auto-shop, 183, 185

Barbrook, Richard, 160
Barron, Brigid, 33
Barton, David, 59
Bateson, Gregory, 60
beer, 19, 20, 188, 193
behavioral residue, 171–72, 176–77, 180, 210. *See also* leaked constructedness
Belmont Report, 110, 122
Benjamin, Walter, 42, 176, 179
Bennett, Jane, 203n4
Betty Crocker, 179
Bezos, Jeff, 101
Bic for Her, 86, 202
big ego design, 38, 109. *See also* expertise, restoratively nostalgic
binge watch, 188–89
BioLite, 43, 202
biomedical ethics, 110, 150–51
biomedical healthcare, 109–11, 114, 125, 150
*Biopresence*, 194
biopsychosocial healthcare, 111, 150–51
Black, Anthea, 48, 73
Bonilla, Yarimar, 178
bootstraps narratives, 143, 186
Bottura, Massimo, 171
boundary object, 146, 147, 149, 152–53, 154, 161
Bowen, Robert, 159
Boym, Svetlana, 7, 17, 26, 44, 67, 118; on types of nostalgia, 9, 30, 52, 112, 142, 197
Brandt, Deborah, 69, 154
Bratich, Jack, 70
Bratton, William, 178
Brawer, James, 116
*Breaking Bad*, 188–89
Bretzel, Raoul, 192–93

brief, design, 149
Brisebras, Thomas, 169
*Broken White*, 182
Broockman, David, 135–36
Brooke, Robert, 56
Brown, Tim, 53, 59, 199–200
Brush, Heidi, 70
Buchanan, Richard, 4, 12, 36, 64, 81–82, 167, 213n4
Budweiser, 193
Burisch, Nicole, 48, 73
Burkean parlor, 87
Burke, Kenneth, 8, 87–89, 91–92, 103, 114, 135, 144
Burke, Peter, 27, 214n6
Burton, Neel, 171
buzz, 175, 221n5. *See also* narratability; tellable
Byrne, Rhonda, 111

Cabbanes, Yves, 39
Candy, Linda, 141
capitalism, 53–55
Capps, Lisa, 172
Carlile, Paul, 146, 149
Carrey, Jim, 114–19
Casakin, Hernan, 94
Castiglione, Baldesar, 174, 179
CDC (Centers for Disease Control), 119, 128, 134, 218n11
Ceccarelli, Leah, 109
cemetery, 193–94
Chachra, Debbie, 185
chain-referral sampling, 215n1
Chan, Priscilla, 31–32
Chan Zuckerberg Initiative, 31–32
*charrette*, 23, 208–9
*Chef's Table*, 171
Cheston, Richard, 182
Chicago, Judy, 47
chief complaint of medicine, 112, 125
chief concern of medicine, 112, 125
chocolate, 187–88, 211
Christen, Kimberly, 72–73, 216n8

Christopher, Gary, 182
chronic illness, 111, 151, 209
Cialdini, Robert, 88, 134
Citelli, Anna, 192–93
class tourism, 184
Clear RX, 94
client, 36, 138–62, 209, 219n5
client-centered design, 139
client criticism, 152–54, 209
client education, 146–48, 157
client feedback, 152–55
client stories, 144–46, 150–52
Clinton, Hillary, 119
coffee, 42, 157, 189
Cold Stone Creamery, 185
collective decision-making, 114
collective memory, 7; community of,
    65, 89; designing with, 145–46; as
    literacy gateway, 69–70; memory
    studies, 27–28; of an object/design,
    170, 180, 187–88
collector, 171–72, 175–77. *See also* behav-
    ioral residue
communities of nostalgia: collective
    memory, 65–73, 99; creating new,
    113, 119, 121, 179, 182, 186; rheto-
    ric and, 84, 86; stability, 108
connoisseur, 182, 186–93, 210, 211
connoisseur activism, 189–199
conspiracy theory, 118, 128
constitutionality, 129–32
consubstantiality, 87–88, 98
consumer-citizen, 170
contact zones, 31, 51–52; antagonistic,
    190–93; failure to see, 177–78; me-
    diation, 39, 109–10, 114, 133, 140,
    149, 153; redesign from, 58, 62, 72,
    99–102, 143, 145, 206
contract, 160–61
Cope, Bill, 58, 197
Costello, Brigid, 141
counter nostalgia, 10, 57
Covert, Bryce, 185
Covino, William, 109

Coxon, Ian, 173, 180
craft, 19, 35, 47–59, 51, 94–95, 172–73,
    210; care, 179–80; class, 184–86;
    connection, 178–86; ethics, 73,
    184–86; fair, 216n7; labor, 53–56,
    179, 185; pleasure, 62–63, 158, 178;
    rights, 53, 158; stewardship, 9, 42
craftivism, 49
craft revival, 51, 55, 66–67
craft UX, 178–86
craftwashing, 73, 185
Crawford, Matthew, 55, 61
Create West Virginia, 10–11
crisis of confidence in the professional,
    142
critical nostos, 51–53, 58–59, 63–65,
    67, 70–73, 77, 199
critique v. complaint, 153, 209
Croce, Arlene, 155
*Crochet Coral Reef*, 71–72
*Crocheted Environment*, 47
cross-stitch, 50, 57
Crowley, Sharon, 36
Csikszentmihalyi, Mihaly, 62–63, 117,
    166, 182
Cuff, Dana, 138–39, 140, 219n5
cultural capital, 175, 186, 211
cultural probes, 95–96, 124
curing, 42, 116–17, 121, 137, 150. *See
    also* healing
curiosity, 171. *See also* surprise; wonder
customer is always right, 38, 97, 126,
    155. *See also* participationism
customer loyalty, 173, 181, 183, 193
customization, 166, 210
cybernetics, 60

dark design, 201
data-oriented design, 86
Davis, Fred, 7, 65, 215n6
Deacon, Aaron, 18, 213n1 (chap. 1)
death, 23, 41, 193–94
deceleration, 6, 167
decision-making we, 81, 88, 206–7;

mediation, 98–99, 117–19, 124–26, 129, 134–36; not we, 91
deep canvasing, 136
Delagrange, Susan, 173
Delbanco, Tom, 127
deliberation, 77–105
deliberative duty, 135, 217n12
delighter, 173–74, 179
deliverable, 152–54
democracy, 77–80, 83–84, 87–89, 92–93, 97–102, 108, 217n12
democratic design, 135–36
democratization: design, 23, 77; expertise, 23, 38–39, 140; history, 27–28; medicine, 108, 111, 148; memory, 27–28, 48; science, 78, 108; technology, 23, 32, 58, 77, 108
Dennett, Daniel 154–55
design, 23; v. art, 139; as indeterminate, 81; rhetorical (see rhetorical design). See also the names of individual types of design
design-after-design, 169
designing for the political, 99, 203–4
designing for politics, 99
design research, 12, 64, 85, 94–96, 196
design thinking, 12–13
design for time, 4, 189, 181–84, 187–190
detached self, 165–66
diagnosis, 118, 128, 147, 149–50
digital activism, 175–78, 221n6. See also slacktivism
Digital Artisans Manifesto, 160
digital divide, 18–19, 22, 32
digital inequity, 18–19, 22, 33, 54–55, 214n11, 216n8
digital stories, 175–78
diplomatic recognition, 152, 155
direct-to-consumer advertising of drugs, 110
DiSalvo, Carl, 12, 22, 99, 101, 213n4, 215n16

disaster communication, 10–11, 143
Disney: measles outbreak, 108, 128, 130; UX, 174, 191
Dissanayake, Ellen, 178
DIT (Do-It-Together), 184–85
DIY (Do-It-Yourself), 61–62, 64, 118, 148, 179, 184–86
Donati, Kelly, 190
Dorst, Kees, 149
double-listening, 113, 116, 118, 137, 205
Draper, Stephen, 84
Dunne, Anthony, 95–96, 99–100

Easter egg, 173–74, 211
eavesdropping, 93, 190. See also rhetorical listening
ecology of care, 180–81, 182, 184, 189
Edwards, Derek, 69
efahrung, 167, 221n3
Ehn, Pelle, 38, 39, 77, 79, 170, 217n11
Ehrenreich, Barbara, 110
ekklēsia, 83
elderly, 94, 95–96
Elemental Coffee, 157
Elliott, Anthony, 165–66
Elk River chemical spill, 143
emotion: control, 6–7, 121, 130; designing for, 166, 201; feedback loop, 59–65, 215n4; mediation, 113, 126, 136; as weakness, 10, 59, 97, 123–24. See also specific emotions
emotional design, 59–60, 63–65, 165, 201
emotional labor, 185
emotional othering, 122, 124, 129
empathy, 37, 92–97, 151, 216n7
empathic design, 94–97, 115, 124, 150
empathy for experts, 151
empathic modeling, 94
enchantment, 221n4
English, Deirdre, 110
English major, 11–13, 90–91, 195–96, 208, 219n2

enthymeme, 37, 83–84, 86
*entschleunigung. See* deceleration
environmental communication, 36–37,
    143, 197–98
epideictic rhetoric, 84, 86–87, 89
*epistemic technê*, 38–39, 102, 109, 112,
    127, 141, 215n15. *See also* expertise
*erlebnis*, 167, 221n3
ethnography, 64, 85, 196. *See also*
    design research
ethos, 143, 145, 206–7, 220n6. *See also*
    trust; voice
evidence dolls, 99–100
experience economy, 165, 185
expertise, 38–40, 141–43; democrati-
    zation of, 23, 82, 140; dualistic,
    115, 116, 119, 133; explicating, 142,
    146–48, 153; layering, 58, 128, 135,
    144, 148, 157; repertoires of, 58–59;
    reflectively nostalgic, 39, 93, 126,
    127–28, 140–41, 151, 152, 157, 158,
    207; restoratively nostalgic, 36,
    121, 124, 126, 140, 150
expert novice, 54
exploration, 174–75. *See also* surprise;
    wandering; wondering
Eternally Yours, 42, 165. *See also* slow
    design; SlowLab
"Everyday Voting," 203
Eyal, Nir, 40–41, 180

Facebook, 4, 17, 40–41, 123, 180, 182;
    depression, 41; envy, 41; Lookback,
    177; memorials, 182, 198, 206; On
    This Day, 17, 41, 176–77
fading affect bias, 181
fake news, 124
fandom, 188–90; resistance, 190–91;
    forensic, 188
FDA, 128
fear, 107, 122–24, 128–30, 133
feedback, design, 152–54
feedback loop, 60–61, 64
Feenberg, Andrew, 22, 79, 82, 214n10

Fields, Corey, 56
filter bubble, 134–35
Fleckenstein, Kristie, 143
Fleischmann, Carly, 120
flow, 62–64
focusing illusion, 134, 181
Forester, John, 101
forgetting, 27, 41
fractal recursivity, 58
Fuad-Luke, Alastair, 12, 23, 42, 181
Fukuhara, Shiho, 194
fundamentalism, 36–37, 45, 97–98, 109,
    124. *See also* restorative nostalgia
Fuss, Diana, 57
future workshop, 89–91

Gal, Susan, 58
gamergate, 214n13
Gardner, Jeff, 149
Gaver, Bill, 95–96
Gee, James, 54, 70
geek, 190–93
Geller, Sarah Michelle, 119
generative magic, 109–10. *See also* reflec-
    tive nostalgia
George, Anders, 12
ghostwriter, 154
Gilligan, Vince, 188–89
Gilmore, James, 165, 185
Glenn, Cheryl, 177
global warming, 36–38, 198
god memory, 89, 114–15, 118, 122, 131,
    145, 154
god term, 89, 91, 170
Goldberg Rule, 150, 153
Goldstein, Jan, 142
Goodnight, Thomas, 112, 123
Google, 18–19, 54, 146; medicine 108,
    114, 148, 220nn9–10
Google Fiber, 18–19, 203, 213n1 (chap. 1)
Gosling, Samuel, 171
great unfriending, 4
Greer, Betsy, 49
Ground Zero memorial, 135

Guaman Poma de Ayala, Felipe,
51–53, 57
guilt, 117, 118, 122, 126

Haagsma, H. T., 150
habitus shock, 157, 159. *See also* refusal
Haidt, Jonathan, 37, 197–98
Halbwachs, Maurice, 7, 65, 89
Halton, Eugene, 166, 182
Harry Potter, 190
Harry Potter Alliance, 190
Hartelius, E. Johanna, 111
Hawisher, Gail, 40, 215n1
healing, 116–17, 119, 120, 132, 137, 150.
*See also* curing
health: healthism, 127; personal, 122,
126–27, 129, 130, 133–34; public,
122, 129, 131–32
Hennessey, James, 58
Hepper, Erica, 43
herd immunity, 130
heroic medicine, 110
Heroku, 94–95, 172–73
Hertz, D. G., 179
Heijdens, Simon, 182
*High Fidelity*, 179
Hirschberg, Baruch, 152
Hitler, Adolf, 28
Hobsbawm, Eric, 187
Hoendervanger, J. G., 150
Hoey, Brian, 11
Hofer, Johannes, 5, 24–25
Holland, Mary, 131–32
Hollwich, Matthias, 42
homesickness, 5–6, 24–26
HomeStove, 43
hope, 60, 108, 113, 114, 116, 120, 137
Hornsby, Nick, 179
Horváth, Ödön von, 210
Hsu, Eric, 165–66
Hull, Glynda, 70
human-centered design, 12, 85, 96–97,
195–96
humanities, 11–13, 195–96

Huppatz, D. J., 72
Hurwitz, Mitch, 191
Hutcheon, Linda, 10, 29
Hutchinson, Tom, 116
Huyssen, Andreas, 27, 60
hyper-serialization, 188

Ice Bucket Challenge, 175–76
identification, 87–88, 93, 126, 131, 135,
144, 154
IDEO, 12, 53, 195–96
iFixit, 183, 211
IKEA effect, 178
informed consent, 110, 122, 131
informed dissent, 101, 121, 125–28,
148, 152–53, 177, 203–4. *See also*
adversarial design; agonism;
provotype
ingroup identity, 37, 117, 197. *See also*
consubstantiality
inheritability, 181–84, 211
initial concept fixation, 150, 153–54
innovation, 11, 20, 58, 77; v. tradition,
18, 77, 107, 179; user, 199
Instagram, 17, 177, 180
interface design, 22, 64, 93, 202–3
invented tradition, 187
iPhone, 176, 184
Irvine, Judith, 58

Jackson, Hannah-Beth, 129–34
Jameson, Fredric, 20, 29, 203, 214n8
Jenner, Edward, 106
*jidoka*, 168
John Deere, 183
Johnson, Robert, 38, 86
Jones, Doug, 197
Jørgensen, Marianne, 48
Jungk, Robert, 89–90

Kalantzis, Mary, 33, 59, 197
Kalla, Joshua, 135–36
Kano, Noriaki, 173
Kansas City, 18–19, 213n1 (chap. 1)

Kantor, Jodi, 54–55, 102
Kaphar, Titus, 31
Keightley, Emily, 221n3
kids these days, 201
kill fee, 160, 161
knitting, 19, 35, 48–50, 56–57, 63, 65–71
knowledge boundary, 149–51
Kurlinkus, Krista, 66, 143
Kurlinkus, William, 179, 180
Kyng, Morten, 38–39

labor, 53–59, 160, 181, 184–86
Ladino, Jennifer, 10, 30, 57
laggards, 20, 58
Lankshear, Colin, 70
*Larry King Live*, 114–19
Lawson, Bryan, 138
lead users, 20
leaked constructedness, 180. *See also* aura; behavioral residue; provenance; wabi-sabi
lean management, 54
liberal democracy, 98
liberal tradition, 97–99
Light, David, 191
Lippmann, Walter, 102, 217n12
Listening to the City, 135
literacy: access, 31, 33–35, 70; equity, 31, 33, 35, 70; violence of, 70, 214n12
literacy gateways, 33–35, 69–72
literacy sponsors, 61–62, 69–70
localization, 19, 43–44, 135–46
logical fallacy. *See* rhetorical fallacy
London, Kerry, 157
longing 4, 6–7, 26, 67
loss, 7; of control 11, 116, 122, 160; digital, 55; emotional feedback loop, 59–61; mediation, 113; of time, 26, 189
Lowenthal, David, 28
Lupton, Julia, 85, 86
Lyon, Arabella, 85, 217n10

maintenance of copyright clause, 160–61
Make America Great Again, 8–9, 29, 84, 195
Maker's Bill of Rights, 183
makerspaces, 183, 185
manufactured scientific controversy, 109
Manzini, Ezio, 23, 37, 38, 97, 165
Marinker, Marshall, 111
Marx, Karl, 9, 53
Massumi, Brian, 60
May, Ernest, 150, 153
McCarthy, Jenny, 106, 114–20, 218n7
McDonalds, 185, 189
McMurria, John, 186
McQuitty Shaun, 184
measles, 108, 122, 128, 130
mediation, 106–37
medical exemptions, 128, 130, 133
medical rhetoric, 117, 119, 132–33
medicine: history, 110–11; on the internet, 108, 114, 148, 220nn9–10; as personal responsibility, 126–27
*Medscape One-on-One*, 131
melancholia, 6, 7, 58
memorial, 30–31, 41, 135, 182, 193–94
memorial interactivity, 141–43, 144, 146, 152, 161, 207, 221n2
memory boom, 27
memory crisis, 27
memory studies, 27
memos, 154–55
Mercury, 128
metaphorical design, 94–95, 172–73
*métis*, 38–40; mediation, 112, 134; redesign, 49, 51–53, 58–59, 72, 109, 128, 169; rejecting, 178, 190
Meza, James, 127
Middleton, David, 69
millenials, 201
Miller, Carolyn, 77
Mittell, Jason, 188
mixtape, 179–80

MMR (measles, mumps, rubella) vaccine, 107, 114
Mochon, Daniel, 178
Mogensen, Preben, 100, 104
Moisio, Risto, 184, 186
mommy instinct, 106, 114
Monk, Gerald, 106, 113, 114, 119, 205
mono no aware, 42, 181–82
Monteiro, Mike, 138, 155, 157
mood boards, 146
Moore, Roy, 29, 197
moral foundations, 37, 118, 134, 197–98
Mouffe, Chantal, 22–23, 88, 97–101, 104, 123, 129, 216n8
Mountain Mama, 117
Moynihan, Daniel Patrick, 136
Mulgan, Geoff, 23
Müllert, Norbert, 89–90
multiliteracies, 32, 40, 59, 70, 200
Muniz, Albert, 193
musealization, 40
mutirão, 39
Myers, Jacob, 161
#myNYPD, 177–78
mystery, 174–75. See also secret

narratability, 171–78, 210, 221n5. See also buzz; tellable
narratable UX, 171–78
narrative complexity, 188
narrative depth, 173–74
narrative medicine, 111, 118, 120–21, 123, 127, 151. See also chief complaint; chief concern
narrative of illness, 113, 118
National Council of Teacher's of English (NCTE), 160–61
neoliberalism, 97, 123, 184, 186
neostalgia, 22, 33–35, 47, 49, 69–72, 116, 172–73
Netflix, 188
neurological diversity, 120–21
Neustadt, Richard, 150, 153
Neville-Rehbehn, Daniel, 203–4

new capitalism, 35, 44, 54–55, 57
Nikolaj Contemporary Art Center, 48
Nilsson, Elisabet, 39, 77, 170
No Coaster Please, 169–70
Norman, Donald, 3, 59, 84, 96–97, 165, 166, 168
Norman doors, 84–85
Nora, Pierre, 27–28
Norton, Michael 178
nostalgia, 5–8, 30; Alzheimer's, 182; appropriation, 44, 52, 72–73, 200; boom, 17, 26; chicken pox, 134; combative, 191; control, 51, 108, 116, 119; creativity, 63; dismissing, 5, 9–10, 20, 28–30; empathy, 37, 40, 52, 84, 92–97, 151, 216n7; familial, 61, 65, 179, 182; feminism, 47–51, 57, 65–66; history of, 5, 24–30; homeostasis, 6, 20, 27, 108; identity, 7, 18, 27, 37, 48, 56, 65, 144, 173; international, 43–44, 51–52, 72; omnitemporal, 6–7, 25, 58; psychology, 6, 20, 27, 37, 40, 60, 63, 84, 108, 171, 182; resistance, 6, 11, 19, 26, 30, 47–59, 72, 190–93; stress relief, 62–63; tensions, 6–7, 25, 40, 57, 58, 62, 72; therapeutic, 63, 182, 184
nostalgia mapping, 208
nostalgia for nature, 107, 115–16, 126, 134, 189–190
nostalgia priming, 144
nostalgia-typing, 116, 205
nostalgic contact zones, 31, 51–52; design, 145–46, 206; identity, 58, 62; mediation, 115, 143, 149
nostalgic design, 3–4, 11, 20–22, 24, 27–28, 194, 196
nostalgic localization, 18–19, 43–44, 135
nostalgic loss aversion, 180–81
nostalgic other, 66, 119, 184, 190
nostalgic rupture, 4, 67, 159, 167, 172–73, 177

nostalgic stasis, 36, 109, 111–13, 204
nostalgic user experience architecture
  (N-UX), 167–70, 210
Nunes, Paul, 191
NYPD, 177–78
Nyhan, Brendan, 133, 158

objects of legacy, 72–73
obsolescence, 26, 165, 183–84, 211
Ochs, Elinor, 172
Odyssey, 26
Offit, Bonnie, 125–26, 127, 137
Offit, Paul, 106, 108, 121–26, 218n9
O'Guinn, Thomas, 193
Olbrechts-Tyteca, Lucie, 84
omission bias, 126, 131
On This Day, 17–18, 41, 177
Opel, Douglas, 45, 127
OpenNotes, 127–28, 137, 146
oppositional brand loyalty, 193
Oprah, 111
overwork, 54–57, 64
Oz, Dr., 111

Pacenti, Elena, 95–96
Palmer, Katie, 123
Pan, Richard, 128, 130, 133
Papanek, Victor, 58
Pariser, Eli, 134–35
participation-ism, 97. See also customer
  is always right
participatory design, 38–40, 79–80,
  89–92, 109–11, 135, 216n5
participatory medicine, 109–11
Passerman, Daniel, 127
Patient Self Determination Act (PSDA),
  110
Paton, Bec, 149
peer review, 208
Perelman, Chaim, 84
personalization, 166, 169–70, 176, 182,
  210
Petrini, Carlo, 189–90
Pfaffenberger, Bryan, 200

Phillips, Kendall, 214n9
photography, 176–77
phronesis, 83
Picard, Rosalind, 63
Pickering, Michael, 221n3
Pine, Joseph B., II, 165, 185
Pink Tank, 48
pink-washing, 34
playground, 206
Portlandia, 170
Portniari, Folco, 170
"pouch phone," 210–11
Pratt, Mary Louise, 31, 51–52
Prelli, Lawrence, 84
pride, 6–7, 34, 60–61, 113, 159–60
Princeton University, 31
profession, 142, 149, 162. See also
  expertise
propaganda, 8–9, 28–29
Proust, Marcel, 172
provenance, 179–84, 189. See also aura;
  behavioral residue; leaked constructedness
provoke, 99–101, 193–94. See also agonism; informed dissent
provotype, 100–101, 135, 156, 193,
  203–4. See also agonism; informed
  dissent
public intellectual, 136
public opinion, 102, 132. See also vox
  populi
public safety, 129–32. See under rights,
  communal
Putnam, Robert, 119–20, 134, 219n14

Raby, Fiona, 99–100, 101, 201
Rams, Dieter, 158
Ratcliffe, Krista, 92–93, 96, 103, 150,
  190, 216nn6–7, 217n9
rationalism, 10, 89, 97–98, 121, 123,
  125, 214n10
Reardon, Ken, 79–80
Redström, Johan, 169
reflective nostalgia, 30–31, 38, 52; re-

sistance, 11, 34, 190; sensitivity, 67,
171; taste, 186. *See also* expertise,
reflectively nostalgic
refusal, 114, 124, 127, 155–61, 209;
agonistic, 158; antagonistic, 158;
medical, 158–59
Reiss, Dorit, 130–31
remediation, 22, 70, 93
repair, 183–86, 211, 221n8
restorative nostalgia, 9, 30, 111–12;
community of, 89, 115, 117, 118;
professional, 142; refusals, 157–58;
scientific, 36, 108, 109, 120. *See also*
expertise, reflectively nostalgic
retro branding, 170, 191
rewatchability, 188
Reynolds, Simon, 20, 47
rhetoric, 35, 83–84, 87–89, 92–93,
97–99; and technology 77, 213n4
rhetorical design, 4, 12, 73, 80–82,
102–5, 201, 213n4
rhetorical designer, 81, 93
rhetorical fallacies, 10, 36, 157–58, 197
rhetorical refusal, 155–56, 157, 209.
*See also* refusal
rhetorical listening, 92–93, 121, 150,
152, 216nn6–7
Riechers, Angela, 20
rights: communal, 98–99, 129; individual, 98–99, 120; negative, 130;
positive, 130
Right to Be Forgotten, 41
Right to Repair Bill, 183
risk, 121–22, 133–34; dread, 123, 126;
individual, 126–27, 134; sharing,
126
rites of passage, 134, 181
Rittel, Horst, 82
ritual, 42, 186–88, 211
rock climbing, 183
Rosa, Hartmut, 6, 167
Rosa, Jonathan, 178
rotavirus vaccine, 123
Routledge, Clay, 6, 20, 30

ruptures of the present, 172–75, 180,
194. *See also* surprise
Ruskin, John, 26, 53, 55

Sander, Thomas, 134
Sanders, Bernie, 181
Sanders, Elizabeth, 64
Sartwell, Crispin, 28
savoring, 171, 186–90. *See also* slow
design; taste for time; wandering
SB277. *See* Senate Bill 277
scapegoating, 29, 88, 114, 118, 197
Schapiro, Miriam, 47–48
Schilb, John, 155
Schleifer, Ronald, 112, 125
Schmitz, Thomas, 83
Schön, Donald, 142
Schultz, Pit, 160
science communication, 35–37, 108–12,
119–23, 126–28, 133–36
secret, 173–75, 188
secret urbanism, 175
Sedikides, Constantine, 6, 17, 27, 40,
60, 63, 175
Selfe, Cynthia, 22, 32, 40, 93, 195,
215n1
Selfe, Richard, 22, 93
selling out, 191
Senate Bill 277, 128–36
Sennett, Richard, 54–55
sensitivity v. sentimentality, 67
shared decision-making, 111. *See also*
decision-making we; participatory
design
Silva, Vesta, 127
Siva, Jessica, 157
sketches, 150, 153–54. *See also* boundary object
skeuomorph, 3, 22, 93, 180
Skowronski, J. J., 181
Slack, Andrew, 190
slacktivism, 176–77, 178, 221n6
slow consumption, 30, 167, 171,
187–189, 193

slow design, 42, 167, 170–71, 181–82, 210
slow food, 170, 189–190
slow food manifesto, 170
SlowLab, 42
slow storytelling, 171–75
slow virality, 175–77
Smith, Kimberly, 9–10, 29–30, 97, 204
social capital, 119–20, 134–35, 219n14
social currency, 176
social media, 4, 17–18, 40–41, 175–77, 180, 182. *See also* Facebook; Instagram; Twitter
South Korea, 184
souvenir, 171
speculative design, 96, 99–100, 201, 203, 210
speed, 26, 41, 54, 165–68
Spinuzzi, Clay, 79, 216n5
sprezzatura, 174, 179
Starbucks, 44, 157
Star, Susan Leigh, 146
Star Wars, 191
STEM, 31–35
Stephan, Elena, 171
stewardship, 42, 181–84
Stewart, Susan, 5, 171–72
stitch n' bitch, 50, 65–67
Stoller, Debbie, 50, 65–66
street market, 80
Streitfeld, David, 54–55, 102
Stuckey, Elspeth, 214n12
"Students' Right to Their Own Language," 160–61
Sun, Huatong, 22, 43
Super Bowl, 185, 193
surprise, 172–75, 221n4. *See also* curiosity; rupture; wonder
Swann, Cal, 142

Taimina, Daina, 71–72
taste, 169–70, 182, 186–193, 211
taste for time, 170, 182, 186–87, 189, 193

Taylor, Summer, 144
technocracy, 12, 23, 48, 79
techno-logic, 32–33; access and equity, 35, 44, 69; resisting dominant, 51, 177, 195; mediating between, 78, 114, 126–28, 131, 177
technological determinism, 22, 109
technology of memory, 17, 41, 176–77
Teich, Oren, 94–95, 172–73
tellable, 172. *See also* buzz; narratability
temporal anchoring, 60–61, 187–88
temporal reorganization, 187–88
Terrio, Susan, 187–88, 211
*The Secret*, 111
thimerosal, 128, 130, 132
third way, 58, 101, 115–16, 119–121, 133, 205
*This American Life*, 36, 213n2
*This Old House* 186
Tilburg, Winjnand van, 63
Tiki Room, 191
tomato harvester, 78
Topgaard, Richard, 39, 77, 170
Toyota, 54, 168
transactive memory system, 142, 144–46, 148, 149, 151, 161–62, 207
transphobia, 135–36
Tremmel, Georg, 194
Trump, Donald, 4, 8–9, 29, 213n1
trust, 118, 143, 145, 147–49, 150, 154–55, 206–7. *See also* ethos
Turan, Zeynep, 72, 213n2
Twitter, 34, 117, 177–78, 218n13

Umar, Sanda, 182
underlife, 51, 56–57, 59
universal design, 42, 206
University of California, 78, 89, 216n1
user audience, 81
user-centered design, 52–53, 84–87, 124
user error, 84
user experience architect, 168
user experience design, 168–70

user-friendly design, 86
user persona, 85, 86. *See also* design
    research
UTOPIA, 38–39, 79
UX. *See* user experience design

vaccine, 106–7; court, 132–33; forced,
    131; history, 106–7; injury, 131–33;
    mandatory, 130; preventable illness,
    121–22, 126; schedule, 114–16, 130
Valentine's Day, 185
values, 10, 84, 97–98, 204
Vannatta, Jerry, 112, 125
virality, 175–76
Virilio, Paul, 41
Vohs, Kathleen, 187
voice, 158–61, 209, 220n11
Von Hippel, Eric, 20, 58–59
voting, 18, 77, 99, 136, 203–4, 217n12
vox populi, 4, 135, 217n12

*wabi-sabi*, 42, 180, 182. *See also* leaked
    constructedness
Wakefield, Andrew, 107–8, 218n3
Walker, Jan, 127
Walker, Stuart, 210
Wallace, Amy, 126
wandering, 26, 173–74. *See also* wonder
Waramungu, 72–73, 216n8
Waza, 94–95, 172–73
Webber, Melvin, 82
WebMD, 111, 125, 148, 220nn9–10. *See
    also* under Google

Wegner, Daniel, 142, 144
Wen, Leana, 128
Wertheim, Christine, 71–72
Wertheim, Margaret, 71–72
West Virginia water crisis, 143
who are we?, 80–81, 84, 87, 98, 104,
    113. *See also* decision-making we
wicked problem, 82, 83, 87, 91, 111
Wiens, Kyle, 183
Wildschut, Tim, 6, 30, 40, 63, 182
Williams, Bernard, 132
Wilson, Woodrow, 30–31
Winner, Langdon, 32, 78, 123
Winslade, John, 106, 113, 114, 119, 205
wireframes, 153–54
Wolf, Marco, 184
Wolsko, Christopher, 198
*Womanhouse*, 47
Women for Life on Earth, 48
wonder, 171–75, 178. *See also* curiosity;
    surprise

Yelp, 186
Yergeau, Melanie, 121
Yochim, Emily, 127
Yongsan Electronics Market, 184
Young, Dannagal, 117

Zanfleet, Tara, 133
Zhou, Xinyue, 24, 37, 84
Zielinski, Siegfried, 17
Zuckerberg, Mark, 31–32
*Zukunftswerkstatten*. *See* future workshop